Praise for
Good Cop, Bad Daughter:
Memoirs of an Unlikely Police Officer

This book is a deeply satisfying read. Karen Lynch's journey from chaotic childhood to the macho confines of the SFPD as one of the city's first female cops will have you rooting for her every step of the way. With great humor and grace, she describes her fraught relationship with her mentally ill mother and her decisions to forge a better life for herself.

Good Cop, Bad Daughter is a testament to the triumph of the human spirit.

—Julia Scheeres, author of *Jesus Land* and
A Thousand Lives: the Untold Story of Jonestown

Who knew that a childhood alongside an unstable mother would be the perfect preparation for big city police work? Lynch brings us inside her first year as a San Francisco cop, as she battles not only the dangers and pitfalls of the job but the perils of her mother's mental illness. At once tragic, comic, and uplifting, this is a book for anyone who needs a primer on resilience, or just wants a great read. I only wish Officer Lynch was still on the job; you want a cop with this kind of empathy, insight, and toughness to be responding to your 911 call tonight.

—Caroline Paul, author of *Fighting Fire*

Good Cop,
BAD DAUGHTER

Good Cop,
BAD DAUGHTER

Memoirs of an Unlikely Police Officer

Karen Lynch

NOTHING
BUT THE
TRUTH,
LLC

SAN FRANCISCO

Nothing But The Truth, LLC
980 Magnolia Avenue, Suite C-6
Larkspur, CA 94939

GOOD COP, BAD DAUGHTER™ and GOOD COP, BAD DAUGHTER Cover Design are trademarks of Nothing But The Truth, LLC.

For information about book purchases please visit the Nothing But The Truth website at NothingButtheTruth.com
Also available in ebook.

Library of Congress Control Number: 2013956880

Good Cop, Bad Daughter
Memoirs of an Unlikely Police Officer
Eve Batey, Editor. Mickey Nelson, Assistant Editor.

ISBN 978-0-9883754-2-0 (paperback)
ISBN 978-0-9883754-3-7 (ePub ebook)
ISBN 978-0-9883754-4-4 (Kindle ebook)

Printed in the United States of America
Cover design by theBookDesigners, Fairfax, CA
First Edition

This book is dedicated to the men and women of the San Francisco Police Department. *Oro en paz, fierro en guerra.* And to Jim.

Introduction

All persons, living and dead, are purely coincidental.
—Kurt Vonnegut

The events described in this book happened. Of course, memory is an imperfect sense, and memoir is by no means journalism. I have sometimes taken liberties in recreating conversations from long ago. Names have been changed, and in the interest of narrative flow, time has sometimes been compressed. Many people and events that had no impact on the story have been omitted. A few peripheral characters are composites.

Prologue

"**G**raduates Face Worst Job Market Since Great Depression." The headline of the *San Francisco Chronicle* caught my eye while I was waiting for the bus. It was June 1980, and the day's top news story was a depressing reminder that my newly issued college diploma was a useless souvenir of four ambling years.

I put a quarter in the box, dug out a paper, and was skimming the news when an ad stopped me cold. Four uniformed women smiled at me above a caption ordering, "Join the SFPD." The women looked proud and confident, part of a big, happy family. I felt a surge of envy. I'd spent my childhood yearning to be part of a family. For a moment, I tried to envision myself belonging to this group of uniformed sisters.

Then I imagined how Mom would react if she saw the ad. I could almost hear her outrage: "Look at those storm trooper sell-outs. Now they're using women to protect the capitalist pigs!"

I was on my way to Fisherman's Wharf to work my shift as a serving wench at Ben Jonson's Olde English Taverne. Wearing a revealing costume and showing my cleavage for tips had been a lucrative, if sometimes humiliating, way to pay for my last year of college. I had natural double Ds and wasn't afraid to use them. But I'd never intended to make a career of it.

The dismal job market meant that the prospect of spending the rest of my life as a serving wench in a Renaissance-themed bar was a horrifyingly real possibility. I pictured myself decades

in the future, gray haired and shriveled, my sagging breasts flop-
ping inside my corset as I leaned on the table for balance and
cackled, "Now, which of you kids ordered Galahad's Grail of
Grog? Who had the Maid Marian's Mead?"

But being a geriatric wench was not a realistic career choice.
A large corporation had recently purchased the tavern, and the
management intended to close us down. Then what? I had no
safety net, no family to take me in, and no marketable skills. My
biggest fear was ending up homeless again.

I walked from the bus stop to the Cannery, unlocked the
dressing room door, and stuffed myself into my two-sizes-too-
small green velveteen corset. I knotted my burlap skirt high on
the hip for optimum leg viewing, then checked myself in the
mirror and noticed an ugly beer stain on my skirt. I tried imagining myself instead in one of those crisp blue police uniforms, but
dismissed the ridiculous thought of someone like me becoming
a cop.

I had grown up in the Haight-Ashbury neighborhood as the
Summer of Love dawned in San Francisco. Mom had abandoned
her East Coast family, fleeing them as if running for her life.
She spent many years on government assistance because of her
illness—manic depression with overtones of paranoid schizophrenia. She seldom mentioned her New York family, but during
episodes she occasionally ranted in public about her awful
parents, lashing out at strangers, insulting and terrifying them.
Sometimes the police came and took her away. I was glad to see
the police, but Mom hated them.

One of my biggest fears was that I'd end up like her; dependent, reliant upon the Department of Social Services or the generosity of some boyfriend to keep me alive. I had learned from
an early age that relying on the kindness of strangers was a risky
business.

In her lucid days, Mom had always insisted I should become a nurse. She had attempted nursing school herself as a young woman, but her education had ended when she had what she described as her "first nervous breakdown." Maybe she hoped that if I achieved her goal, it would redeem her in some way. Or maybe the lines between us were just so blurred she couldn't see me at all. And for my part, I suppose I believed that if I did everything she asked, Mom would finally be happy.

For four years I'd given Mom's dream my best shot, scrambling for Cs in chemistry and physiology and failing organic chemistry twice. Now I had graduated from college, and in spite of my terrible science grades, I had been tentatively accepted into the fall class of nursing students at Emory University in Georgia. The university required I take organic chemistry yet again in summer school and this time get at least a C.

The school had optimistically sent me a box containing a nurse's cap, stethoscope, and name tag. When I put everything on and examined myself in the mirror, I cringed. I hated the ugly cap, and the harsh squawk of my name tag, Nurse Nassberg, recalled Nurse Ratched from *One Flew over the Cuckoo's Nest*. With the cap propped on my dark bun and my cheekbones free of makeup, I looked severe and a bit scary.

Summer school organic chemistry was proving to be no easier than the regular session had been. Every day before my wench shift, I walked into a classroom in which the professor might as well have been speaking Hungarian. I was failing again, and beginning to face the fact that I would never achieve Mom's dream. All I had ever wanted was for her to be proud of me, and now I felt overwhelmed with the anticipation of her disappointment. I tried rehearsing how I would break the news to her and could already hear her in my head: "The state sure wasted that scholarship money on you!"

At the same time, giving up on Mom's dream felt a little freeing. I had never had a passion for nursing; I was dutifully following Mom's orders. But if I wasn't becoming a nurse, what was I becoming? "A loser," I imagined Mom answering.

On my day off from the tavern I distracted myself by browsing City Lights Bookstore with my childhood friend, Monica. Monica and I had known each other since second grade, and she had stuck with me through everything. She was strikingly beautiful, with caramel-colored skin and long, wavy, golden-brown hair.

I hoped Monica would help me bolster my courage. I had decided not to bother returning to chemistry class, and I knew I could only delay breaking the news to Mom for so long. I would give myself one more day before making the dreaded phone call.

As we came out of the bookstore, we passed Vesuvio Cafe. Although my parents had met there decades earlier, I couldn't remember ever stepping inside. But that day, I felt magnetically drawn in. We chose a table by the window looking out over Columbus Avenue. When our Irish coffees came, we toasted our mysterious futures.

Then suddenly there she was, a young woman with wavy, dark hair driving a black-and-white patrol car up Columbus toward Broadway. She was wearing a San Francisco Police Department uniform and smiling like the women in the ad.

"It's me, Monica. Look! It's me!" I gestured out the window.

Monica looked out in time to spot the rear end of the cruiser. She turned to me and scrunched her eyebrows.

"I know it sounds crazy, but I just saw myself driving that police car! I was wearing a uniform! Monica, I think that's what I'm supposed to do!"

"Whatever floats your boat, honey," she said, toasting me again.

"Women have no place in police work," barked the man at the next table. He downed his beer, grinned, and moved in closer.

"You'll only get yourself killed, or worse still, some man will get killed saving you."

"Let's go, Monica." No doubt the loudmouth thought he was discouraging me, but his words only made me want to prove him wrong.

For the rest of that day and the next, that woman officer, who would soon end up playing an important role in my life, stayed on my mind. It felt so right. The universe had struck me with a lightning bolt, and for that moment my destiny was clear.

I began searching the paper for stories about the new female cops, trying to learn as much as I could about them. Women had been working as patrol officers in San Francisco for only a few years, and the *Chronicle* periodically ran articles reporting on the progress of the rookie females. When the public was polled, few men interviewed thought women could survive as street cops. Some said females were too weak and emotional to handle the stress and predicted the women would run and hide when they were required to fight with a criminal resisting arrest. I felt offended. I was stronger than some of the men I knew, and I had learned to control my emotions, at least outwardly, after years of managing my volatile mother.

The San Francisco Police Officer's Association was energetically fighting the court order compelling the city to hire women. Mom had weaned me on feminist philosophers like Simone de Beauvoir and Gloria Steinem. Now my pride was compelling me to prove the naysayers wrong. I reasoned that if women wanted equal rights, we would simply need to prove we could do the things men do.

But even as I gained certainty about applying to the department, another part of me wondered what the hell I was thinking. My hippie family tribe had lived their lives avoiding the cops. Monica had been my friend forever and would never disown me, but what about my other friends? What about the friends I'd smoked pot with in college at Berkeley? Would they see me as a sellout or traitor? And was I even the sort of woman the police department was looking for? Would the men see me as a joke? Could a former serving wench with 36 DDs walk a beat in the Tenderloin?

Ultimately none of these considerations stopped me. I just couldn't let go of the idea that I was supposed to become a cop. I filled out an application card, and soon the city sent me a packet of information.

The testing process to get into the police academy was three-fold—fourfold if I included the challenge of telling my mother I wanted to be a cop. My first hurdle was the written test. Close to a thousand people were competing for a couple hundred positions, and I had to scramble to find a vacant seat in the Hall of Justice auditorium. I had expected, with all the advertising, there would be more women, but only about one in ten of the test takers was female. Some were older people who'd been forced into second careers by the economic downturn, but most looked about my age, young and eager.

We watched hours of brain-numbing videos depicting ficti-tious crime scenes, then answered hundreds of multiple-choice questions. The test focused on our observational skills and ability to recall details. No actual knowledge of the law was required. It seemed fairly straightforward, and I was confident I'd done rea-sonably well.

The agility test had me more nervous. I wasn't sure what level of physical fitness was expected or how stiff the competi-tion might be. To be on the safe side, I decided to attend the free training offered by the city.

The training class met in the evening at the Hall of Justice gym. The two female officers in charge were attractive and very fit.

I'll call them Thelma and Louise. The group of fifteen academy hopefuls, all women, varied in age and fitness. While I was not particularly sporty, I had done weight training in college and was strong. If you created a fitness chart with the Pillsbury Dough-boy on one extreme and a Navy SEAL on the other, I would have fallen somewhere in the middle.

The agility test consisted of an obstacle course where we were to run a few laps around the gym, hop onto a low balance beam, run along it without falling, jump over a six-foot wall, drag a 150-pound dummy-shaped sandbag fifty feet, and hoist the dummy onto a low table, folding his arms and legs over him. Finally, we would take a grip-strength test. The whole event was timed, and we would be ranked according to speed.

Louise started us working on the dummy drag first. I tied my long hair back in a ponytail and hoisted the dummy under his armpits without much effort. I hauled him across the room, heaved him on top of the platform, and folded his legs in record time. I nodded in satisfaction. Months of toting trays of fishbowl-sized margarita glasses and manhandling drunken customers had paid off.

The wall was another story. I had never before attempted to hurdle myself over a six-foot wall, but after displaying my superior dummy-dragging skills, I was a bit full of myself. I got in line for my turn. So far, no one ahead of me had made it over. The wall was a smooth, solid hunk of golden wood. Its glossy, shellacked finish offered no footholds or traction.

When my turn came, I ran to the wall and jumped to grab the top as I'd seen the others do, but I struggled to pull myself all the way up. Hanging there, feet dangling uselessly, I tried again and again to haul myself over. Finally I surrendered and dropped to the floor like rotten fruit. I watched as the women in line behind me also failed. We each took our turn. We jumped, hung, gave up, and dropped. After each turn, we whined, groused, and commiserated.

"This wall is too high! This wall is too slippery! This wall is sexist! This wall hates people who have breasts!" I wondered if the naysayers were right. If I couldn't even get over this wall, maybe I didn't deserve a spot in the department.

Thelma and Louise had been watching us do our routine for some time without comment.

"You girls can get your asses up over that wall just as fast as the guys can," Thelma finally said. We looked at each other, skeptically. "You just have to know the trick. Women can't do things the same way men do. Our strength is in our legs, ladies. Thunder thighs! There's a reason why God gave us big muscles in our legs." I then noticed Thelma's firm, well-defined thighs, the approximate size and shape of HoneyBaked hams. "I want you to watch very carefully how I do this. Later, I'll do it in slow motion, and that's the way you're going to start: real slow. Then you're going to practice a hundred times a day until you can get over that wall in three seconds. You hear me?"

We nodded pessimistically, still not convinced the wall was scalable.

"When I say, 'You hear me?' you say, 'Yes, ma'am!' You *hear* me?"

We answered together. "Yes, ma'am!"

"That's how it's gonna be if you ever get your sorry asses into the academy. 'Yes, ma'am' and 'Yes, sir!' You got that?"

"Yes, ma'am!" we replied. A joker behind me said, "Yes, sir," but Thelma missed it.

Thelma then ran to the wall full speed, leaped, and grabbed the top deftly while simultaneously planting her right foot in the middle about three feet up. Throwing her left leg over, she bounded off in pursuit of her imaginary criminal. A jump, climb, swoop combo.

"Go get him!" yelled Louise. "Get that bad guy!"

Watching Thelma, I suddenly saw there was more than one way over that wall, and I knew I could do it too.

"Girls, I want you to remember this. In the academy you are going to have to master many skills. Men will teach you these skills and the ways they do them. You are not men. Sometimes you are going to need to find your own way to do things. Sometimes, your way will be even better than their way."

She and Louise spent the remainder of class breaking the steps down slowly. Jump, climb, and swoop. Jump, climb, and swoop. It took us many tries that night, but by the end of class we had all mastered the wall.

When test day finally came two weeks later, the wall was a cinch. I jumped, climbed, and swooped. It amazed me that I could climb over it in seconds.

The third challenge was the oral exam. When the day came, I couldn't decide what to wear. It hadn't occurred to me to invest in a decent suit, and I hadn't thought to ask anyone what women wear to such interviews. I finally settled on a gingham dress and black four-inch heels.

Unlike the agility test, I'd done nothing to find out how the oral exam would actually be administered. I had, however, mentally planned the entire thing, imagining the questions the board would ask, and although no one had told me to do so, I'd prepared a fifteen-minute speech about why I would be a great police officer.

I was seated before a panel of three men whose faces revealed none of the milk of human kindness. My outfit had seemed adequate as I dressed that morning: business-like, but feminine. But now, before these men, it felt ridiculous. The dress's neckline was embarrassingly low, and I'd worn too much lipstick and my long hair was loose.

A few minutes before I walked into the room, a monitor handed me a scripted scenario involving a dispute between neighbors. One neighbor was displaying a swastika poster in his front window. The other neighbor wanted the poster taken down. Every time I told the interviewing sergeant that I would ask the offending neighbor to take down the poster, the sergeant replied, "He's not doing it!" When I suggested the complaining neighbor could live with it, the sergeant screamed, "He wants it taken down!" I had no idea where the law stood on this issue and could think of no alternative solutions. I mentally reviewed First Amendment rights, not knowing if the police could force a citizen to take down an offensive sign.

The whole time, I resisted the urge to tug at the lacy fabric near my neck and stretch it to cover my cleavage. *Why had I thought playing up my femininity was a smart idea?* These men wanted to see a man sitting in front of them, or at least someone dressed like a man. I felt exposed, like they were giving me a gynecological exam without even supplying me a paper gown.

My fifteen minutes finally came to an end, and I never had the chance to tell the board a word about why I'd be such a great cop. I left knowing the only way I'd make it into the academy was if I had a high enough score on the written and agility tests to make up for this disaster. I skulked down the stairs of the old hospital, certain I'd failed.

A few weeks later, I opened an envelope with a return address from the City and County of San Francisco. The hiring list had hundreds of names ranked by overall score. While I was far from the top, I'd scored enough cumulative points to be in the hiring pool and would move on to an academy class when they reached my number.

Knowing Mom would be furious, I avoided telling her for months as the city worked their way down the list and finally reached my number. Two weeks before my academy class was due to begin I worked up the nerve to call. I braced myself to deliver the news. No matter what awful things she said or did, I held out hope for our relationship.

"Hi, Mom. How are you?"

"OK, I guess. John still sits like a lump all day," she said, speaking of her current husband. "Honestly, I don't know what I was thinking, marrying an older man. He has no sex drive whatsoever."

I'd heard this complaint before and rapidly changed the subject before she volunteered grisly details. "Yes. Well, I have some good news."

"Let me guess, you're getting married," she said, without enthusiasm.

"Well, no." I worked to keep my tone upbeat. "I've decided to join the San Francisco Police Department. They're doing a big hiring drive and opening the doors to women."

"Are you out of your mind?" she shrieked. "How could you even think of joining them after everything they've done to me? They've been persecuting me for decades! I knew you hated me, but this is the worst thing you've ever done to me! Why not just drive a stake through my heart?"

I took a deep breath.

"Mom, this is not about you. It's just something I have to do."

"Well, isn't that the world's greatest news! My daughter's becoming a fucking Nazi!" She slammed down the receiver without saying good-bye.

I sank onto the couch. Maybe I was being crazy. Why did I want this so badly? Why had I worked so hard to put myself through college, only to subject myself to the police academy? Was I doing all this to rebel against my mother? No. That was ridiculous. Then I considered everything I'd been through with Mom, and the answer was obvious.

My whole childhood, Mom had been training me to be a cop.

PART ONE

Beatniks

I was committed to a mental institution before I was born. I was Mom's placental passenger, floating obliviously in utero at Agnews State Hospital for the Mentally Ill. I obviously can't describe our time in the hospital, but when I was a small child I remember Mom sometimes screaming at Dad for sending us there.

"You shipped me off to Agnews with your unborn child, you bastard!" she would howl. It was hard to believe Mom and Dad had once loved each other.

My parents migrated separately to San Francisco in the mid-1950s. Lured to North Beach by Ferlinghetti, Kerouac, and the specter of Jack London, they were beckoned by a San Francisco that was romantic and fog-shrouded, the air savory with Barbary Coast brine. Both were striving writers; like many before them, they dreamed, as Mom put it, "of escaping the intolerable dullness of bourgeois existence."

My mother, Ann, was of Scotch-Irish, Catholic, working-class descent. She had left home at eighteen and enlisted in the army to get away from her family. By Mom's account, her father, Vincent, was an alcoholic, and her mother, Catherine, was cruel and resentful. Eugene O'Neill couldn't have imagined a better cast.

The McNeil family's point of pride was that Vincent had helped build the Empire State Building. The story of my grandfather's role in the construction varied depending on Mom's level of intoxication. Some nights he was the architect, other nights the chief engineer. In truth, he was but one of hundreds of construction workers who helped raise the iconic tower.

Mom's brief army career ended unexpectedly. The night she lost her virginity at age nineteen, she became pregnant. She told me that her own mother had never shared even the most basic mechanics of reproduction with her. Mom placed her baby for adoption and headed to Los Angeles, where she briefly enrolled in nursing school before moving north to San Francisco.

When my father, David, came to San Francisco, he left behind his German-Jewish family, a family he resented for sending him away to a school for gifted children shortly after his eighth birthday—or at least that's the story my mother told. Drafted from an Ohio public school, he had allegedly scored 160 on a standardized IQ test. This accomplishment caught the attention of school administrators who, with my paternal grandparents' permission, determined Dad's gift would be best nurtured in a state-sponsored boarding school. Once they'd sent him away, my grandparents showed little interest in having him return home, believing their parental obligation had been satisfied by raising him to the age of eight.

My father was handsome, in a swarthy way. Mom was pale in contrast, with icy blue eyes and light brown hair. After my parent's marriage at San Francisco's City Hall, they moved into a Haight-Ashbury apartment, spending their days at City Lights and Caffè Trieste, sipping espresso and discussing world events and philosophy with other beatniks. Nights, they tapped their feet to jazz at the Purple Onion, attended poetry readings, or shot pool at Mike's. I don't think my father ever wore a black beret, but I like to picture him in one.

I never knew what precipitated the breakdown that landed

us in Agnews State Mental Hospital—Agnews was but one of many psychiatric hospitals Mom would reside in throughout her life. We were released in time for Mom to deliver me at Mount Zion Hospital in San Francisco. Mom often reminded me that while she was in Agnews the doctors had encouraged her to have an abortion, practically begged her, but that she had forcefully declined.

"I always wanted you, Karen. My own mother never wanted me," she said, the smoke from her Marlboro veiling her long chestnut hair. "Do you have any idea how lucky you are?"

While Mom and Dad still proudly considered themselves bohemians, parenthood inspired Dad to find full-time work as a technical writer. To a casual observer, our lives wouldn't have appeared very different from those of other neighborhood families. Mom cleaned, cooked, and spent her days reading history while I played beside her with my imaginary friends on the floor near the blue chenille couch.

Every morning I would ask Mom how much she loved me.

"More than all the tea in China. More than all the coffee in Brazil. More than all the grains of sand at the beach," she'd answer. And I loved her more than all the stars in the Milky Way.

"I would never, ever leave you, Karen. The worst thing a mother can do is to abandon her child," Mom would sometimes say, and I couldn't help but wonder if she was considering that option.

If the observer had peeked through the window, the scene would have seemed benign. Mom was the most beautiful, kindest woman in the world, and I wanted nothing more than to play on the floor beside her.

But if the observer had listened closely, he might have grown suspicious. Though I was only five, when Mom came to a particularly compelling passage chronicling medieval tortures, such as the rack, the drawing and quartering of heretics, or perhaps the guillotine and the French Reign of Terror, she read to me aloud. The stories terrified me, and many nights I dreamed I was awaiting my turn at the guillotine, watching heads rolling into a basket.

"If we'd lived in Germany during the war, you and your dad would've been killed in the gas chambers," she sometimes casually mentioned. "But there is no way I would have let them take you from me. I would've gone in with you." Though I could tell she was trying to make me feel better, I found little comfort in Mom's offer to join me in my hypothetical asphyxiation. I hadn't yet discovered that our mother-daughter conversations were unusual. Had I even thought about it, I might have assumed all mothers spoke about concentration camps with their children.

Mom and I would stroll through the neighborhood, then down the hill into the Panhandle of Golden Gate Park, the misty air redolent of eucalyptus. It was 1963, Haight-Ashbury was a quiet working-class neighborhood, and the flower children had yet to arrive. The neighborhood merchants smiled as we passed. Mom turned heads with her curvy figure. On our way to the park, youthful mother and cherubic child, the baker greeted me with a cookie, the florist with a Gerbera daisy, and the barber with a lollipop. At the playground, we met other children and housewives from the neighborhood. The kids played on the swings and climbed tree stumps while the mothers sat on the green park benches chatting and reading paperbacks.

The highlight of our day was the arrival of the SFPD horse patrol. To the children in the park, the San Francisco mounted police officers were rock stars. Squealing with delight, we rushed to them as soon as we heard the clomping of approaching horseshoes, begging to pet their horses. The cops were always kind, showing us spots between the ears where the horses liked being scratched. When the uniformed men were around, I believed nothing bad could ever happen. They were as solid and stoic as the bronze statues of cavalrymen that were planted throughout the park.

Dad came home reliably at six o'clock, and we ate dinner as a family. Inspired by Julia Child, Mom cooked Dad elaborate gourmet dinners: beef bourguignon, veal scallopini, and a 1960s favorite, probably not Julia Child's recipe—tuna noodle casserole dappled with a potato-chip crust. In the evening, as they were cleaning up the kitchen, Mom and Dad pretended they were going to put me in the oven to cook me. One of them would carry me over while the other opened the oven door. I would giggle and scream, never revealing my terror. I always feared the game would go too far and they would actually cook me. The look in Mom's eyes made me wonder if the thought had occurred to her.

Then, almost overnight, that thin veil of normalcy over our family was pulled away. And suddenly, we were nothing like the other families. Mom became less interested in reading to me. She told me to stay in my room, and I spent hours lulling myself into a trance on my rocking horse. I began to miss the days of the scary history stories. I was curious about what she was doing and I missed her. When I finally snuck out to find her, she was often in bed and would tell me to go back to my room. I noticed the color of her eyes had faded to whitish-grey. When I was five, I didn't yet grasp the significance of Mom's change in eye color. Years later, I would grow to recognize and fear that first aura of an oncoming episode.

She began disappearing for hours on mysterious errands. "I'm running to the corner store, Karen," she would say, already on her way out. "I'll be back in a little while. Don't open the door for anyone." So began my early police training. To keep the gnawing fear of door-knocking strangers at bay, I would pretend I was invisible. From my vantage point in the bay window facing Masonic Avenue, awaiting Mom's return, I performed my first surveillance operations. I counted people going into St. Agnes' church, telling myself Mommy would return after one hundred had entered, knowing she would actually be back long before ten had come and gone. It was a small parish. Overestimating the length of time she would be away was a mental game I played to stay calm.

Mom would return, disheveled and smelling of wine, always just in time to start dinner before Daddy came home. One evening she ran in from an interminably long shopping trip. She tossed the groceries on the counter, threw me the peeler, and we began readying potatoes for stew. Soon a pot was simmering on the stovetop. I'd particularly missed her that day, so I hovered close, eager for her attention.

"Can I stir?" I reached up toward the spoon.

"You don't touch this!" she snapped.

She offered her thin, veiny fingers as I gave her my chubby starfish hand. I looked up into her eyes. She seemed about to caress my hand, then all at once swerved toward the aluminum pot, pushing my palm onto the hot metal.

I remember screaming, "No!" and trying to pull away, but she pushed back harder, overpowering my childish efforts. My hand seemed stuck to the pot, as if melting into it. I sensed if I kept pulling she wouldn't stop, so I let my body go limp as my hand absorbed the heat. When she let go, I threw up, retching long after my stomach was empty. She must've realized what she'd done at some point and called the doctor. I whimpered as he applied ointment to the burn and wrapped my hand in white gauze. My hand throbbed against the bandage, pulsing with each beat of my heart.

When Daddy came home at his usual time he said, "Karen, I hope you learned not to play with the stove." His slender fingers were shaking as he examined the dressing on my hand. *Had I really done this to myself?* "You should have known better."

Mom nodded in agreement. "Poor baby," she said. "You won't make that mistake again." Then she wrapped her arms around me and pulled me close. I melted into her and began softly crying with relief that she still loved me.

"Home Is a Place from Which You Run Away"

When I was a child, Mom's mood swings were mysterious, unpredictable storms. But by my teens, I started deciphering a pattern. Mom would be depressed but functional for a long while, sometimes for years at a time. During those periods, she smoked cigarettes by the carton, read furiously, and preferred to stay home. Then suddenly she would begin drinking heavily, and a manic episode would immediately follow.

When Mom was manic, I had no way of predicting what she might do next. So I began to only feel safe when Mom was depressed. Because Mom seemed happier when she was manic, I developed a near phobia of anyone who seemed too happy. I tended to feel safest with introverts and less exuberant personality types.

Mom seemed calmer after the kitchen episode, and I began to hope she was returning to her old self. I clung to the memory of the kind and beautiful mother she had once been. We returned to our old park routine.

My neighborhood friends were now old enough to play on the salvaged cable car in the larger children's playground at Golden Gate Park. At the small farmyard near the antique carousel, we fed chickens birdseed and shared our carrots with the goats. On special occasions, our mothers treated us to rides on the ornate merry-go-round. My favorite carousel pony was a caramel beauty. With his oatmeal-hued mane, he resembled my beloved mounted patrolman's horse. As the carousel revolved, I imagined riding through the park with the policemen.

Then my childhood exploded. I never really saw the baby; she was swaddled inside her carriage. We kids were on the cable car when it happened. I was pulling the rope on the bell.

"All aboard! Get your tickets!" *Ding, ding, ding!*

Suddenly, Mom howled, a long, primal cry. She stood with her hands in the carriage, shrieking, a look of horror on her face.

Just minutes before, I'd been sitting with Mom on the bench when a mother I'd never seen before asked her to watch her baby while she ran to the store. Everything had been fine. Now, dozens of mothers materialized from all over the park, circling the carriage.

"Call an ambulance!" shouted one. Another ran to the phone booth.

"Don't let the kids over here!" said a chubby blonde. She rushed to us, her blue gingham housedress flapping behind her like a superhero's cape, sliding to a stop with her hands on her hips.

"You children stay here and play. Don't go over there!"

"What's going on?" A choir of five-year-olds, we were desperate to know.

"Nothing. Don't worry. Just play!"

We pretended to play while spying on the proceedings. Telling us not to worry was a sure sign there was something to worry about. A police car and ambulance arrived. A paramedic tenderly lifted the baby from the carriage, wrapping her in something. *A blanket? A towel?* The officers stayed in the park, interviewing the mothers and writing in their little brown notebooks. Mom was chattering to a policeman, frantically waving her arms in the air.

When the baby's mother returned, the only sound in the park was her high-pitched keening. As she collapsed to her knees onto the gravel, two officers caught her beneath her arms and helped her to the bench. Sitting beside my playground friends, still believing myself to be one of them, a disturbing thought occurred to me. Had my mother done something to that baby?

I would never know exactly what happened that day, and I would never work up the nerve to ask Mom. Though it wasn't my best investigation, the baby in the park was my first suspicious death case.

The next morning, after Dad left for work, Mom dragged two gray suitcases from the closet and began a frenzy of packing. A half-hour later, we were in a Yellow Cab on the way to the Grey-hound station.

"Those bitches in the park are blaming me for that blue baby's death. We're getting out of here. We're leaving that bastard and going on an adventure, Karen. You're going to meet my family in New York." She glanced at my face. "Don't be sad, I'm doing you a favor. If you grow up with that neurotic bastard you'll end up as screwed up as he is. He's nuts because they shipped him off to that crazy school for genius kids. There is nothing more boring than a neurotic. But now we'll be free of him, thank God. I'm the only one who loves you. You don't need anyone else." She seemed very alive, full of energy. I hadn't yet learned that when Mom was at her most energetic she was deadly dangerous.

I had mixed feelings about the trip. Even at five years old, I understood we were running away from something and I wasn't sure how to feel about it. And what were we running from? The bitches in the park? Dad? I felt like a traitor for abandoning Dad. Though I didn't see him much because he worked long hours, I had never spent a night away from him before. Would we ever come back?

But part of me was excited by the idea of an adventure, and of meeting my relatives. Not only had I never met Mom's relatives, she'd never even shown me pictures of them. I'd never even seen a picture of her as a child.

"Yay! Will I meet my grandparents?"

I knew I was taking a chance by bringing up the subject. My park friends had grandparents, and I had always been a little envious. The one previous time I'd asked if I had grand-parents, Mom had snapped at me and told me not to waste my time thinking about them. But I couldn't stop longing for a big, extended family, other people I could rely on and maybe turn to when Mom was being mean. When Mom mentioned my grand-mother, she always called her "that bitch who never wanted me." She said her dad had spent his life drunk to escape "the bitch." But now, I felt a glimmer of hope that Mom might be willing to give her parents another chance.

"Maybe. You can meet Aunt Connie, maybe your Aunt Jean. Who the hell knows where your Aunt Kay is?" Mom took a long drag on her cigarette and gazed out the taxi window.

"Connie's a saint. She was my ally when I was a kid and had to put up with all the crap," she said, blowing smoke toward the roof of the cab. Hearing about my aunts was news to me. I couldn't remember Mom mentioning she had sisters.

We had been on the bus for three days when Mom met Nick. He was tall and sturdy, with a full head of curly black hair. The two of them stayed in the smoking section at the rear of the bus, kissing and hugging. I sat up front near the driver and gazed out the window, wondering if Mom and I would ever see Dad again and feeling horrible that I hadn't even said good-bye to him.

The driver told us we would stop in Chicago for an hour. We piled off the dark bus into the dark garage, then stepped into the bright yellow glow of the depot. Light bounced off the white tile floors and walls. The station reeked of ammonia; it was as if we'd stepped into a giant bathroom. I followed Mom to the snack bar, climbed onto a black vinyl stool and spun around three times for luck. When I stopped, Nick had disappeared.

"Where did Nick go, Mommy?"

"He went to get a shot."

I gasped, feeling panicky. I couldn't imagine what sort of place Chicago was where people were shot for no reason. *Was it like Germany?* Mom had told me that before the Nazis started killing people with gas, they'd shot people. *Was Nick being taken somewhere to be shot?*

Two police officers were sitting at the lunch counter, laughing and sipping coffee, oblivious to Nick's situation. I wondered if I should tell them. But I had no idea what to say. Maybe Mom meant Nick had gone somewhere to get a vaccination. I looked around for some clue.

"What the hell's the matter with you?" Mom asked. I stared down into the swirling milk clouds in her coffee, avoiding her eyes.

"I'm just worried about Nick getting shot."

Mom snorted out a laugh, some coffee dribbling out her nose.

"No, dummy. He's getting a shot of whiskey at the bar next door."

I hated when she laughed at me, but at least Nick was going to be OK. He seemed like a decent guy, and I always felt safer with Mom when witnesses were present.

"New York is a city and a state, so you say it twice," said Mom. But Nick had a house in New Jersey, so we got off there instead. "You only have to say New Jersey once," said Mom.

"We're going to live with Nick now. If anyone asks, say he's your father. Don't say one word about that bastard in San Francisco. Tell everyone your last name is Olsen. You're Karen Olsen, not Karen Nassberg. Understand?"

"Yes."

"Repeat your name."

"Karen Olsen."

"Good." She nodded and seemed relieved. Karen Olsen was my first undercover alias.

Nick's house was a ramshackle two-bedroom bungalow. The rooms were void of furnishings except for a couple of mattresses on the bedroom floors. Mom and Nick spent most of their time in their bedroom drinking wine. I figured they were doing the naked wrestling I had once accidently seen Mom and Dad doing. So I stayed out of their way, spending hours playing on the front steps, coloring, and reading the *Classic Comics* Nick bought me. *The Prince and The Pauper* was my favorite. Nick treated me kindly, but it annoyed me that Mom now had so little time for me.

"Karen!!" Mom was calling me from the toilet again. I knew this monthly ritual and a wave of revulsion hit me. I stepped into the bathroom and she handed me her saturated sanitary napkin.

"Put this in the trash." I walked to the kitchen carefully folding the pad in half and holding it as far from me as possible, holding my breath so I wouldn't have to smell it. I was never allowed to complain or say "yuck." Mom told me that only weaklings were squeamish about natural bodily functions. Fearing I might be a weakling, I buried the gruesome evidence at the bottom of the trashcan, then returned to my spot on the wooden stairs outside.

Sometimes, as I played, a policeman drove by in his black-and-white car and smiled at me. I waved at him every day, until Mom caught me.

"What the hell are you doing? The cops are not our friends! Do you want me to go to jail?"

After that, I didn't wave anymore. I couldn't imagine why the police would take Mom to jail. I wondered if it had something to do with the dead baby. Then I worried about what would happen to me if the police did take her to jail. I doubted Nick wanted to get stuck with a little kid. I had no idea that as far as Dad and the law were concerned, Mom had kidnapped me.

As we came out of the dime store one morning with some new comics, some people had stopped to watch a gray truck rolling slowly down Main Street. Some kind of creepy contraption was strapped onto a platform in the raised truck bed. Wires and a brown leathery hat hovered above an uncomfortable-looking wooden chair.

"Nick, what's that scary-looking thing?"

"That's an electric chair. Police kill bad people with it. The people driving the truck are protesting, showing everyone how awful it is. They don't want anyone killed in it anymore."

After that I couldn't stop picturing Mom in that chair, wearing that ugly helmet, and I was terrified for her.

Just as I was growing used to Nick, Mom told me we were ditching him and heading to New York. Mom said that Nick had turned out to be another bastard.

"When are we going home?" I asked.

There had always been certain words I was forbidden to say. Among others, I wasn't allowed to say *home*, *cozy*, or *cocoa*. Occasionally I forgot which words were forbidden.

"Dammit, Karen. Don't say 'home'! That word reminds me of your father and his idiotic poetry."

During their beatnik days, Dad once wrote a poem called "Home Is a Place from Which You Run Away." But it seemed to me Mom was the one who did the running.

From the city, we took a Port Authority bus to Brooklyn and found Aunt Connie's house. I was excited to learn I had a cousin, Stephanie, who was thirteen.

"I've always wanted my very own kid sister!" she told me.

Brooklyn was hot that summer, and we cooled off by running through water spurting from open fire hydrants. In the afternoon, when the Good Humor truck circled the neighborhood playing calliope music, we'd race behind the truck with our dimes clenched in our sweaty palms.

One time the Good Humor man wordlessly took my money, closed the back window, and drove off without giving me my ice cream.

"The Good Humor man took my dime and didn't give me anything!" I shouted.

"Hold this!" said Stephanie. She tossed me her Drumstick and took off in hot pursuit. Minutes later she ran back, holding up my Popsicle like an Olympic torch. The entire ice cream–eating crowd cheered for her. I hugged her hard. For the first time in my life I had backup, and I loved the feeling.

"When you gave the man your dime, did you ask him for anything?" Aunt Connie asked later.

"No, I didn't have a chance!" I replied defensively.

"Karen, you must always ask for what you need," she advised. It would take me decades to learn that lesson.

From the first day of the adventure, I harangued Mom, asking when I would meet my grandparents.

"You'll meet them soon. Stop nagging me!" Mom had said in New Jersey. But when we got to Brooklyn, her story changed. "Your grandparents are dead."

"What happened to them?" This was shocking news. I wondered if they had died recently or if they had been dead for a while and Mom had just heard the bad news.

"That's enough of your questions. Believe me, you're not missing a thing." She lit another cigarette with quivering hands and stormed out of the room.

That afternoon, I asked Stephanie how our grandparents died.

"Our grandparents aren't dead, silly! They live in Long Island. What made you think they were dead?" I thought it best to remain silent about that. *Did Mom lie to me? Did I misunderstand? Had Stephanie not yet heard the tragic news?* A new open case: The Missing Grandparents. "Do you have a picture of them?" I asked. Stephanie searched for a photo album. My childhood was full of mysteries that required detective skills to solve.

"I need to take care of some grownup business," Mom said before disappearing and leaving me with my aunt. I quickly grew to love Aunt Connie and even wished she were my mom. Sometimes I fantasized about Mom not returning and felt some relief at the idea. I could stay here and grow up with Stephanie; we could pretend to be sisters. Then I immediately felt guilty for thinking such a thing.

Mom returned from her mystery trip a few days later, never saying where she'd been. That night I tossed and turned in my sticky bed, missing foggy San Francisco and my Dad. As I cried, Aunt Connie stroked my hair and sang softly, "Too-ra-loo-ra-loo-ral, Too-ra-loo-ra-li."

"Everything will be OK," she promised.

How could she know how far from the truth that was? I finally fell asleep. But minutes later, Mom was screaming.

"We need to get out of here right now. He's coming! Get up! Now!"

A minute later, the doorbell rang. In the darkness, I could barely make out the silhouettes of two policemen in the hallway. A third man walked beside them, and I trembled with fear, thinking the police had brought some crazy bad man to get us. Then I worried maybe they had come for Mom to put her in that electric chair.

"Balls! Why the hell did you let him in, Connie?" yelled Mom.

"I had to, Ann. He brought the police."

Then I recognized the third man. It was Dad. I wasn't sure if I should hug him. Would she be mad if I did? Would he be mad if I didn't? Not certain what to do, I remained very still. But secretly I was relieved to know our "adventure" was over.

Lifesavers

We rode the Greyhound back to San Francisco with Dad. Mom wasn't happy about it, but she said we were broke so we had no choice. She barely said a word during the five-day trip. She just stared out the murky window, chain smoking. Dad sat on the aisle seat beside her and told me to sit behind them. He never let her out of his sight.

When Mom got up to use the toilet in the back of the bus, Dad hopped into the seat beside me and started his interrogation.

"How long were you at Aunt Connie's?"

I had no idea. Weeks? Months? I didn't have a chance to answer before Dad picked up the pace of his questioning.

"Where did you go before Aunt Connie's?"

I was nervous about telling him. I didn't know all the rules about marriage, but I knew enough to think Dad would not like Mom kissing another guy and changing my last name to Olsen. I hesitated. Dad looked at me expectantly.

"Well?"

"New Jersey."

Luckily Mom returned to her seat before his questioning continued.

Dad had to abandon our apartment when he started searching for us. But he'd purchased a new Volkswagen Beetle, and I was excited about that. We found a sunny studio apartment on Grove Street with big bay windows and the three of us moved in. I jumped up and down on my parent's double bed to celebrate their reunion.

"Don't get your hopes up," Mom warned.

I really wanted to get my hopes up. I hoped Mom and Dad would stay together forever and that Mom would not take me on any more adventures. I continued believing Mom would eventually return to the way she had once been.

Mom had put on some weight since New Jersey. Her belly protruded over the elastic waistband of her stretch pants. We'd only been home a few weeks when she woke up screaming in the dark, doubled over with pain.

"Dave, take me to the hospital!"

We ran to the car and Dad sped to the emergency room. We rushed through the hospital door, blood gushing from between Mom's legs and flooding her favorite loafers. The red was garish and startling on the fluorescent white of the hospital floor. As I ran behind Mom, slipping in her blood, a nurse grabbed my hand and hurried me to the waiting room.

"Sit here and wait for your dad."

A policeman was the only other person in the room. He was sitting in a plastic chair, leaning over his magazine, and looked up as I came in. I noticed his hat in the seat beside him. I had never seen a hatless policeman before. He seemed naked without it, an imposter.

"How are you?" His voice was deep and raspy.

During the adventure Mom had warned me not to talk to the police. I wondered if it would be OK to talk to him now that we were home.

"Would you like a Lifesaver?" he asked, holding out his pack. That settled it.

"Sure. Thank you." He let me take cherry, my favorite. "I don't like the green ones," I said.

"Me neither. Nobody likes them. Why do they even make green ones?" He had a generous smile. "You might as well sit down. Looks like we might be here a while."

"I'm scared," I quietly told my shoes. My formerly white sneakers were now mottled with red splotches. I was worried Mom would be angry I got my shoes dirty.

"Don't worry. It'll be OK. Here, take the pack."

I wondered how he could be so sure Mom would be OK, but I figured since he was a policeman he might have some inside information. I took the candy and decided to think about something else.

After a while, Dad came in. His face was white and his hands were trembling. He took my hand and stared into my eyes.

"Your mommy is very ill. She may die. Do you understand what that means?"

"Like the baby in the park?"

"Yes, like that. Do you want to come with me to see her?"

"OK."

He led me into the treatment room. It smelled terrible, like the Mr. Clean my mother used to mop the kitchen floor before she stopped doing housework. And there was another smell—a sensation, lingering, filling my mouth with a coppery metal taste.

The nurse shook her head at Dad. A white sheet covered all of Mom except her ashen face. Dad looked over at Mom and let out a small yelp. Then he covered his mouth with his hand, as if to keep more from escaping.

"Say good-bye to your mother, Karen." Slow-motion tears snail-trailed down his cheeks. I bent down and briefly put my lips on Mom's cool cheek. Her eyes were creepily glassy, and she didn't move when I touched her.

"I love you, Mommy."

A week after our trip to the hospital Mom was back home, and Dad and I were perched on the end of her bed.

"Let me tell you. Bleeding to death is a horrible way to die!" Mom always said "haarrible" with her New York accent. "I was so thirsty! I was dying of thirst! Then I was floating around above my bed, looking down at my body and the doctors and nurses trying to save me. I could have just floated away. But I thought about you, Karen, and I knew I had to come back. I came back for you!"

Wow! Mom turned down heaven for me? I felt a surge of relief that Mom had kept her promise to never leave me. But I had some questions about the incident.

"How does blood just start pouring out of a person for no reason? Do people die that way all the time?" I wanted to make sense of this seemingly random disaster, afraid this mysterious bleeding might strike me next.

"Your mommy had a miscarriage. That's when a mom is going to have a baby but it doesn't survive and it comes out."

"Bullshit, Dave. Tell her the truth. It was the botched abortion I had in New York."

I didn't know what that meant, and I knew better than to ask.

"We're leaving that bastard for good now," Mom announced out of the blue one morning a few weeks later. "I'm divorcing him, and you'll get to see the son of a bitch on weekends. The judge says he only has to pay me $125 a month for child support. No alimony. But thank God, we won't have to live with him anymore!"

A hot surge of panic shot through me. Alone again with Mom? Mom had told me nearly every day how unhealthy it was for me to live with Dad, but I still loved him, although I pretended to be

aloof when Mom was nearby. Any affection I displayed toward
Dad would be seen as a blatant act of betrayal.

We moved a few blocks away to a boarding house for single
mothers and their children. During her army days, Mom had
been trained to operate a switchboard, so she began searching
for work and was hired by an insurance company in the financial
district.

"How do they expect people to survive on this kind of salary?"
Mom said as she read her first pay stub. "Karen, when you grow
up, you should be a nurse. I wanted to be one, but it didn't work
out for me. Nurses can work anywhere in the world and they
will always be needed." That was true. Throughout Mom's life,
nurses would be needed more times than I could count.

When she was in a good mood, she read me *The Wind in
the Willows* in our top bunk while we munched peanut brittle.
Sometimes she put her arm around me and we snuggled against
the pillows. Though I missed Dad, in those moments I loved
having her all to myself. I wanted the two of us to stay huddled
together in that bunk forever.

At first, Dad came every weekend and took me to the Presi-
dio, where we explored the old army base and plucked wild mint
from the hills. Then we headed to Chinatown for savory seaweed
soup, or to Caffè Trieste, where he sipped strong black espresso
while I guzzled Italian soda. But soon his visits dwindled, and
some days my chest ached from the pain of his absence.

"Karen, I have some exciting news," he said one day while we
were snuggling on the lumpy boarding house sofa. I held my
breath, bracing myself. In my life so far, exciting news had never
been good news.

"I enlisted in the army, and they're sending me to Germany.
Do you know where that is?"

"No. Is it far?" I only remembered Germany as the place where Mom said Dad and I would have been killed for being Jewish.

"Yes, it's in Europe, very far away. You have to fly for hours to get there."

"Will I ever see you again?"

"Of course, Bunny! I won't be there forever!" He laughed, shaking his head as if he'd never heard such a crazy question. Breathing in his sweet, spicy scent, I hugged him for an extralong time, then kissed his scratchy cheek.

The next time I saw him, I was in high school.

The Kindness of Strangers

Mom didn't stay single long, and a few months later I had a new alias. Alan Crenshaw was dashing, at least according to Mom. He was tall, blond, and suave, and she fell in love with him on their first date when he jumped out of his Porsche convertible in front of a florist and filled her arms with dozens of roses. But I never fell for him. I eyed him with suspicion and viewed him as a new rival for Mom's attention. His feeble attempts to woo me with cheap paper dolls fell flat.

One evening, he arrived at the boarding house bearing a gift I couldn't ignore. I was six years old and had opened my share of presents, but this one took my breath away. Inside a foot-tall glass case stood a spectacular geisha doll. Her kimono was red satin, and her obi, sparkling ivory. I named her Ami. I would never love Alan, but I had to hand it to him, he did have good taste in dolls. However, my relationship with Ami was fraught. Confined for eternity to her glass prison, she was a doll only to be admired, not touched.

Soon Alan flew us to Japan, where he was living and doing business. Floating above the Pacific for what seemed like days, we traveled regally on Pan Am from San Francisco to Tokyo. When we stopped to refuel in Hawaii, beautiful island girls greeted us with plumeria leis, as if we were honored guests staying for weeks, instead of just passing through. At the airport bar Mom treated me to a coconut drink topped with a paper umbrella.

"Wow! Is this coconut juice?"

"No, coconuts have milk. That's pineapple juice."

She lifted her coconut to the room in a toast. "This is how it looks to be in love!" The bar customers applauded

Alan booked us into the Palace Hotel in Tokyo, the most elaborate building I'd ever seen. From our room's window, we looked down on the grounds of the Imperial Palace.

"Will we get to see the Emperor and Empress?" I asked.

"Maybe. We'll see."

Jetlagged, I fell asleep as soon as I lay down on my cot beside their bed.

Ravenous hunger and the squeaking of bedsprings woke me a few hours later. Alan's naked behind rose and fell mere inches from my face. Mom was invisible, but was whispering, "Oh God!!"

As great as my hunger was, I wasn't foolish enough to interrupt naked wrestling. But finally, I could not stand it any longer. I felt my stomach devouring itself.

"Mom, I'm hungry," I said, softly. When she didn't answer, I waited.

"Mom, I'm hungry." I increased my volume a notch. They continued bouncing like circus clowns on a trampoline.

"Mom! I am very hungry!" I was shouting. Alan and Mom stopped for a moment.

"Go down to the restaurant and order breakfast," said Mom, slightly out of breath. "Tell them to charge it to your room." The squeaking resumed as I pulled on my dress.

I inched toward the elevators, unsure what to do. The thought of walking into a restaurant alone petrified me. And I didn't even know where the dining room was. I rode down to the lobby and wandered around hesitantly until, by luck, I happened upon the restaurant. I stood by the door pretending to read the menu. One side was in English, the other Japanese, and I could only read a few words. Despite my hunger, I couldn't gather the courage to enter. I felt embarrassed, as if I would be committing some sort of crime. I was afraid people might laugh at a six-year-old just walking in and charging breakfast to her room. I couldn't remember ever seeing a child do something like that, even in San Francisco.

I wandered back to the lobby and stood staring at the young, pretty elevator operators. If I returned to the room too soon and interrupted again, Mom would be furious. But I was so hungry.

"Good morning to you!" said one of girls. When the operators were waiting for calls, they passed their time chatting, keeping the doors open until the next customer rang. I decided to stay on the elevator with Miko—that's what her name tag said—and spent hours riding with the girls. They seemed to welcome the diversion, or maybe the opportunity to practice their English, and they taught me a few words of Japanese during our time together.

"Say *arigato-go-zei-masu*," said Miko. "That means 'thank you.'"

I repeated, "Arigato-go-zei-masu."

"Say *ohayou*. That means 'good morning.'" *Good morning* was easy to remember because it sounded like the American state Ohio.

Foreigners were still rare in Japan, and my unusual appearance attracted attention. The girls paraded me through the hotel like a newly adopted exotic pet. They called me Karen-san, and I began fantasizing Miko and her friend might keep me and allow me to live and work with them. They treated me to a bento lunch at the café, then took me to the gift shop and outfitted me with a red kimono, obi, and slippers. I was thrilled that I looked just like Ami. By the time I returned to the room, Alan and Mom were asleep, and I was dressed like a geisha and had acquired taste for sashimi.

Alan rented us a house in a town called Ogikubo, and Mom enrolled me in kindergarten. My new alias was Karen Crenshaw. I practiced writing *Crenshaw* over and over. Mom said I was to tell anyone who asked that Alan was my father. This proved to be easier than in New Jersey, because here, if anyone spoke to me, I only stared blankly. It would take months before I understood even elementary Japanese.

At lunchtime, the other children in their freshly pressed blue uniforms all brought out bento boxes filled with hard-boiled eggs, fish, rice, and fruit. I had nothing. But it wasn't hunger that made me uncomfortable; it was the embarrassment of not conforming. I came from a strange planet where mothers did not pack lunches for their children.

Ogikubo was a verdant paradise, full of pastoral open spaces and fields of wildflowers where children ran free and chased butterflies with nets. I loved the fragrance of the tatami floor I slept on and the fragile, hypnotic light that peeked at me through the shoji screen. Mom and Alan mostly ignored me, and we lived a peaceful life in the town for several months.

We did our food shopping in an open-air market with a crowded, flea-market atmosphere. It was a humid day, and I was sweaty and a little whiny. Mom was becoming irritated with me. I looked up and saw that the color of her eyes had changed. My hair stood on end, and I immediately stopped whining. We'd been standing in the sun at the fishmonger's, and I looked away briefly. When I turned around, Mom had vanished. I roamed through the vegetable stalls and soon realized I didn't know my way back home. I was seized with panic, realizing I was lost in a foreign country and could not speak the language. All at once the emotion of the past year overwhelmed me in a wave of something like exhaustion. Although losing my dad had been upsetting and confusing, until this moment I had never before felt abandoned. Now, in the middle of this market surrounded by people I couldn't understand, I was completely alone. Mom had been right. The very worst thing that could happen would be my mother abandoning me. I swore to myself if she found me I would never whine again. But would she even look for me? Could I survive without her? I became frantic. My head bobbled, searching in every direction. Then I spotted a teenage boy riding up to me on his bicycle.

"Are you lost?" He asked in perfect English.

"Yes." I couldn't even tell him my address, but described my neighborhood and a few landmarks. He gently lifted me onto the seat of his bike and hopped back onto the pedals. He placed my hands around his small waist. I wasn't afraid of him at all. He seemed kind and gentle. Even at six, Mom was the only person I was wary of. By comparison, everyone else was calm and predictable.

"Hold on!" he said, and I'd never felt safer. My sadness suddenly evaporated as we came upon a huge field of sunflowers. We turned onto a path and soon we were lost in the tall, yellow flowers.

"I didn't know flowers could be so big!" I shouted. They billowed over our heads and smiled down at us. They seemed to have individual personalities. We were both laughing with joy.

He escorted me to the door of our house, and Mom slid back the shoji screen, barely acknowledging my rescuer. She did not seem at all surprised to see me. I wondered if she'd even noticed my absence. My new friend waved good-bye and rode away.

"We're going back to San Francisco," Mom said. "Pack your stuff."

"Can I say good-bye to my friends?"

"There's no time for sentimentality. That bastard burned my book!" Mom had occasionally mentioned she was working on a book of historical fiction about Lady Jane Grey, though I couldn't recall ever seeing her write. "He threw it in the fireplace and burned it to a crisp. Years and years of my life's work, gone! Ruined! We're getting out of here right now." She pushed a suitcase toward me.

During the months we'd lived together, Alan and I rarely spoke. After Nick, I had learned it was not a good idea to care much about my make-believe fathers. Anyway, it was obvious from the beginning Alan would have preferred it if I had not been around. I could hardly blame him. He hadn't signed up to be my dad. He had a real daughter back in San Francisco. So when we left, I wasn't sad to leave him, but I was sad to leave my friends and the beautiful town, and I dreaded what adventure Mom might have in store next.

"Pack!" urged Mom.

The next day we were back in San Francisco.

When we returned to the boarding house, I was relieved Ami was on the shelf where I'd left her months before. I dusted her case, then modeled my kimono for her and told her about my adventures in Japan.

"See? We're twins now!"

A few days later, I came home from school and found Ami missing from her shelf. I searched our room, and fearing the worst, ran downstairs to find Mom. She was sitting in the front room under her usual veil of smoke.

"What happened to Ami?" I tried to make my tone nonchalant. If Mom had taken her as some sort of punishment, I didn't dare show her how much I cared.

"Oh, Alan came by today. He took the doll and said he was giving it to his real daughter." She puffed smoke with irritation and paused. "He said you didn't deserve it." A smirk flickered across her face.

Chinatown

It didn't take long for Mom to become miserable at the boarding house.

"I was not meant to live in some ridiculous communal situation! The women in this house are illiterate boobs! I have to find a way for us to get out of this dump, Connie." She often called me by her sister's name.

After returning to the switchboard, she saved enough money to move us away from the illiterate boobs. She found a studio for rent just over the hill from Chinatown. The back gate of Spring Valley, my new elementary school, was directly across the street from our apartment.

When I took my seat for the first day of second grade and looked around, I noticed everyone else in my class was Chinese American. After school, my classmates attended yet another two hours of Chinese school. Though I longed to be like the other kids, I doubted Mom would enroll me.

The children at Spring Valley had formed their cliques by kindergarten, and I was a round-eyed Janey-come-lately. This was my first conscious experience with a caste system. I soon figured out if that I wanted any friends, I would need to identify the other outcasts and misfits and attach myself to them. The American-born Chinese kids, or "ABCs," had the highest status. Many of their families had been in California since the Gold Rush, and most spoke English only. The newer immigrants were called "FOBs," for "Fresh Off the Boat." The ABCs looked down on the FOBs, mocking their old-country ways and unfashionable clothing. It didn't take me long to deduce which caste might consider me for membership.

Mom said she couldn't afford to give me lunch money, so she suggested I just grab whatever was in the house. Given that Mom had stopped shopping, and we tended to survive on chow mein from the local deli, my lunch-bag choices were limited. But when our teacher, Miss Connor, announced that the school cafeteria needed help and mentioned that volunteers received free lunch as payment, I jumped at the opportunity. Each day at noon I scooped canned string beans and entrees featuring Spam onto my classmate's plastic trays, then sat down for lunch with my mostly FOB coworkers.

After school, we played foursquare and Chinese jump rope in the schoolyard until the yard duty monitor kicked us out. Then I headed across the street to watch family sitcoms until Mom got home from work. I passed the time in half-hour segments brought to me by mountain-grown Folgers and Palmolive soap. Watching *Leave It to Beaver* led me to believe that the rest of the country lived quite differently than we did. I interpreted television sitcoms as documentaries and studied them with rapt fascination, like an anthropologist observing a newly discovered tribe. I believed if I could learn to mimic their behaviors I might eventually pass for normal. I defined "normal" as anyone who was the opposite of Mom.

I noticed many of the FOBs at Spring Valley were also friendless. The new immigrants did not play together much, maybe trying to camouflage themselves among the other students. The recent immigrants, already fluent in Chinese, did not attend Chinese school. Their afternoons were free, as were mine, and many were also latchkey children. Their parents juggled multiple jobs, and the kids were expected to take care of themselves.

One day as I came into class I noticed a new girl, beautiful, with very round features and a friendly smile.

"Mae has just immigrated here from the Szechuan province," Miss Connor said. "She speaks Mandarin, not Cantonese. We should all help her feel welcome and help her get used to the way we do things."

I could feel my chest puffing as our teacher spoke. Yes, now I had a mission. I appointed myself Mae's ambassador, knowing the other kids weren't going to be fighting to play with her anyway. Whether Mae liked it or not, she was going to be my new best friend. Well OK, not new or best—let's face it, she would be my only friend.

Mae lived up the hill, and from that day on, we played together, communicating with gestures and our own version of sign language. Before long, we were racing back and forth to each other's apartments scrounging snacks, doing our homework, and collecting rubber bands to fashion our Chinese jump ropes.

Mae's mother worked nights in a restaurant, so she always left Mae and her sister a big pot of soup simmering on the stove and a steaming rice cooker on the kitchen counter. Full of bok choy and pork, delicious and savory, that soup was our comfort food. I never knew if Mae's mother was aware she was feeding an extra child.

Some days we ran over the hill to Chinatown and played at the Chinese Recreation Center. Other days, we explored near Cameron House, a social-service agency for Asians, searching alleys, trying to find the secret passageways to San Francisco's underground tunnels. One of the entrances was rumored to be inside Cameron House. We would casually look around for the entrance, pretending to be spies.

An old man from the neighborhood often asked us if we wanted "white pennies," then gave us handfuls of dimes. We used the White Penny Man's spare change to purchase our favorite snacks: salty red ginger, preserved plums called *moy*, and dried sweet and salty fish. The flavors reminded me of Japan, and I liked them right away. In my latest imaginary movie, I was playing the role of a Chinese American girl who had been stolen away from her real family. Someday, I hoped, they would find and reclaim me.

Mom and I often spent the evenings with a tribe of Bohemians we had joined at A Big Little Store, a used bookstore on Polk Street. The owner, Jim, told us he chose the name so the bookstore would be the first one people would notice when they opened the Yellow Pages. Jim was a big, handsome man who reminded me of a slightly overweight Richard Burton. He had two children who were often at the store. Steve was three, Barb was five, and I was seven when we first met. During the week they lived with their mom in Mill Valley, and I looked forward to the weekends when we would all play in the bookstore under Jim and Mom's relaxed supervision. We amused ourselves in the back rooms of the store, climbing mountains of boxes of used books, pretending we were summiting "Mount Never-Rest." I embraced Steve and Barb as long-awaited siblings.

While we kids played, the adults relaxed on folding chairs near Jim's cash register, drinking wine and talking politics. On rare occasions, someone would purchase a book. After he closed for the night, Mom and I had dinner with Jim, and sometimes with my new pretend siblings. As his marriage ended, Jim began spending nights at our apartment.

I had a different feeling about Jim than I'd had about the other men in Mom's life. Jim seemed to actually like me. One day, I stayed home from school with a sore throat while Mom went to work. All day, as I lay in bed, I imagined cool, soothing refreshments. Just as I was dreaming of popsicles, Jim let himself in with his key. He delivered a shopping bag full of Campbell's soups, popsicles, and ginger ale, unloading everything onto the kitchen counter. He must have locked up his bookstore to go to the store for me. Miraculously healed upon seeing the contents of Jim's bag, I bounced up and down on my bed. He laughed, watching me.

"How did you know? How did you know? I was dying for a popsicle!"

"Your mom said you had a sore throat, so I took a wild guess," he smiled.

Wow! I felt like hugging him, but restrained myself. After all, who knew how long he would hang around?

When Mom and Jim decided to try living together, we found a new apartment just around the corner from the bookstore. The front room alone was larger than our entire studio had been. They agreed that marriage was just a meaningless piece of paper and said they didn't need a document to legitimize their partnership. Jim used to say, "We'll stay together as long as it's good." But it never seemed all that good to me. They bickered and fought from the start, and Mom rarely showed him much affection. When Jim wrapped his arms around her, she often stood coldly motionless. They referred to each other as "partners," and as the new business grew, they actually did become partners of a sort.

The young people who virtually lived in the store began multiplying. They wore their hair long, smoked marijuana, and called themselves "flower children." Jim noticed they sometimes wore buttons pinned to their jackets with political opinions printed on them, so he decided he'd try selling a few in the bookstore. Within days, flower children were flooding the store, clamoring for buttons. Jim, Mom, and the tribe now spent their days bouncing around ideas for new button slogans.

"'Ayn Rand is Ronald Reagan in drag,'" quipped Mom.

"'Go intercourse thyself,'" suggested Jim.

"'Once you've seen one redwood tree, you've seen them all,'" Mom said. She hated Ronald Reagan and loved quoting the governor's faux pas.

"'Jesus is God's atom bomb!'" yelled a tribemate.

"'Chastity is its own punishment!'" said another.

"'I am a human being; do not fold, spindle, or mutilate,'" replied Jim.

"'Support mental health or I'll kill you!'" said Mom. The group laughed, a bit nervously.

This was the nightly show at A Big Little Store. They passed around a jug of Mountain Red wine, filling their coffee mugs. When they passed a joint, the button ideas grew even more random. Mom and Jim guzzled wine but rarely smoked pot. Mom said she didn't like the way it made her feel. Secretly, I wished she'd smoke more of it. She was calmer and kinder the few times I'd seen her stoned.

Then Mom and Jim would close the store and move us on to a tribemate's apartment. Leaf and Sparrow, two of the hippie kids who worked for Jim, rented a studio in the neighborhood. The partying went on late into the night, and sometimes I fell asleep on their couch. When it was finally time to go home, Jim would lift me over his shoulder in a fireman's carry. Floating comfortably, I pretended to be asleep as he toted me home. I enjoyed being close to him and didn't want him to put me down, but when I was not "asleep" I kept my distance. Though I hadn't cared much about leaving Nick or Alan, and had pretended to be nonchalant about Dad's absence, losing Dad had hurt me deeply. I still believed that someday he would return for me. I desperately wanted him to love and miss me, and I was afraid if I showed Jim any affection I would somehow be betraying Dad. I also suspected Mom might dump Jim without warning, so I was wary of becoming too attached.

When we got to our apartment, Jim would tuck me in, and I'd continue pretending to be asleep as he kissed me gently on the forehead. Then the part of the night I hated would start.

"Why don't you just go back to Sheila? All you really want is some mealy-mouthed yes-woman! You can't handle a real woman! 'Yes dear, no dear, you're absolutely right, dear!'" Mom could continue like this for long stretches.

"Come on, Ann. That's enough. Let's go to bed," Jim said.

"For once, I wish I could have an intelligent conversation with my intellectual equal! Dave may have been neurotic, but he had an IQ of 160. I wouldn't even guess what you scored on an IQ test, if they even gave them in your hillbilly town!"

"Ann, knock it off." Jim refused her bait. This would only frustrate her more.

"A battle of the wits with an unarmed man! God help me! Why do I keep ending up with loser after loser?"

One night Mom struck an unusually low blow.

"No wonder Marge killed herself! Who wouldn't, after living with you?"

In my bed I cringed when she said that. Jim had made the mistake of sharing the sad story of his long-ago first marriage, and now Mom would repeatedly use it against him. But this time, she had pushed him to the brink.

"You're *evil*, Ann!"

That particular exchange haunted me. As I grew older, I sometimes reflected on Jim's assessment of Mom's character that night, and I wondered if Mom was truly an evil person. Was she evil or mentally ill? I wrestled with that question for decades. If she were evil, then I would be justified in escaping her. If she were ill, wouldn't I be a bad daughter if I abandoned her?

During their fights, I often pretended to sleep. But when their voices became too loud, I sidled into the front room and stood between them. When I was small, the simple presence of a sleepy eight-year-old was all that was needed for effective conflict resolution. But as I got older and less cute, I had to develop other tools of intervention.

Mom quit her job at the insurance company switchboard, saying she was tired of working for the capitalist pigs anyway, and she began working full-time with Jim. They were selling buttons faster than the factory could produce them, and Jim's store was finally making decent money. On days the store was closed, we walked picket lines with Cesar Chavez's farm workers, trudging around supermarkets passing out buttons bearing La Huelga's logo. Other days, we marched in Vietnam War protests, often selling buttons to the crowds. Overnight we had become capitalist-pig hippies.

My First Steady Partner

Mae eventually moved to another neighborhood, and I found myself searching for a new best friend. Then Monica transferred to our school, and we bonded because of our mutual outcast status as the only non-Chinese kids in our third-grade class. Her mom, Janette, was Mexican American, and Monica had inherited her beautiful café au lait complexion. They lived in a one-bedroom apartment above Jim's bookstore.

Within days of meeting, Monica and I became inseparable, migrating up and down the stairs between her apartment and the bookstore. Janette was a single mom and worked swing shifts as a nurse. She hired a young woman named Mona to watch Monica during the evenings. It didn't take us long to deduce that Mona was a complete airhead. After school, we would tell Mona we were going to the playground, then disappear, not returning until 8:00 p.m. or later. Jim and Mom were too busy running the store to notice our absence, and Mona believed whatever we told her.

Some days we really did go to the playground, where we spent hours on the swings, floating beside the traffic speeding into the Broadway tunnel. But we spent most days playing "Harriet the Spy." Inspired by the children's novel, we identified certain neighborhood suspects and clumsily followed them through city streets, logging arbitrary evidence of imaginary crimes into our notebooks. Since we lived in Polk Gulch, we could walk in any direction and find interesting spots to perform our intelligence operations. Monica was my first steady patrol partner.

We seldom saw anything truly suspicious, so we were forced to concoct stories about the lives of the strangers we observed. We decided one man in Chinatown was a former bank robber on the run from federal authorities. We "investigated" a North Beach artist for fraudulently reproducing famous artwork. We never brought a case to the District Attorney, but for years two small girls walked a volunteer foot patrol through the streets of San Francisco.

Buttons were taking over our lives. Jim closed the bookstore, deciding it would be more lucrative to operate the button business as a mail-order operation from our apartment. We moved his handmade plywood bookshelves into our front room, where they lined the walls, now brimming with button containers instead of paperbacks.

Jim took us shopping at the neighborhood supermarket, Cala Foods, and I was stunned at the vastness of the store, having previously only shopped with Mom at corner markets for a couple of items at a time. When Jim took us shopping he bought more than twenty different items. I was excited at the prospect of having supplies. It had never occurred to me that most people shopped for enough food to last a few days or longer.

One night, when the three of us had stopped at the corner Baskin-Robbins after dinner, Jim noticed the clerk tossing dozens of round cardboard ice cream cartons into the dumpster behind the store.

"Hey, those would be perfect for storing buttons," Jim told Mom.

When Jim asked the storeowner if we could take them, he said, "Go ahead, knock yourself out." Monica and I were then assigned the weekly task of collecting as many discarded ice cream cartons as we could carry. The owner was happy to get rid of the debris, and we were happy to do the errand because Jim paid us in ice cream.

After school, Mom and I pulled the orders for delivery. On Mondays, we shipped out mass mailings of catalogs, then filled the orders each day as they came in. On the front of each recycled ice cream carton, we pinned a sample of the button inside. Mom opened the mail and called out titles and quantities. I located the bin and counted the buttons into manila envelopes, doing my best to avoid being jabbed by the pins. Bloody fingertips were a job hazard, but I didn't mind because Mom was grateful for my help.

"Three 'Ban the Bra,'" Mom read.

"Three 'Ban the Bra.'" I repeated each order to ensure quality control.

"Ten 'Hell No, We Won't Go.'"

"Five 'God Is on a Trip.'"

"Four 'War Is Unhealthy for Children and Other Living Things.'"

"Ten, 'Make Love, Not War.'"

"Thirty 'Jesus Is Coming, and Man, Is He Pissed.'"

"Fifty 'What if They Gave a War and Nobody Came?'"

"Twenty 'I Love Mankind. It's People I Can't Stand.'"

For months, this was how we spent our afternoons. When we were done, we addressed envelopes and marked each one "hand cancel" so the buttons wouldn't be squished in the giant stamp-canceling machines. Then we headed to the post office before it closed. I couldn't remember ever having more fun with Mom.

Occasionally, Dad would send me a postcard. When I was nine, I received one from his base in England showing Queen

Elizabeth perched, in all her regalia, on the edge of her throne. He'd scribbled a note: "Isn't this a pretty picture of the queen? Love, Dad."

His postcard left me feeling vaguely insulted. The message felt condescending, as if in his mind I remained chronologically where he had last seen me, forever frozen at age six. I had long since stopped thinking of myself as a child. It annoyed me that he didn't realize I was now a mature working woman.

Jim opened a head shop on Grant Avenue, kitty-corner from the legendary bohemian hangout Caffè Trieste. He named the store Up Against the Wall, in parody of the saying made famous by Los Angeles cops, "Up against the wall, motherfucker!" The name was also a fun play on words, since the store's main staple would be posters. Jim loved puns, yet another reason Mom was forever annoyed with him.

After run-ins with the law as a young man during civil-rights protests in Georgia, Jim had no great love for police. He had spent time in jail in Atlanta and told us the police there had sometimes beaten him. Then the army forced him to be in the Military Police because he was big and strong. He hated being an MP and resented being assigned to work he despised. He deplored machismo and bullying of any sort and he found some of his fellow MPs sadistic. But Jim never approved of people referring to cops as "pigs." Though it wasn't unusual to hear one of our hippie tribe talking about some harassment they'd endured from the "pigs," I never heard Jim use the word, and we kids knew better than to say it.

Crammed with thousands of colorful posters, bumper stickers, and buttons, the Grant Avenue store became our playground. It was stocked with Zig-Zag rolling papers, hookah pipes, and love beads, and scented with sandalwood and musk oil. To add to the atmosphere, we shared space with Gorilla Records, where hard rock blasted night and day.

Barb and I sat behind the counter with Jim, stringing love beads to sell at the peace marches. Jim had rigged a black-light room in back, where he displayed dozens of Day-Glo concert posters from The Fillmore and Avalon Ballroom. We kids loved playing in that room. If one of us wore a white shirt, it was especially fun to watch each other glow in the dark. We danced to the Rolling Stones and played freeze tag, switching the black lights on and off. It was 1967, and we were loving the Summer of Love in San Francisco.

When Jim delivered merchandise to the shops on Haight Street, I sometimes tagged along, wearing my poncho, love beads, and peace symbol necklace, pretending to be his assistant. As we walked the Haight, street dealers announced the type of acid they were selling without a care they were advertising LSD to a nine-year-old and her presumed father.

"Windowpane," the dealer sang, as we passed.

Jim also let me work behind the counter at Up Against the Wall, and I enjoyed feeling useful. My desire to help was in part fueled by my suspicion that Mom was not pulling her weight in the Jim and Ann so-called partnership. Mom talked a lot about feminism, suffragettes, and equal rights, but Jim was apparently doing all the work. And Mom was so mean and Jim so forgiving that I feared he would get sick of her awful treatment and kick us out. I became good at operating the cash register and making change, hoping to make myself indispensable to him and earn our keep.

One night, after I sold a woman some buttons, Jim looked over at me with his eyes wide and eyebrows raised. Had I given someone the wrong change?

"Do you know who that was?"

"No, who?" I asked.

"That was Janis Joplin!"

"Wow!" At nine years old I was more into folksy Joan Baez and Joni Mitchell, but I'd heard Joplin's name, and from the frenzy of excitement coming from the guys over at the Gorilla Records counter, I figured she must be a big deal.

Mom loved to go to the gay piano bars and sing show tunes with the boys. Some nights Jim and Mom took me with them to the Improv club on Broadway. Those were always good times. We loved calling out skit suggestions to the actors on stage. The club had a two-drink minimum, but neither of them ordered more than two because of the inflated prices, so they both stayed relatively sober and enjoyed themselves.

But carefree nights were exceptions. Though peace and love were the buzzwords of the day, at home Mom had been escalating the violence with Jim, almost as if she wished he would actually hurt her. During their fights, she often goaded him to "go ahead." One afternoon, Mom lifted her pillow to show me a steak knife she'd hidden there. I had never seen her do that before, and it seemed like a very bad idea.

"Don't worry, I'm ready if that bastard attacks me again."

Again? I had never seen Jim raise a hand against her. As days passed I felt increasingly nervous about Mom keeping that knife in her bed, and I fretted about warning Jim.

"You're undersized!" she screamed at him during a fight a few nights later.

Oh no, I thought. *This might be it.* Though I was only nine, I suspected that what Mom had said was a very bad thing to say to a man. Mom had already told me virtually everything there was to know about sex, giving me much more information than I needed or wanted, including her masturbation techniques.

"Come on, Ann. That's enough."

"And you look like a damn hick with your broken teeth. Why don't you go to a dentist? And look at the belly on you! Jesus, you could easily be in your third trimester! I can't stand sleeping with you anymore!"

Jim hadn't taken good care of himself; that was true. But he was handsome in his way. I was worried Mom might do something with the knife, but I figured as long as he was awake he could overpower her if she tried. But what if he passed out? I was growing to love Jim and now I worried Mom might kill him.

There was no stabbing that night, but I obsessed over the knife for days, hardly sleeping the nights they fought. Then finally, home alone one afternoon, I lifted Mom's pillow. The only thing there was the tag that it was against the law to remove.

As I grew older, Mom began consulting me as a family therapist, confiding about her relationship with Jim, asking for advice and, sometimes, intervention.

"Karen, tell Jim he's an alcoholic," she would say right in front of him. "Isn't he? Don't you agree with me that he's a raging lush?"

I usually played it safe, offering, "You've been working really hard, and I think you're both tired." I'd learned by trial and error that sometimes I could calm them down with similar suggestions. Other times, nothing I said made a bit of difference, and I stood between them as they yelled over my head, fearing Jim might finally lose control and kill her. There were nights when I almost wished he would.

Then one afternoon they suddenly announced they would be taking a three-week trip without me. I was elated. Their get-away was a welcome vacation from my job as couple's counselor. Leaf and Sparrow, who had just returned from a spiritual quest to Nepal and India, would be staying in our apartment to baby-sit me. I liked them both and looked forward to hearing more of Leaf's travel adventure stories.

The day they arrived at our apartment, the only thing I remember Leaf bringing in the way of supplies was a gallon-sized baggie full of pot. I'd never seen so much marijuana in one place. Leaf spent his days weeding through his bag, pulling out seeds and stems, and rolling perfect joints.

"Check out this one!" He proudly displayed his work to Sparrow and me. When he wasn't processing his weed, he prepared bizarre meals inspired by his persistent munchies. "I'm making vindaloo for dinner tonight," he told me when I got home from school. We'd had vindaloo every night, but I wasn't complaining. He combed through the refrigerator daily, mixing virtually anything he found into stew, then adding curry powder.

"*Vindaloo* is Hindi for 'chef's surprise,'" said Sparrow when Leaf left the room. We giggled. Leaf's lethargic pot addiction had the unexpected benefit of causing me to actually miss the alcoholics who'd left me.

Mom and Jim returned from their trip with suitcases full of duty-free cigarettes and liquor. Jim unpacked cartons of his beloved unfiltered Pall Mall Reds and Mom's Marlboros. Curaçao was one of the ports they'd visited on their trip, and they'd purchased bottles of the island's liqueur, a syrupy blue confection. They poured me a glass, but even at nine years old I found it too sweet.

"Ugh! Tastes like mouthwash mixed with cough syrup and urine." I just threw in the urine to make them laugh.

"Everyone loves a smartass," Jim laughed. That was always his favorite thing to tell me.

The Floating World

Soon after their return, Mom pulled me out of school and made me her adventure companion again.

"I've always had wanderlust," Mom explained to Jim. And it was true she'd always had an aversion to "home." Since Japan, Mom had developed a fear of flying. We would travel on ships or trains. Mom said her Hebrides clan was a seafaring people; surrounded by ocean on the barren Isle of Barra, the McNeils had a genetic need to sail the seas.

Jim took me to Macy's two days before we left on the European adventure she had planned. Mom hated shopping and tended to wear her clothes until they disintegrated. She'd even kept the blood-saturated loafers from her near-death experience. I sometimes examined the burgundy stains with ghoulish fascination, instantly transporting myself back to that terrifying night when I nearly lost the only person in the world who loved me.

"You can't travel the world in torn jeans and a poncho," Jim said. "Choose anything you want."

I tried on a few paisley dresses and a blue coat with gold buttons. Jim sat on a bench outside the dressing room as I came out and modeled. He gave me the thumbs up on each outfit I tried.

"Get them all, and the coat. You'll need it."

"Are you sure? It's a lot of money. I don't want Mom to be mad."

"It's fine, Karen." He looked me in the eye. "This is my money. This is how I want to spend it."

"Thank you, Jim." I was so grateful to him, but still I held myself back. *Why can't I hug him? What is wrong with me?*

After shopping, he took me to lunch. Jim rarely spoke of his childhood, but he'd had a couple of beers with his burger, so he was unusually talkative.

"My dad was a real son of a bitch. Never wanted me. My mother was the one who wanted to adopt me. My dad used to make me pull a switch off the chinaberry tree whenever he wanted to give me a whippin'. The switches were never thick enough. He'd send me back to that tree over and over until I picked the one he liked."

Jim had no trace of the South in his speech, but when he said *whippin'* I could almost hear vestiges of Georgia. He took another slug of beer.

"Son of a bitch."

That was all he said about it. He'd once shown me a picture of himself at age three, wearing tiny overalls and looking so sad. Now, watching him bite into his burger, I wanted to cry, imagining that small boy being whipped.

Jim gave Mom some money, and we left on our journey. I was not looking forward to being alone with her, but I hoped maybe this trip would work out better than the others. As I would for much of my life, I hoped this time would be different. *This time will be better. This time will be better.*

As we crossed the country on Amtrak, it seemed to take weeks to pass through the never-ending cornfields. The passengers in the bar car joked that America consisted of two coasts, framing one gigantic cornfield.

We were excited when we learned we would stop briefly in Gary, Indiana. Fans of *The Music Man*, we knew the lyrics by heart. As the conductor announced the station, Mom began singing, "Gary, Indiana, Gary, Indiana," and I joined in. But our singing trailed off as the train crept into the station and I pulled the curtain from the window of our Pullman, revealing the town. Gary was a dismal, industrial sprawl, the yellow air pea-soup thick with pollution. It was hard to imagine the Gary that might have once inspired a composer to write such a cheerful song.

"Sometimes art is just better than life," I said, eliciting a rare laugh from Mom.

The train's bar car was our main residence for the next five days. Mom chatted with passengers, drinking and smoking, while I amused myself playing solitaire and pestering the old black porters. The porters fascinated me, spending their lives aboard the train, seldom seeing the families they left behind.

"Where did you grow up, Sherman?" I asked our barman.

"Louisiana 'riginally, but my people mostly all moved away from there. All three my brothers is workin' for Amtrak, each on a different line. Only times we sees each other's at the station. We wave to each other as the trains go by."

I figured he was pulling my leg, but I loved hearing him speak. He would say "Loooo . . . zeeanna" and the result was musical.

When we arrived in New York City, we took a taxi to the pier where HMS *Queen Elizabeth* was berthed. Mom told me she was the second-largest passenger ship in the world. Her sister ship, HMS *Queen Mary*, was just a bit larger. Mom said Britain's Royal Navy had used the ships to move troops during the Second World War. Cunard was the shipping line, and everywhere we looked we saw signs with their advertising slogan, "Getting there is half the fun." *The person who dreamed up that slogan never traveled with my mother*, I thought.

The ship's horn bellowed three long bursts.

"All ashore that's going ashore," a ship's officer sang, a cockney lilt to his voice. As the tugboat pulled us from the dock, everyone celebrated on deck. We threw streamers over the ship's railing, aiming for people waving on the pier. The deck was festooned with streamers, and confetti swirled around us in the wind. Crossing the Atlantic was still an event. Passengers toasted with champagne and some threw empty glasses into the harbor. Mom said it was a tradition to do this, if you hoped to return to that port someday.

We floated past the Statue of Liberty, then under the Verrazano Bridge. Standing on deck, the wind in my hair, I pretended I was a movie star. A casual observer might have assumed we'd won a lottery or suddenly inherited a fortune. But our financial circumstances hadn't changed. In San Francisco, we still rented an apartment in a working-class neighborhood, we didn't own property of any value, and I worked in the school cafeteria to earn a free lunch. We were traveling on the fruits of Jim's labor.

Mom told me she'd saved every penny to pay for this expedition. It was true that she had been a lifelong hoarder of cash, socking away a little all the time and then coming up with an envelope full of hundred-dollar bills out of the blue. She'd complain how broke we were for months, then—poof!—money appeared for an adventure, no doubt much of it donated by Jim. It made little sense to me at the time. At home, we often lacked necessities. Yet, now, we were drinking champagne on a gigantic ocean liner. Well, she was drinking champagne. The chorus of "If They Could See Me Now" from *Sweet Charity* popped into my head.

The ocean liner was divided into first and second class. Passengers jokingly referred to second class as steerage, because second-class passengers were not allowed to visit first-class public areas unless accompanied by a first-class passenger. We traveled second class, though by the end of the trip Mom had found her way into every bar on the ship, including those in first class.

I was asleep in the top bunk the first night when Mom stumbled in, very late. All the rooms were called "cabins," never "staterooms"; the ceilings unabashedly displayed clunky steel pipes and sturdy hardware. This ship was proud to be a ship, not a floating hotel.

"Ha!" she shouted, slamming the cabin door behind her. "Those stupid, ugly Americans! I fooled the hell out of them!"

"What?" I kicked myself for not pretending to be asleep.

"I told those idiots in the Lookout Bar that I was Lizzie Borden's daughter!" She laughed venomously. "And the fools believed me!"

"Why wouldn't they?" I knew it was chancy. If I asked the wrong question, I'd become the subject of her wrath, lumped together with the other fools, idiots, and nincompoops who inhabited Mom's world.

"Jesus, Karen. You're as bad as they are. Lizzie Borden never had children. Don't you know that? Anyway, it was hysterical. I told them my whole sad story about being an ax murderer's daughter. And my grandparents! The loss. They fell for the whole ridiculous story. Boobs!" She kicked off her shoes and then passed out on the lower bunk seconds later.

After that, I lay awake for a long while, wondering which passengers we would have to avoid for the remaining days as we crossed the Atlantic. It was good to know these things in case at some point we had to take to lifeboats.

The next morning while Mom slept, I stayed in a deck chair under a blanket, staring out at the endless, gray, roiling ocean, nothing but water and the curved arc of the horizon before me. We never even seemed to pass another vessel. A wave of anxiety rolled through me as it dawned on me—there was no way off this ship.

Most of the day, I meandered through the public rooms alone until, hours later, Mom finally woke up and found me. We spent the remainder of the day playing bingo and trivia games, sipping afternoon cream tea and eating petit fours while listening to a string quartet.

"What happened last night?" Mom asked. "Were you with me in the bar?"

"No, I went to bed around ten. You were talking to some people from Texas."

"Wow. I can't remember a thing. I'd better watch my drinking for a while. Those blackouts scare me," she said. *Me too,* I thought, but didn't dare say it. Only Mom could comment on Mom's drinking.

By five o'clock Mom was drinking in the Promenade Bar. She wasn't buying me alcohol yet, but I got the impression that if I'd ordered a drink, the stewards would have served me one. There seemed to be an "anything goes—we're on the high seas" attitude shipboard. One six-year-old entertained us for hours after his parents let him drink beer until he was staggering. He sang, danced, and told jokes. He had the whole bar in hysterics and was by far the best floorshow of the trip. My "usual" was tomato juice spiked with lemon and Worcestershire sauce. Mom's was Cutty Sark and soda.

By the second night, Mom attached herself to a group of veteran World War II Royal Air Force pilots. She came back to the cabin at night telling stories about the pilots, their heroic missions, one pilot's experience as a prisoner of war. She respected the men deeply and held them in higher esteem than she did the "ugly Americans." The fact that we too were ugly Americans never seemed to bother her. According to Mom, we weren't like the others. They were mere tourists—we were travelers.

It was May 1968. We spent a month touring Europe, arriving in Paris just as the student rioting ended. I was thrilled to see the Eiffel Tower, having loved the *Madeline* books.

At first Mom stayed sober, making friends with our tour-bus companions. Mom and the younger tourists laughed that we were on the "If it's Tuesday, this must be Belgium" tour because our bus stopped in a new city every morning. We saw Paris, Rome, Venice, Lucerne, and the Black Forest.

But I felt uneasy during the trip. Every statue in Paris had been eerily painted red during the student riots, and the vandalism gave me a creepy feeling. Mom became friendly with our bus driver, a middle-aged man who was missing his right ear. Each time we boarded the bus, the driver was already in his seat, and I couldn't help but notice the gaping hole where his ear had once been. Mom chatted with him during one of the stops and learned he'd been tortured by the Nazis. Though I knew the war had ended more than two decades before our trip to Germany, Mom's continual references to it throughout my childhood made me dread being there.

By the time we reached the Black Forest, Mom was on a tirade. We had stopped at a border checkpoint and now were back on the bus.

"Didn't you see how that customs official looked at us when he read your Jewish name on your passport?" said Mom.

I hadn't noticed, but now I had something else to worry about.

"Jesus, Karen! Are you completely oblivious to your surroundings?"

Not certain if she expected an answer, I remained silent. I was slowly coming to understand that Mom was a bully and that I was cowed by her. I thought, *I used to know how to love my mother, but now I don't even know how to like her.*

A couple of nights later, Mom got into a screaming match in the hotel lobby with an older Austrian man. As I walked into the bar to meet her, Mom turned to me, howling.

"This man said the United States is an abortion on the face of the earth!"

The man had a smirk on his face, as if he was enjoying riling Mom up. I tried to think of some way to calm her down. *Just agree with her.*

"That's terrible, Mom."

The Austrian left the lobby, and Mom decided she'd come back to the room with me. I was relieved the scene was over but expected she would direct her drunken rant at me next. Mercifully, she passed out.

During the return trip on the SS *France*, Mom complained she hated sailing on the French Line and said that the crew was snobby. She said she preferred the chummy feel of British passenger liners. Instead of chow mein, we were now living on consommé, quenelles, crudités, and other foods I'd never heard of before. The seas were particularly rough during our return crossing. For three days, even the ship's crew was green. In every public restroom, passengers could be found heaving. I was no exception. Inexplicably, Mom never became seasick. But after enduring days of my nausea, Mom was exasperated.

"We come from a seafaring people! What the hell's the matter with you? You did not get this from my side of the family! It must be the Nassberg genes. Knock this off right now! It's mind over matter!"

Though I tried willing myself out of seasickness, I was unable to do it, and my wimpiness disappointed Mom. When we finally set foot in San Francisco, I was relieved to see Jim and prayed I'd never have to board a ship with my mother again.

The Brig

It was around midnight, and Jim was pounding on our apartment door. Mom wedged her back against the door, waving me away.

"Now he wants to come in here and sleep off his three-day toot! Well I have no intention of letting that bastard in!"

"Ann, open the door! I lost my keys. I got a heat on and got rolled."

Jim had been "rolled" so often over the years that Barb, Steve, and I had incorporated the routine into our childhood games. We took turns playing the parts of the passed-out rolling victim and the officers driving the paddy wagon.

Jim continued pounding. Then, as if the idea had just occurred to her, Mom suddenly ran to the phone.

"There's a maniac breaking into my apartment. He's going to kill me—and my infant daughter! He's kicking down the door!" When the officers arrived, Mom had Jim arrested, convincing them if they didn't arrest him, the blood of an innocent child would be on their hands. I stared out the window at the paddy wagon, double-parked in front of our building. The cops came out with Jim in handcuffs and led him to the wagon's back door. I watched as he climbed in and felt so sad. He wasn't even that drunk. He could still walk.

Two days later, Jim returned home and Mom let him in. His ex-wife Sheila had bailed him out of county jail, and Mom was incensed. Mom's anger made no sense to me. Jim had been no drunker the night she'd had him arrested than she herself had been on many previous nights. It seemed to me that Jim should have been the one who was mad at Mom. But somehow she'd managed to turn the tables on him.

"I knew you'd go crawling back to her! Well you can have each other as far as I'm concerned! I'm going to live in England for a year. I want my half of the money from the business. I've had enough of this crap. You've been using me as a slave and I've gotten absolutely nothing from this so-called partnership!"

This wasn't the first time I'd heard about Mom's England plan. She'd been a lifelong Anglophile with a remarkable memory for every historical detail of the British monarchy. For years, she had dreamed of living in a quaint English village. The idea usually came up after she read an Agatha Christie novel.

Though I was wary about traveling with Mom again, I was also excited at the idea of reinventing myself in a new country. On the cusp of adolescence, I hoped that upon my return my classmates would view me as a sophisticated world traveler. I began to portray our previous trips as exciting adventures, not the terrifying, drunken ordeals they had actually been. Maybe this trip would be different, I told myself. I even imagined that by the time we returned to San Francisco, I would have acquired an English accent that might impress my American classmates.

When Mom wanted something from Jim, she never resorted to feminine wiles or subtle manipulation. Though he outweighed her by a hundred pounds, Jim never once physically threatened her or even said "no" to her. He simply could not change his kind, generous nature. Business had not been great lately, but without any argument, he gave Mom half their savings, and we took off for another adventure.

This time we would sail on a P&O ship. Unlike Cunard, this shipping line promised no fun while getting there. The ship was the *Arcadia*, and we boarded her in San Francisco. The plan was to sail all the way to Southampton. We would be traveling through the Panama Canal, docking in Florida, then crossing the Atlantic. The whole trip would take three weeks. Once in England, Mom planned to find an apartment and enroll me in school. I was twelve.

For the first few days, we attended meals in the ship's dining room with the other passengers and participated in various group activities like a costume party and a scavenger hunt. For the costume party I dressed as a gypsy, and Mom fashioned herself a toga from the cabin's bedsheets. I befriended a few teenagers—British citizens sailing back home—and mostly stayed with them in the teen bar, the Pop In. Though I was not yet a teen, I easily passed for one.

In the first port, Acapulco, Mom and I browsed outdoor fruit markets and silver jewelry stands, masquerading as normal tourists. Mom was still lucid. But as we sailed out of harbor, she turned to me in a panic.

"Two of the passengers are trying to kill me, Connie."

My skin crawled.

"What are you talking about, Mom?"

"They've been putting LSD in my drinks."

This was my first experience with what I later learned were Mom's paranoid delusions, but at the time I was confused. I wondered if what she was saying was true. I still believed much of what Mom told me, and in all her years of erratic behavior, she'd never before thought she was being poisoned.

I had begun to notice that Mom's mental breakdowns often followed a period of heavy drinking. The booze set off a manic cycle. Then, once she reached critical mass, she no longer needed liquor to continue her high. Now in Panama, her eye color was fading again.

"*Non carborundum illegitimi*. Don't let the bastards grind you down," she sang continuously as she roamed the ship's public rooms, insulting anyone who had the misfortune of stepping into her path. The smallest thing could set her off, and her outbursts were vicious. She developed a particular rage toward any passenger who chose to rest sunglasses on top of his head.

"I'm going to get a little hammer and bash in those phony sunglasses they all wear on the top of their heads!" she said threateningly, raising her fist to a random young man who'd innocently stepped into her line of fire. As I tried coaxing her to our cabin, an attractive French woman approached, advancing toward the dining room.

"Oh, you think you're so special, with your fancy clothes and jewelry. Well you're not going to kill me as easily as you think, you snail-eating bitch!" Mom lunged toward her hapless victim, fingers poised like claws. I grabbed Mom's arm and pulled her back as the passenger hurried away. I tried leading her to the cabin, but she yanked her arm back and pushed me hard. I stumbled for balance on the swaying ship.

"So you've joined their team now, Karen! I knew they would get to you. You always were a traitor!"

Passengers watched as I stood paralyzed, unsure what to do. It was mortifying. I wanted to jump off the side of the ship—anything to escape. I couldn't control her, so I abandoned her, only returning to our cabin to sleep and never finding her there. I lived in the Pop In, with other teens who were avoiding their parents for more ordinary reasons.

As the ship entered the first lock of the Panama Canal, Mom disappeared. It occurred to me I hadn't seen her for hours, though I have to admit I hadn't been looking for her. I worried about what sort of trouble she might have started and I began wandering through the public rooms, not really wanting to find her. After an unsuccessful search, I decided to go to bed. I had just pulled my nightgown over my head when I heard a knock on the cabin door. Thinking it was Mom, I opened it. An elderly Englishman in a white ship's officer's uniform stood in the doorway. Reflexively, I crossed my arms across the neckline of my flimsy nightgown.

"I'm Dr. Wilson. Are you Ann McNeil's daughter?"

"Yes."

"Your mother has been placed in the brig."

I took in this information. The brig? Like something from a pirate book, from *Treasure Island*? I imagined Mom walking the plank.

"She attacked another passenger, and we've had no choice but to restrain her. I have diagnosed your mother as manic-depressive with overtones of paranoid schizophrenia."

Oh. I was beginning to understand. Mom was under arrest. This was no joke. But this stranger's assessment seemed premature, and he seemed overly impressed with his own diagnostic insight. *Hadn't she just been drinking too much? What kind of doctor works on a ship anyway?*

"She will remain in the brig until we reach American soil, at which point you and your mother will be removed from the ship. Do you have a family member who might collect you from Fort Lauderdale?"

I was at a loss. My mind was reeling. A minute ago we were headed to England for a year. I had no backup plan! Mom, as scary as it was to acknowledge, was all I had. The only person

I could even think to call was Jim. But hadn't Mom left him? Were they even a couple anymore? I had no idea if Mom planned to go back to Jim after the year was over. It felt presumptuous of me to ask him to help us. But who else was there? I hadn't heard from my father for years and wouldn't even know how to begin to find him. Mom hadn't spoken to her New York family since the police had come to Connie's house. I did have an adult cousin on my father's side of the family, Pat, who lived in Florida. Mom had always liked Pat, and they'd stayed in touch by mail over the years. Before we'd left San Francisco, Mom had spoken about looking her up while we were docked in Fort Lauderdale. She was one of the few members of either of my parent's families I'd ever met. I scarcely knew her and I felt horribly embarrassed at the idea of imposing on her.

For the next three days, while Mom was a prisoner in the brig, I drifted around the ship, posing as a petulant adolescent avoiding her parents. I stayed with the teen passengers, acting nonchalant about Mom's whereabouts. No one noticed I was a free agent, walking around like an adult—albeit a short, penniless adult.

On Mom's second day in the brig, I searched for Dr. Wilson. When I found the infirmary, I stood in the doorway, looking around for something brig-like. The room was quite small, everything painted a soothing eggshell white. There was an examination table, a chair, and a desk. No signs of a mini-prison. The doctor sat at his desk, writing.

"Can I see my mother?"

Dr. Wilson dropped his pen, startled, and looked up. "That won't be possible. She is safe, and you don't need to worry. We've made contact with your cousin in Florida, and you will be disembarking there when we arrive."

"Where is she?" A panicky sensation crawled up my chest.

"The brig is essentially a padded cabin with a bunk and lavatory. Your mother cannot hurt herself or others now. But you will not be able to see her. I'm sorry." He did not sound sorry in the least.

"You said she was a 'manic-depressive with overtones of paranoid schizophrenia.' What does that mean?" I had heard each of the words separately before, but never in one sentence. I knew paranoia meant believing people were out to get you. I thought manic meant full of energy. I thought I knew what it meant to be depressed. But I had a vague and confusing idea of schizophrenia. *Wasn't that where you thought you were many different people?*

"It means your mother is severely mentally ill. It's quite complicated and, I'm sure, hard for you to understand. Ask your family doctor to explain it to you when you return home." He returned to his writing.

Family doctor? We had none. The only doctor I had ever seen had been someone from the Department of Public Health after I failed a school-administered tuberculosis test in sixth grade and needed a chest X-ray. The idea that we had a family doctor presumed that we had a stable family. I left the infirmary and returned to my cabin. This was before the days of freewheeling cruises with nonstop buffets. Passengers were assigned a specific table for meals and a place, time, and group of people to eat with and were expected to be there for every meal. If I returned to our table, I would risk having to answer concerned questions about Mom's health and whereabouts. I couldn't face the idea of lying to them, or, even worse, telling them the truth. Besides, I suspected Mom was already the talk of the ship, and I was deeply embarrassed for both of us.

Afternoon tea was served at four o'clock. It was the only meal offering informal seating, so for three days, I grabbed sandwiches and sweets from the tea trays. I was ashamed of the relief

I felt that Mom was locked away, relief from the burden of her behavior and worrying about what she might do next. Then I felt a wave of guilt for wishing for my mother's incarceration.

As we neared port, I packed our suitcases and waited. Mom was lethargic and medicated when the doctor reunited us. She barely said a word. Once we were docked at Fort Lauderdale, we were hastily ushered off the ship by several officers. Packs of passengers gawked as we descended the gangway. Pat and her boyfriend, Eric, were waiting at the dock. I was overcome with gratitude to have real adults take over the care, feeding, and containment of Mom.

Cheyenne

Eric drove us to the emergency room of a Fort Lauderdale hospital where a doctor examined Mom and gave Pat a prescription to fill. Leaving the pharmacy, we drove past hundreds of palm trees until we reached a modern, sunny apartment complex.

Pat was in her twenties, pretty and full of life—the good kind of life, not Mom's brand of scary, manic life. I instantly loved her for rescuing us and tried to come up with some way to stay there with her. *Could she adopt me?*

Pat's apartment overlooked the swimming pool, and as soon as we stepped inside, Mom headed out onto the balcony and lit a cigarette. I followed her because the way she was staring over the railing was giving me the creeps.

"I should just fucking kill myself! Not that any of you would care. I should just throw myself off this balcony right now!"

"Let's go back inside," I said, sliding the glass door open and grasping her elbow. For some reason she allowed me to lead her inside.

I spent the night with one eye open, making sure Mom didn't carry out her threat. Jumping from the third story wasn't much of a suicide plan, more a daring high dive, but still.

On the third day, Jim arrived to rescue us. The cigarette-smoking, Colt 45–drinking knight in tarnished armor had flown to Florida from San Francisco as soon as he could get on a flight. I was overwhelmed with relief when he came through the door. When Mom heard Jim booking our flight to San Francisco, she screamed, "I am not getting on a plane, dammit! If God intended us to fly, he would have given us wings!" For reasons I still don't fully understand, Jim allowed Mom to insist we return by train to San Francisco. Later I would blame myself for not warning him. For six days, the three of us would be confined to a small sleeper compartment. It's hard for me to grasp what he was thinking as he purchased our tickets, but since he had not witnessed Mom's behavior on the ship, he must not have fully understood what we were facing. I had no idea what information, if any, the shipping company had revealed to Jim, but he must have believed he would still be able to control Mom.

The next morning we said good-bye to Pat and Eric and boarded the train. As the tranquilizers wore off, Mom became increasingly agitated, and though we had bottles of medication from the emergency room doctor, she refused to take it. After a few hours, she complained about being trapped in our small compartment and convinced Jim to take us to the bar car. A foolish mistake, but by then, I'm sure, Jim needed a drink. It didn't take long for him to realize his error.

"What the hell are you looking at, you mental midgets?" Mom screamed at the bar patrons. "I'll give you something to look at." She launched into her Gershwin repertoire: "I'd like to be like that gal on the river, who sang her songs to the ships sailing by. She had the goods and how she could deliver, The Lorelei . . ." Mom was no Ella Fitzgerald, and the bar car quickly evacuated. Jim downed a double shot of whiskey and tried edging Mom out of the bar, but she gripped the bar with both hands, refusing to budge. I can't remember what ruse we finally came up with to lure her back to the compartment, where it was clear we would have to confine her for the remainder of the trip.

Once back in our Pullman, I placated Mom by singing show

tunes with her. Jim thought if we plied her with enough liquor, she might pass out. At the next station he hopped off the train to buy a bottle of Cutty Sark. Minutes became hours as I waited for his return, part of me fearing he might never come back. I shuddered at the thought of being stuck alone with her again. It was finally hitting me how desperately I needed Jim. Mom and I sang through the scores of *Cabaret* and *Fiddler on the Roof* and were halfway through *Gypsy* by the time Jim returned. He filled a water glass with scotch and gave it to her straight. But the alcohol did not produce the effect he hoped for. It somehow energized her.

"Let me out of here, you assholes! I'm going back to the bar!"

She tried pushing past us. Jim held her in a bear hug and signaled me with a nod of his head to block the door. I leaned my back against the compartment door and crossed my arms over my chest like a centurion. He struggled with her for what seemed a very long time. Then all at once, she broke away and lunged headfirst toward me. I reflexively volleyed her shoulders back with both of my palms. Jim grabbed her again, this time pulling her to the ground. She swung at him wildly, scratching him with her long fingernails, gouging his neck and face. I dove to sit on her legs while he restrained her arms. She shrieked for a long while, then, eventually, she stopped writhing. I looked up and saw blood was running down Jim's cheek. It looked as if he was crying blood.

"You can let me up now. I'm not going to do anything," she said flatly. Jim's blood dribbled onto her yellow blouse. I stared into Jim's eyes, sending him a telepathic message: *Don't do it! Don't fall for it!* We kept our weight on her, burying her alive like an accused witch, for what felt like days. Finally we negotiated her cooperation by bribing her with the promise of a cigarette.

Jim and I incarcerated Mom in that compartment for six days.

This was my first prisoner extradition. Someday, I would be paid for custody escorts, but none would ever be as difficult as this. In this scenario, the guards had become the prisoners. Mom held us hostage and raged relentlessly, raving that we were part of the group of ignorant fools who had infiltrated the government and imprisoned her.

Occasionally I crept out to the dining car to gather supplies, though Mom rarely ate when she was manic and Jim and I had lost our appetites. But Jim didn't dare leave the compartment for a minute. There was no way I had the strength to restrain her alone.

On the fourth day, we decided to mix some Thorazine into Mom's scotch. I don't remember which of us came up with the idea, but I'm not sorry for it. During one of Mom's brief catnaps, Jim furtively crushed pills into her drink in our swampy toilet stall. When she awoke, he gave her the drink. By the time we reached Cheyenne, Wyoming, Mom was in a deep sleep. I took a real breath for the first time in days. The train would remain in Cheyenne for four hours, enough time to walk away from the station and get dinner somewhere. We left Mom asleep in her bunk and wandered into town. By this point I was too exhausted to care what happened to her. If I'd been the accomplice to her homicide, so be it. *Take me to jail. Go ahead.* I'd already been held prisoner.

I was mystified by what motivated Jim to rescue Mom. At the time, I believed he was driven by some strange obsession with her. I couldn't yet understand why he was willing to put up with her mean temper or why he would have crossed the country to subject himself to more of it. *Did he have any idea how messed up Mom was when he got on that plane to Florida? Would he still have come, if he'd known?*

It wasn't until years later, when I examined all the evidence, that I finally understood. Jim was rescuing me, not Mom. But at age twelve, I simply didn't understand what drove him. Maybe I even thought of him as a bit of a sucker for being so easily taken in by Mom's antics. I had felt trapped with Mom for years, and all I wished for was to find some means of escape. It baffled me that Jim, or anyone, would actually choose to be near her.

We stumbled into a cheap Chinese restaurant in Cheyenne. The menu was nothing like in San Francisco. The dive offered chop suey, egg rolls, and egg foo young—all of the frozen, Chung King variety. Not that we were hungry. We just craved a few hours of peace, relief from the monster.

"Have an egg roll, Mr. Goldstone," Rosalind Russell's voice sang in my head. Even during disaster, my interior musical-theater soundtrack played on. For the two hours we sat in Chop Suey House, I couldn't stop thinking, *Let's just leave her on the train*. Now, years later, I wonder if Jim might have been thinking the same thing.

As we crept back to the station, Jim gently put a hand on my shoulder but didn't keep it there long. Part of me prayed Mom had wandered off somewhere so we'd be free of her. On the other hand, losing Mom in Cheyenne might prolong the agony of the journey. I was sure Jim wouldn't just abandon her there. He'd come so far to save her. I loved her and I hated her, but mostly I just wished she would evaporate. Not die exactly, just float away. I needed some bolstering and felt like hugging Jim but still wasn't sure how to treat him. Now, a lifetime later, I am haunted by regret. If I could relive that moment, I would hug Jim and tell him how grateful I was that he had come to get us. But then, all I could do was trudge up the train steps, already exhausted by the thought of what was waiting for us.

We returned to the tiger's cage, and Mom was right where we'd left her, still asleep. Relief flooded over me until I realized we were still three days from San Francisco—three long days. At least now that Jim and I had figured out how to spike her drinks, we might get some sleep.

Getting There Is Half the Fun—Again

Once back in San Francisco, Jim brought Mom to a psychiatrist and filled out her paperwork to apply for supplemental security income (SSI), public assistance for the disabled. Her psychiatric history qualified her to receive the benefit, and she was so heavily medicated she could no longer work. Jim continued to run the dying business and lived with us, though I sometimes wondered why he stayed. He put his arm around her one night as she sat between us on the couch watching *Rowan & Martin's Laugh-In.*

"Stop that!" Mom pulled his arm off her shoulder. "I've finally figured out why I hate to be touched. I'm autistic. The idiot doctors should have seen it sooner. It's obvious. I have all the symptoms. That's why I don't even like you to hug me," she said to me. "It was one thing when you were small. But now it just gives me the creeps." I wanted to storm out of the room and shut myself in my bedroom. But it wasn't worth paying the price of one of her tirades. As pathetic as it made me feel, there were still times I wished she would hug me.

Mom hated the lethargy her medications induced as a side effect. The doctor initially prescribed lithium, but she'd refused to let us take her for the frequent blood tests required.

"Psychiatrists are bourgeois, neurotic, sophomoric know-it-alls, and talk therapy is self-indulgent poppycock!" she screamed at the doctor the first time we dragged her there. But at least on

Thorazine she was calmer. Her manic phase passed like a hurricane, leaving us exhausted and with little spirit to rebuild.

Meanwhile I was dealing with my own adolescent issues. I was in the seventh grade at Marina Junior High, and my chest was beginning to draw attention. I'd inherited Mom's overly ample bust line, and at twelve I wasn't happy about it. The daily ritual of changing for PE had become a miserable ordeal. The idea of being naked in front of my peers was so humiliating that I avoided it at all costs. When they made us jog laps, I did everything I could to avoid breaking a sweat and, therefore, the need for a shower.

With puberty, I developed an embarrassing crush. While my classmates adored Bobby Sherman and Donny Osmond, I had fallen hopelessly in love with Jack Wild, the pint-sized actor who played the street-smart pickpocket the Artful Dodger in the film version of *Oliver*. My attraction to him was inexplicable, and fearing the derision of my peers, my lifelong friend Monica was my sole confidant. I even joined his fan club—surprisingly, he had other fans—collected his photos and memorabilia, and fantasized that one day, the tiny actor would return my love. Yes, I was in love with the Artful Dodger, never imagining I would soon become him.

Mom stopped drinking and gradually weaned herself off Thorazine. Since returning from Florida, she'd been in her depressive mode, reading dozens of books, chain-smoking cigarettes by the carton, and seldom leaving our apartment. But her dream of moving to England had not died in the brig of the *Arcadia*. The money earmarked for the year was squirreled away in envelopes under her bed. Exactly one year after our aborted trip, she decided to set off on the adventure again. This time I was completely terrified at the idea of another disastrous trip, but I knew it was useless to try to talk her out of the idea. Again we departed, this time boarding a train in San Francisco. Jim rode through the Rockies with us on the Canadian Pacific train. The three of us spent a few days in a New York hotel before the ship set sail.

Always looking out for me, Jim went to Manhattan's garment district alone and returned to the hotel with new clothes for us. He handed me a shiny shirtdress in gunmetal-gray satin. He knew Mom wouldn't buy clothes for me and whatever I had would have to last me the entire year. When I wore the gleaming dress I felt beautiful, like Princess Caroline. Jim gave us bags full of clothes and enjoyed our trying on one outfit after another. When the ship sailed from harbor, I leaned over the railing and watched with sadness as his form became smaller and smaller.

It was assigned seating in the dining room of HMS *Queen Elizabeth II*. The maître d' led us to our table. Two attractive young women were already seated, white linen napkins draped over their laps. They were professional ballerinas from New York's corps de ballet, in their early twenties, traveling to Europe for their first big adventure. By the time we joined our tablemates, Mom was already flying high from the bon voyage party. Trying desperately to distract the women from her intoxication, I handled introductions and attempted to control the conversation.

"We're from San Francisco," I said. They smiled politely.

"What ballets have you danced in?" I asked.

"*Swan Lake* and *Coppélia*," answered the younger brunette.

I tried to think of other questions to ask them. If I could keep things moving, and upbeat, Mom might stay in a celebratory mood. But it was a pointless effort. Mom, already in her dragon mode, had focused in on her prey.

"You're both too damn short and fat to be prima ballerinas! You'll never make it in the ballet. Why even bother?" She let the line land, puffing on her long cigarette. "Bother" came out "baaatha" with her accent. For this evening's performance, she was playing an inebriated, charmless Auntie Mame. "My grandmother was Anna Pavlova, the greatest ballerina of all time, so I know whereof I speak!" She lifted her glass to them in a little toasting motion, and then drank.

This was the first I had heard of my legendary faux-ancestor. The ballerinas were beyond polite, staring silently with disbelief as Mom continued her critique of their lives.

"Neither one of you is pretty enough either! Just face it, you're wasting your youth." She gulped more scotch as punctuation. Mom's attack became increasingly virulent as dinner dragged on, course after interminable course. All I could think of was abandoning her at the table. Yet, perversely, I felt the need to stay and try to shield the ballerinas from Mom's assault, though helpless to stop it.

After the girls left the table, I followed. It was impossible for me to force Mom into the cabin. She would have kicked and screamed until she landed in the brig again, and I knew better than to suggest she'd had enough to drink and might want to go sleep it off. No matter how kindly I phrased it, she would only lash out and cause a bigger scene. Several passengers were already inspecting her with disapproving expressions. I imagined their voices judging Mom, and judging me. As I fled the table, she shouted, "You have a fat ass!" The taller brunette ballerina glanced over her shoulder at me, and something like sympathy flashed across her face.

Mom woke up the next morning with a vague sense she'd done something wrong.

"What happened last night? I blacked out."

"Do you remember dinner?"

"Not much. We were seated with two girls, right?"

"Yes." I wasn't sure how much to tell her. Mom seldom was embarrassed, but I sensed this time she knew she'd stepped over a line.

"What did I do?" I felt her embarrassment as if it was my own and was overcome with shame.

"You told the girls they were too short to be professional ballerinas, and some other stuff." Minimizing, not delivering the full report, I still couldn't bear to hurt her.

"Ugh. Do you think I should I apologize?"

"That might be a good idea."

I briefly fantasized about being on a lifeboat with Mom and the dancers, conspiring with them to throw her to the sharks, then kicked myself for being a bad daughter. But Mom had scared herself straight with that opening-night debacle. To my surprise, she apologized to the girls. Though returning to the table for dinner was excruciating, the women accepted her apology graciously. They could easily have requested other seating, but they smiled at me sympathetically as the steward seated us.

Mom was on her best behavior for the rest of the Atlantic crossing. She even managed to control her drinking. This time, she was determined to make it to England.

Rottingdean

By the second night aboard the *QE2*, Mom had started a shipboard romance with a dining room steward named Adam. He was a rather bland man, a few years younger than Mom, blond, with glasses. They spent his off-duty hours together in our cabin, and I avoided them by attaching myself to a roaming tribe of teenagers.

After five days at sea we disembarked in Southampton. Adam had a farewell dinner with us at his favorite Southampton restaurant, German Edie's. Edie was famous for cutting the neckties off the men who came into her restaurant and decorating the walls with them. Adam knew the routine and wore no tie. Mom loved Edie's jokes and for weeks she told anyone who would listen Edie's story of the woman who swallowed a razor blade.

"Did you hear about the woman who swallowed a razor blade?" Mom would ask her unwitting audience. "She gave herself a tonsillectomy, an appendectomy, and a hysterectomy. She castrated her husband, circumcised her lover, cut two fingers off a casual acquaintance, and there were still three shaves left on the razor."

We left Adam and hopped a train to London, where we stayed at a bed-and-breakfast near Paddington Station. We rode the underground all around town, toured museums and cathedrals, and visited all the places Mom had spent her life studying.

One Sunday afternoon, we boarded a river ferry and spent hours floating aimlessly up and down the Thames. The main attraction of the riverboat was that alcohol was available on board when the landlocked pubs were required by law to be closed. We shared a window booth with three young men, beer mugs lined up in front of them.

"Where are you guys from?" asked Mom. I was gazing at the riverbanks as we drifted past Hampton Court. The skinny redhead might have been twenty and the two dirty blonds looked in their late teens.

"Do you really say 'guys' in the States? Like on the telly?" said the redhead.

"Sure, it's the same as 'blokes' or 'mates,'" said Mom.

"We're from Liverpool. It's our first time in London. We've never met Yanks before," said the youngest.

"Well hold your hats and hallelujah!" sang Mom.

The boys found our accents hilarious, and we liked theirs because they reminded us of the Beatles. Mom ordered a pint of beer and I ordered a half-pint of Watney's Red Barrel. She smiled her approval. We spent the day telling jokes, pointing out sights, and singing Beatles favorites. Mom, playing the part of a newly tenured professor, gave us history lessons as we passed each land-mark. She was thrilled to be the center of attention. She identified sites of historically significant beheadings with terrifying precision and knew the history of each tower, describing the gruesome demise of various monarchs. The boys were captivated by Mom's ad-lib history class.

After a few weeks in London, we traveled by train from one English village to another, looking for an affordable furnished apartment. Mom settled on a town called Rottingdean, a seaside village seven miles east of Brighton. Mom liked the fact that Rudyard Kipling had once lived there and she found the town charming, so she signed a rental agreement for an apartment above the sweets shop on High Street.

For me, living above a candy store was a childhood dream come true, and Rottingdean was enchanting in a vaguely macabre way. There were tea shops brightly decorated in chintz on each block, and the town maintained its quaint Tudor architecture and cobblestoned sidewalks. But it took little imagination to envision the hundreds of women who had once been accused of witchcraft being tortured in the village pond. Mom told me witch hunting had been a regular sport in England for almost 300 years until the mid-18th century. The pond where the accused had been drowned dominated Rottingdean's village green, giving it an eerie, melancholy air.

We stayed in a hotel on Queen's Road in Brighton until our apartment became available. During the daytime, we ambled along the rocky beach eating ice lollies. Sometimes we stopped in at Virgin Records to listen to music on headphones. In the evenings, we strolled the Victorian pier and visited the Dance Palace, a formal dance hall turned disco where Mom and I met and danced with people from all over the world. Then Mom discovered a gay piano bar in the neighborhood, The Galleon, and we befriended some of the drag queens who performed there. Mom had always adored gay men and had been very proud of herself for inventing the button slogan "Better Blatant than Latent."

By then I'd graduated to lager and lime pints. No one ever questioned my age when Mom bought me a drink, though I was only thirteen. Pub customers would say, "If the top of your head can touch the bar, you're old enough to order a drink." I chose lager and lime because the flavor reminded me of 7-Up. The taste of alcohol didn't much appeal to me, but Mom was usually more congenial when I joined her.

On Mom's fortieth birthday, we met a young man named Clyde who was staying in our hotel. We celebrated with him, barhopping the dozen pubs on Queen's Road, picking up new friends like an impromptu conga line as we moved along.

"It's a long way to Tipperary, it's a long way to go!" Mom joined the pub sing-a-longs, surprising me with a new repertoire of songs I'd never heard before. There were lifetimes of Mom I didn't know.

Our conga line included men of all ages. In the past, I'd assumed they were drawn to Mom, but now I sensed some were also interested in me. I felt both fear and a sense of excitement at this realization, as if I'd discovered a previously unknown superpower without being given instructions on how to use it. Mom was flirting with Clyde, but I caught him looking at me when she wasn't watching. I was terrified she would notice and turn on me.

Our apartment was a short bus ride from my school, Longhill. The novelty of being aboard a double-decker bus never wore off, and for the whole school year I climbed the spiral staircase for a seat on the top deck. By the second day I realized the curriculum was much more difficult than the San Francisco school's had been. These eighth graders were doing trigonometry, and I'd barely started algebra. When the teacher rambled about sine and cosine, I stared at her blankly.

The math teacher, Miss Green, was an angry beet of a woman. She took an instant dislike to me, though my crime was inadvertent. One evening, Mom had told me to make do with the only pen we had, so I'd done my homework with red ink. The next morning when I turned in the assignment, Miss Green was livid. "I'm the only one who uses red ink here!" she fumed, her face as red as the ink. "I mark the corrections with red ink! Do you understand?"

"Yes, Miss," I answered, imitating the response I'd overheard my classmates use when addressing a teacher. She was outraged, as if I'd intentionally set out to defy her, and she carried her grudge for the entire school year.

The language arts classes were less traumatic. Mr. Hart liked my essays and forgave my cultural ignorance. The differences were simultaneously subtle and obvious. When Mr. Hart took attendance the first day, each student responded with a crisp *Sir!* To my American ear, it sounded like *Suh!* It took me a moment to figure out what *Suh!* meant. By the time they reached my name, I was able to imitate the syllable but was embarrassed to be faking an English accent. I waited for one of my classmates to stand up and shout, "Imposter!"

Rottingdean was far from a cultural melting pot. Most of my classmates had last names of British origin and nearly every student was Caucasian. My German-Jewish last name set me apart and provided material for mockery. Some of the meaner boys simply called me Iceberg. Every time this happened, I cringed, feeling somehow the person could see through me and knew how standoffishly I had treated Jim. Now that we were away, I missed him terribly.

Corporal punishment was still a common occurrence at Longhill, a fact that simultaneously intrigued and appalled me. The headmaster could give a student the cane anytime he so desired. My classmate, Donna, whispered to me with barely suppressed glee, "They make them pull their pants down and spank them with a stick across their naked bums!" After Donna's revelation, I was haunted by the creepy vision of some poor schoolboy, pants around his ankles, bent over the headmaster's desk, a picture at once repellant and oddly titillating. During the school year, rumors of caning victims occasionally circulated through campus, eliciting terrified excitement from the students.

I continued unwittingly breaking rules for weeks. Once I was called in for wearing dangly earrings when only flat posts were allowed. When I entered the headmistress's office, I was unsure of what crimes constituted capital offenses and feared I might be caned. I was relieved when she told me I only had to stay for detention. With time, I learned to camouflage myself.

There were five bars, or public houses as they're known in Britain, in Rottingdean. It took some months for Mom to wear out her welcome in each. Her favorite was the Plough, a pub next to the witch-torturing pond. Upstairs from the Plough was the Loft, a dimly lit teen bar in a rustic attic, my new part-time residence. No one over the age of twenty-two frequented the place; the majority of customers were under eighteen.

Adam appeared on our doorstep in late autumn. Mom hadn't mentioned he was coming, but she didn't seem surprised when he rang the bell.

"Adam's Cunard contract is over, and he doesn't have anywhere to go. He'll be staying with us on and off," Mom announced after he'd left for the pub. Unlike with Nick or Alan, this time Mom didn't ask me to pretend Adam was my father. Maybe she sensed my loyalties were now with Jim.

While Mom and Adam mingled at the Plough every night, I stayed upstairs with my new Loft friends. These teens were more like adults than San Francisco teens. Many had left school at fifteen or sixteen and already had full-time jobs. They worked days as mechanics or shop girls and met at the pub almost every night.

I figured Adam must have imagined he'd landed a rich American divorcee. *Boy, was he in for a disappointment.* He came and went, rather harmless and nerdy. Even after a couple of months, I could have barely picked him out of a lineup.

Then, just before Christmas, the coal miners went on strike. The entire country was plunged into periodic rolling blackouts. The perpetual darkness accentuated Rottingdean's gothic quality. Undeterred, we continued our nightly pilgrimage to the Loft and the Plough, using candles to light our trudge through the frosty pitch. In the candlelight, shadowy specters loomed over the village pond.

Mom's eye color began turning milky again that spring, and I dreaded what might happen next. Adam had noticed Mom changing too. The last time I saw him, I was waiting at the bus stop across the street from our flat. He came out carrying a white duffel bag. The man traveled light. His posture ramrod-straight, his gait rapid and focused, he looked my way for a moment, then went on. He didn't bother saying good-bye or even waving, but I knew we'd seen the last of him. When my bus came, I climbed the spiral staircase to the upper deck and watched as Adam trotted down the cobble-stoned High Street toward the water-front. I felt nothing.

When I came home that afternoon, Mom was pacing and muttering.

"Karen, the people in this village are planning to drown me. They've figured out the truth about me." Her eye color was near translucent. "And I have news for you," she continued. "You're a witch too." I said nothing. I knew we were now in dangerous terri-tory. I hoped for some miracle that might bring her back to reality. But her hallucinations and chanting went on all night long.

I continued attending school but spent my days obsessing about what she was doing. While I sat in my classroom, Mom purged my belongings, throwing away most of my clothing. After school, I went straight to the dustbin to rescue and hide what I could. She began telling me she was Joan of Arc and babbling incomprehensibly, claiming she was speaking French. At times she was so convincing I almost believed her. I wondered about the difference between hallucinations and miraculous visions.

Mom claimed she saw angels in the distant hills. *Hadn't Joan of Arc claimed something similar? Where was the line?* I knew Mom was not really speaking French. I was studying French in school, and her gibberish could not be mistaken for even arcane dialect. I hung on to this idea as if it were my only evidence that she was not in fact Joan of Arc.

On Sunday Mom insisted we go to church and, fearing her wrath, I went along, as if attending Sunday mass was our weekly ritual, though Mom hadn't considered herself Catholic since childhood. We barged in, Mom pushing me inside, the heavy door slamming behind her. Every pew was full, and the priest was deep into his sermon. As we made our noisy entrance every parishioner turned to inspect us. My cheeks were burning even before I spotted several of my Longhill classmates.

Mom led me in front of the congregation, handing me a candle and insisting I light it. Then she began lighting her own candles. Though I'd spent little time in churches, I suspected we were not supposed to light candles right next to the priest during his sermon. But I had no time to consider that thought as, all of a sudden, my hair was in flames. I turned to see Mom behind me, grinning like a jack-o-lantern, her candle aimed at my face. Mom had set my hair on fire!

I slapped at my head, ineffectually. The acrid odor of singed hair made me gag. I considered sticking my head into the marble bowl of holy water but dismissed that idea, afraid to draw even more attention. But it was too late. The priest had lost his audience, and the congregants stared, mesmerized by us. My classmate Donna watched in horror as I flailed at my sizzling hair and ran from the church. I didn't bother looking back for Mom. I ran the half-mile to our apartment and waited. Hours passed before she finally came through the door.

"I stopped at the convent and met some sisters. They're beekeepers." She unloaded jars of honey from a mesh bag, as if the incident in the church had never happened. I hoped she was somehow coming out of her spell.

Despite all evidence, I continued to hold on to my picture of Mom as a credible person, clinging to the possibility that maybe she wasn't really insane. In retrospect, it's hard to believe I could have been in such denial. But the ship's doctor had been the only one to ever tell me, "Your mother is a manic-depressive with overtones of paranoid schizophrenia." I hung on to the hope that his was not a real diagnosis, that the man had been a shipboard quack. Certainly a real doctor—someone credible, maybe Marcus Welby, MD—would one day appear and diagnose a brain tumor or something.

The next day, Mr. Hart was teaching a lesson on précis when the office secretary came into class. She spoke briefly to Mr. Hart, who led me into the hallway.

"You'll need to collect your things and go with Miss Stewart, Karen."

"What's going on?" I asked. Mr. Hart had always been kind, my favorite teacher.

"I'm not quite sure. But I believe Miss Stewart will explain." He disappeared back into the classroom. Miss Stewart escorted me to the front of the school, saying nothing. Outside, two uniformed police officers jumped up from leaning against their patrol car. The younger cop approached me.

"Are you Karen?"

"Yes."

"Is your mother Ann McNeil?"

"Yes." I dreaded what he might say next.

"Your mother tried to jump from a window. She's at Brighton General Hospital."

"What! How is she?" Our apartment was only on the second story, another poor choice for suicide.

"She's not hurt. She's been put under a psychiatric hold. Please get in the car." He held open the back door of the patrol car, and I got in.

"Are you taking me to the hospital to see her?"

"We're taking you to pack your things. You'll be taken to a children's home."

"What's a children's home? Like an orphanage?"

"Yes." As they drove me to the High Street apartment, the officers discussed what they were having for tea.

"I fancy kipper and chips, and you?" the grey-haired cop asked his partner.

"That'll do," answered the younger. Their conversation meandered to football, Leeds United versus Manchester, Georgie Best, a debate about football players. My mind was racing. A children's home? I pictured Oliver Twist holding his bowl with both hands, begging for more. I went numb, no longer in my body, as if I had somehow stepped outside of myself.

A female social worker met us at the flat. I unlocked the downstairs door and led the growing cast upstairs. Everything felt surreal, like we were in some impromptu stage production.

"You'll need to pack your school things, sleeping clothes, toiletries," the social worker said.

"How long will my mother be gone?" It was a pointless question: How could she know? But I asked anyway.

"You should pack as much as you can fit into the suitcase," she advised.

"Will I be allowed to go to school?"

"That should not be a problem. The children in the home all attend school."

Looking back, it seems odd that my main worry was missing

school. But I was beginning the process of separating myself from my mother. I was starting to perceive Mom as a sinking ship, and I clung to the idea that if I got a decent education, I might not go down with her.

I packed everything I could fit into my small suitcase. On the way out, I noticed Mom's blue leather purse open on the entry-way table with a bundle of cash visible. The officers were in the front room chatting, examining the alleged suicide scene. The social worker ambled in the hallway, miles behind me. I easily slipped out the roll of bills, feeling terrible as I did it. I'd never taken anything from Mom without her permission. I'd never stolen anything from anyone. But now, I was as cunning as the Artful Dodger.

The Children's Home

The Victorian children's home stood on a hill above the craggy Sussex coast, the whitewash blistering from the ravages of the sea-salt air. The building, drafty and damp, reminded me of a set from a horror movie, full of mysterious rambling hallways leading to vacant rooms. Upstairs were two large dormitories. The girls' contained forty small beds in two straight lines, recalling Madeline's little Paris school. But this house was covered in fog, not sunshine and vines.

Mr. Stevens, a gloomy-faced, middle-aged man who ran the home with his family, showed me to the girls' dormitory and pointed out the two available beds. I slid my suitcase underneath one, and when he left me alone, I searched my cardigan pocket for the wad of cash. I counted £200—a decent amount of money. Mom must have made a withdrawal before she was arrested. I told myself she had predicted something like this and left the money for me intentionally. Or maybe she'd been planning to flee the witch drowners. Having the cash made me feel a little safer. I wished I could go back to the apartment and grab our passports, though I had no idea what good they would do me.

The first night at the orphanage was hard. No one had talked to me about what to expect. I wondered how long I might be stuck there and when I might see Mom. I was at a loss to find a way out of the mess we were in.

The next morning, Stevens woke us by barging into the dorm, shouting, "Everyone up! No lollygagging!" The girls shrieked and crossed our arms over our chests, embarrassed at being seen in our nightgowns by a man we hardly knew. I had suddenly become a prisoner. I recalled the stories the Royal Air Force pilots told Mom about prisoner-of-war camps and told myself that people had survived much worse things than my present situation.

Stevens ran the operation efficiently. There were no children begging for more porridge. Meals were served punctually, the fare unimaginative but reliable: white bread with margarine, fish fingers, and chips. Milky, sweet, hot tea was provided to every child at each meal. Each week, a social worker came to meet with the children, who ranged in age from four to sixteen. Many of them were true orphans; I only wished I were one. Unlike my life up to this moment, everything here was prearranged, chaperoned, or supervised. I'd been playing the part of an adult so long that being a child was foreign to me. But I was relieved that I would be allowed to continue at Longhill. The school routine grounded me. While at school, I had the illusion nothing bad could ever happen.

The girl in the bed next to me, Del, was fifteen, an older, wiser woman of the world. I looked to her for guidance in my new life behind bars. Her beautiful caramel-colored skin and dark brown eyes reminded me of Monica, but her hair was short, wavy, and jet black. Where Monica was passive and soft, Del was assertive and tough. Thin and lanky, a bit boyish, Del was a survivor. Though she was skeptical of me at first, she slowly began to share the story of her childhood. The abuse she'd endured at the hands of the foster families she'd lived with made me appreciate that I had little to complain about. Del had adopted a cynical sense of humor during the many months she'd lived in the home. We recognized each other as sister travelers on the road of chaotic childhood and we teamed up to create petty protests against our perceived jailers, the Stevens.

Every Sunday, the entire children's home attended mass as a group, walking together down the High Street. Del had endured this ritual for months, but now that she had me for backup, she found new courage to rebel. That first Sunday, Del and I decided we would not let Stevens parade us into church like a couple of pathetic charity cases. Though the group attended the Anglican Church, not the Catholic Church where the hair-burning incident occurred, the last thing I wanted to do was go back inside any church.

The other girls had already left the dorm with their sweaters and jackets when Del yanked my elbow and said, "Stay here." I stood beside her, unsure of what we would do next. When we didn't respond to his bellow from the bottom of the stairwell, Stevens stormed into the dorm searching for us.

"Sorry, Stevens, we're not interested," said Del. Stevens gawked at Del in disbelief. I was stunned by her courage and shaking with fear. But now it was too late to back out. I wouldn't let myself wimp out on Del.

"Everyone goes. That's the way it's done here. Get your jackets now, we're leaving." He left us alone while he went downstairs to round up the other children.

"Let's tell him we're Hindus," Del suggested.

"Don't you think he'll see right through that?"

"Who cares?" said Del. "Help me set up the shrine."

Soon we heard Stevens plodding up the steps again. When he opened the door, we were kneeling in front of a collection of junk we'd covered with a blanket. Eyes closed, we held our hands in prayer position and rocked back and forth on our knees, chanting "Om" over and over.

"What the bloody hell is all this now?" shouted Stevens. "Get your little arses up off of that floor and come with me!"

Now I was sweating. If you could get the cane in a public school, who knew what Stevens could do to his charges? But Del kept her cool.

"We are Hindus, and you have no right to force us to participate in a religion we do not believe in!"

"What the bloody hell is this nonsense? Come on now and get up!" Stevens looked confused.

"*Nam myoho renge kyo,*" Del chanted. I finally caught on and chanted along with her. When I peeked at Stevens, he appeared to be considering his options. *Oliver Twist*'s Fagin sang in my head, "I am reviewing the situation." I could almost hear Stevens thinking. If he took us kicking and screaming into church, the townsfolk might wonder what was going on in the village children's home. On the other hand, if he let us get away with this silly stunt, the other children might try something similar the following week.

"Alright," said Stevens, caving. "I will allow you to stay this once. But you mustn't tell the others. You are to help the kitchen staff with Sunday dinner. If anyone asks why you missed mass, you are to say I asked you to work in the kitchen. Do you understand?" I looked at Del. She nodded.

"Yes," we said in unison.

He went downstairs, and we danced a victory dance. Later that afternoon, we told the other children we were from India and that Del's real name was Delhi.

After dinner each night, "Delhi" and I washed and dried the dishes as a team. We led the kitchen crew sing-along, and even Stevens sometimes joined in.

"I'd like to teach the world to sing in perfect harmony. . . ." It lifted everyone's mood. After a few weeks, we even seemed to be growing on Stevens; every now and then he'd smile at us, a little shyly.

A few boys in the home were thuggish, borderline delinquents. For the most part they didn't seem dangerous, but a couple of them were beginning to experiment with a life of crime. Ronan, one of the bigger boys, tiptoed into the girls' dorm late one night and woke Delhi and me. At sixteen, he was as big as most adults. He was constantly scheming, coming up with plans to steal food or ways to create mischief in the lives of those he disliked.

"Come with me," he instructed. We pulled on our clothes and followed him like stealthy spies on a mission. Though we had no idea where we were going, we were following him by choice, not coercion. It was late, and the house was deadly quiet. Was he planning to steal food again? He led us into the kitchen, past padlocked cabinets and freezers and down a long, narrow hallway, glancing over his shoulder for Stevens. We abruptly stopped in an empty pantry where two other teenage boys stood waiting. One boy propped a ladder against the white wall. Far above, some sort of ceiling hatch gaped open, and I could see a smattering of stars. It was a clear, chilly night. The fishy sea wind moaned above us, and I felt a surge of dread. This was no petty-theft mission. What did Ronan have in mind here? I had no desire to go outside; the ladder looked rickety and steep, and I hadn't thought to bring a jacket. In the pantry corner, my eye caught a mouse skittering under the wall.

"Come on," said Ronan. "We're escaping!"

Delhi and I scaled the ladder, blindly following our leader. I wondered what the hell I was doing. Climbing around freezing in the middle of the night held no appeal for me. I had never been a risk taker. Living Mom's adventures had been more than enough excitement for me, or so I believed then. I wanted to stay on solid ground, clutching on to things that seemed safe.

We were on the roof now and had to descend one of the ancient rusty fire escapes on the ocean side. Lemmings, we followed Ronan as if we trusted him implicitly. I was panicking. *What if Stevens wakes up? What will he do to us?* I kept my fear to myself.

When we reached solid ground, Ronan blurted, "Run!" We all bolted across the frontage road toward the ocean, though there were no cars in sight. We stopped once we hit the rocky seashore. Ronan hopped up onto the seawall and grabbed a seat. He wrestled some smokes from his jeans pocket and lit a couple. I didn't smoke, but what the hell; I was an escaped prisoner now. *Who knew what I was capable of?* I took one and inhaled, coughing and wheezing.

"So what's the plan, mastermind?" asked Delhi. *That's a good question. We are running away . . . to . . . where? If any of us had a place to go, we wouldn't be in an orphanage in the first place.*

"I dunno," said Ronan. "I just wanted to have me a fag."

"You've got to be kidding," I said. "We escaped for a cigarette? Let's just go back." We filed back across the road, retracing our steps, climbing back up the fire escape and down the ladder, returning through the skylight to our so-called home.

Two nights later, I awoke in the dark, Ronan's full body weight pinning me. His hands cuffed my wrists to the bed as his hot breath washed over my face.

"Don't say a word." He smelled a little minty—like toothpaste.

"What are you doing?" I wasn't going to follow his inane ideas anymore, but he was scaring me a little.

"I'm going to rape you," he whispered, like he was trying out the word for the first time. "If you scream, I will kill you."

This hadn't occurred to me. We'd been friends of a sort, partners in crime. This was the first time I considered his bullying attitude might have been more than bravado.

"Ronan, I thought we were friends," I was trying to come up with a way to dissuade him. Would he really do it with all these girls sleeping just feet from us?

"We *were*," he said, with the emphasis on "were."

"Well, what's different now?" I said, stalling.

"You betrayed me," he said. "We were going to escape together."

This was news to me. We'd never discussed running away from the home together, and if he'd wanted to leave, it was easy enough to walk out. This wasn't Alcatraz.

"Well, I'm sorry." Appeasing him seemed the best thing to do. "I just didn't know where we could go," I was trying to imply that my greatest dream had been to run off with him, it was merely the practicalities that had gotten in our way.

"I had it all planned. You always underestimate me." He said this as if we'd known each other for years instead of weeks and had an ongoing dispute about his competency.

"I know, I'm sorry." I considered asking him what his plan had been, to stall for more time, but it occurred to me that he might not have had any plan at all, and then he'd be even angrier because he wouldn't have an answer. "Can we just try to start over? I'm sorry I didn't trust you," I lied.

He began loosening up on my wrists, and some of his weight lifted off me.

"If I let you go, you have to kiss me."

This was far from the way I'd envisioned my first kiss, but it seemed a small price to pay, and after all, he had just brushed his teeth.

"OK."

He leaned down and gave me a quick, dry kiss on the lips, as if he'd never kissed a girl before, and then he jumped off the bed and ran from the dormitory. Once I was sure he was gone, my whole body began to tremble. Ronan had terrified me more than I would ever let him know. But after years appeasing Mom, I had mastered two invaluable skills. I could calm crazy people, and, more valuable still, I could think fast and mask my fear.

The Exorcist

Mom was committed to a long-term psychiatric facility a two-hour bus ride away from Rottingdean. Stevens let me navigate the bus system on my own a few times, and on one occasion my social worker drove me to visit her. I had expected the hospital to be dismal and creepy, but it was clean and sunny, surrounded by manicured lawns and trees. By my last visit, Mom seemed more lucid.

"I called Jim the other day and told him about the mess we're in. Those idiot cops accusing me of trying to kill myself! What kind of fool would jump from a two-story building? Frankly, I think that landlord on High Street just wanted us out of his flat and had me arrested on trumped-up charges." OK, maybe she was still a bit off, but at least she seemed free of the Joan of Arc delusion.

Two days later, Jim arrived. This time, he'd flown halfway around the world to rescue us. Once again, I was relieved and elated to see him. I threw my arms around his neck as soon as he walked into the children's home. But my happiness waned as I realized what Jim's arrival meant. I was sick at the thought of returning to Mom.

"Is there any way I can stay here?" I asked him.

In the home, I had been allowed to be a child, free of the responsibility for and constant worry about Mom. The idea of returning to a roller-coaster life with her depressed me beyond words. I would have chosen a hundred nights of dealing with the likes of Ronan over going back to Mom. But staying in the orphanage was not an option. I was an uninvited guest of the British government, and England did not need another mouth to feed.

This time Jim was smarter and refused to allow Mom to dictate our means of transportation. When we arrived at Heathrow he began plying her with alcohol.

"You half-wits know I'm afraid to fly!" She began her rant as soon as we sat down at the airport bar. But Jim wasn't falling for it. Now he knew the drill: alcohol and pills, not too much or too little, just enough to knock her out but not kill her.

When we landed in California, their partnership was finally over. Jim would no longer be living with us. He found us an apartment on Bonita Street, a little alley off Polk Street, and we settled into a routine of school and taking Mom to doctor's appointments. Jim found me a weekend and after-school job at a souvenir booth in Fisherman's Wharf.

As the weeks passed, Jim stopped coming around, and Mom became more stable and occasionally ventured out alone.

"I was in North Beach today and ran into Dan Lindberg," she reported when I got home from school. She hadn't mentioned Dan's name in years. When Dad and Mom were married, he'd often spent time with us in the Masonic Avenue apartment. He was one of the beatniks they'd met at City Lights when they first arrived in San Francisco.

"Dan said your father's back in town. He's working as a barker at a strip club on Broadway, the Garden of Eden." She stifled a smirk as she delivered this information. The idea of my father standing outside a strip club trolling for drunken tourists made me shrink with shame. Mom had always said I was a hopelessly bourgeois conformist. Maybe she was right.

Our new neighborhood was full of drinking establishments, all chock-full of ferns and potted plants. Lord Jim's on Polk and Broadway was Mom's favorite fern bar. Some nights I'd barhop with Mom and, as in England, no one ever questioned my age.

"Karen, sing with me! 'What shall we do with the drunken sailor, what shall we do with the drunken sailor, early in the morning.'" We sang some sea shanties, and a few patrons joined in. Lord Jim's was not a piano bar, but the bartender would roll his eyes and tolerate a certain amount of Mom's singing.

I'd begun repeating a mantra to myself: just survive childhood and you will be OK—as if I were serving a sentence, marking off days on my cell wall. If singing with Mom in a bar would keep the peace, I was willing to do it. But even when the mood seemed light, I was in a perpetual state of hypervigilance.

Since the brig episode I'd had a recurring nightmare: Mom and I were at Disneyland, and I was full of excitement, thrilled to be at the happiest place on earth. Then, gradually, the amusement park grew sinister. The attractions began morphing into dark, cold torture chambers. I awoke, silently screaming to escape. I was no psychologist, but even I understood that dream, and I began to believe my survival might depend on getting far away from Mom.

I worked hard at school, hoping to make a high enough grade-point average to be accepted to San Francisco's only public college preparatory high school. That spring, when I found out I had been accepted, my future away from Mom seemed more possible. I would go to college, be a nurse, make Mom happy, and she would get well. Once she was well, I could be free, no longer responsible for her. That was my plan.

I searched the school for my favorite English teacher, and found her in the hallway near her classroom.

"Guess what, Mrs. Dupont! I got into Lowell!"

"Karen, that is wonderful news! You are going to do so well there. You're on your way to college!" But my excitement dwindled as I began wondering where in the world I would ever get the money to pay for college.

When I got home, I decided to bring up the subject with Mom. Almost before I'd finished my question, Mom hopped to her feet, furious. She flailed her arms at the air as if she'd been anticipating this very question for years.

"We don't have that kind of money, you ninny! I'm on SSI, for Christ's sake!"

"Mom, how am I supposed to become a nurse without going to college?" Though I knew we had no money, after years of her insisting I should become a nurse, I hoped Mom had some sort of plan up her sleeve. I had always believed she really wanted me to achieve her missed goal and she would help me figure out some way to do it.

Her outbursts no longer terrified me as they once had. Inspired by Del, my time at the children's home had toughened me a bit. Now I could become the Artful Dodger at will.

"That's not my problem! Join the army or something for all I care! They can pay for it."

Something shifted in me as she said that. Perhaps I should have seen it sooner, but I was finally getting her message. I was one hundred percent on my own.

A week later Mom stopped taking her Thorazine again. She said she hated the way it made her feel. We'd seen *The Exorcist* together, during one of her lucid days, and we both enjoyed the horror movie, though it was the most terrifying thing we'd ever seen. The movie's main characters shared a version of Mom's last name, MacNeil. Initially, we both found that coincidence amusing. But as she slipped into darkness again, the shared name held a portent for Mom. She believed that, like Linda Blair's character, I'd been possessed by the devil. At first she mentioned this casually, but soon she was fixated on the idea.

"You are a witch! They should have drowned you in the pond at Rottingdean!" she shrieked one morning, as I fled for school. Each afternoon, I unlocked our apartment door feeling like I was the movie priest entering Regan MacNeil's room, filled with the same dread I'd felt while watching the movie. I expected Mom to dive at me brandishing a giant crucifix, or something worse.

Her new obsession came to a crescendo on Friday after my choir recital. When I came home wearing the black-and-red dress I'd chosen for the performance, she was livid, my clothing further evidence of my demonic possession. As I came through the front door, she lunged at me.

"Wearing black and red now! You really are a witch. Evil! Evil! I banish you, Satan! I banish you!" She thrashed her arms in my face, banishing me. Though she had considered herself agnostic for years and told me she had lost her faith at age sixteen, a warped version of her Catholic indoctrination surfaced during her manic episodes. I stepped under and around her, into my purple bedroom. At my request, Jim had painted the walls lavender when we first moved in, and I'd decorated my wall with a poster of a giant grape.

"You are the whore of Babylon!" she screamed. All at once, she was in my room, on top of me, pushing. We spiraled toward my purple bed. Her fingers, bony tendrils, were squeezing tightly around my neck. I gagged for air. Now we were wrestling on my bed. I was on my back and she was straddling me, throttling me. She was choking the air out of me, crushing my windpipe. "I banish you! Release this soul from this body," she shrieked over and over. I tried peeling her fingers from my neck, but she had crazy-woman-superpower strength. I couldn't get a breath and I felt myself weakening. By tenth grade, I was as tall as she, but she had fifty pounds on me, a side effect of the lethargy-inducing drugs she'd been prescribed but now refused to take. I thought of kicking her, punching her, biting her, but I couldn't do it. She was my Mom, and I just couldn't hurt her. But I knew if I didn't do something she would kill me.

Carrying her weight on top of me, I pushed as hard as I could toward the edge of the bed, then with great effort turned onto my side. Mom tumbled to the floor, losing her grip as she fell. Then, springing up like a jack-in-the-box, she was back on her feet. I jumped off the bed and rushed her, pushing her out of my room with all my strength. I slammed the door and leaned against it until finally her footsteps faded toward the kitchen.

I wondered what she would do next. Maybe she was picking through the kitchen drawer, choosing a weapon? Mom's footsteps clicked on the linoleum. The rattle of utensils in the kitchen told me she was distracted for the moment. I snuck out the front door and sprinted to Van Ness Avenue to take the bus to Monica's.

When I got to the bus stop, I sat in an apartment building doorway and began sobbing. I prayed for someone, anyone at all, to take me out of this nightmare, to rescue me. As I sat there wailing, a patrol car trolled Van Ness Avenue. I willed them to stop, to come help me, but they drove on past. I was invisible.

I spent that night at Monica's, but as close as I was to Monica, I had never felt comfortable with her mother. Janette guarded Monica as if I was a rival for her love, and as soon as I arrived I felt she wanted me to leave.

I returned "home" the next day. I could think of nowhere else to go. I had no other family, and few friends. The hippie tribe had long since disbanded, my father was by now a stranger, and Jim had moved on with his life, dating and living on his own.

When I returned to the apartment, Mom was nowhere to be found. At first, I was relieved she wasn't there, but then I began to worry.

I gave her until ten o'clock that night, then, when she didn't return, I called the police. If Mom had gone outside in the manic state she'd been in, it seemed likely she would have been arrested. I called the police, and they confirmed she had been taken into custody at Aquatic Park earlier that day after attacking a woman who'd been picnicking on the lawn. I could imagine the scene: Mom on a tirade about sunglasses, pulling at the woman's picnic blanket as if she was performing some kind of tablecloth trick, the salami and sourdough flying through the air.

The dispatcher told me a psychiatric hold had been placed on her. This time she would be sent to Napa State Hospital and would remain there indefinitely. It seemed the cops didn't yet know Mom had a daughter. What had I been thinking the day before, with my fantasies of being rescued by the police? If someone at the hospital figured it out, I'd end up in another children's home. Or maybe I'd end up with some freakish foster family, like the one Delhi had lived with. I needed to get out of the apartment quickly, before some nosy social worker found me.

Then I remembered Mom had said my father was back in town. The postcards had stopped long ago, and it had been years since he'd even called. When Dad never reappeared after his stint in the army, at first I'd mourned him, pretending he'd died in Vietnam, where he served but was never wounded. Then, since he hadn't actually died, but had simply disappeared by choice, I told myself I didn't want him. But now, like it or not, I needed him.

Locating my father required minimal investigative skills. Of course, I'd never bothered looking for him before. But when I finally decided to, all I had to do was call directory assistance.

"Dad?" The word felt foreign, I couldn't remember the last time I'd said the word. "It's me, your daughter. Karen." There was silence on Dad's end of the line. "I need some help."

"Oh. Hi," he said. There was more silence. I shook the phone trying to make it work.

"Did you hear what I said?"

"Yeah. You need help? What do you mean?"

"Mom is in Napa. You know, the state psychiatric hospital? I have nowhere to go. I need somewhere to stay."

"Oh. You know we have a baby now, right?"

I shook the phone again, staring into the speaker. What baby? What was wrong with him? Was he not hearing me?

"Can I come over and talk to you?"

"Yeah, OK, I guess. Let me ask Janice if that works." He put the phone down and I heard the muffled voices of my father and, I presumed, my until then unheard-of stepmother.

Riding the bus to Dad's Mission District cottage, I was seething inside, angry but desperate. I told myself maybe we'd just had a bad phone connection, that he would understand when we spoke in person.

Dad held his baby loosely on his lap as his new wife hopped around the kitchen getting ready for work. Janice was young, blonde, and beautiful. I was stunned my father had attracted such a gorgeous woman. Dad was now billiard-ball bald, with a pockmarked face scarred by teen acne. I'd remembered him as handsome, but the years had not been kind to him.

We spent no time with pleasantries or catching up.

"Mom is in Napa and I have nowhere to go." I repeated, in case he hadn't grasped the situation during our phone call. I paused, letting him jump in and offer to help.

"Oh. This is your half-brother Seth. Do you want to hold him?"

I reached out and took his baby, cradling him on my lap, but refusing to look at him. I wondered if Dad had not heard what I just said.

"Can I stay here with you until I graduate? I can help out babysitting," I said all at once. Embarrassed to be begging, pride stabbed at my gut. Now I allowed myself to look at Seth. He smiled up at me, a cute little guy.

Dad looked at me blankly, then glanced over at Janice, as if she had all the answers. But she was busy on the other side of the kitchen, singing and dancing along to the radio, making coffee. I didn't know if she even knew why I'd come.

"You're supposed to be my father!" I whispered. "I've never asked you for a thing. You haven't even paid child support! I need your help!" I kept my voice low; my anger was boiling over, but I didn't want to upset the baby, or for Janice to hear me.

"Let me think about it," he said. I waited expectantly for a few minutes, then, realizing he had nothing more to say, I handed him his baby and got up to leave. I'd been in my father's home for less than fifteen minutes.

On the bus ride back to Bonita, I puzzled over his reaction. I couldn't believe this was all the man had to say to his only daughter after a decade of absence. I questioned every move I'd made. I hadn't used the right words, I told myself. He, no doubt, sensed my lack of affection for him and knew I was only there out of desperation.

I'd once told myself he'd just given up on seeing me because he couldn't deal with Mom's craziness, that underneath it all, he really loved me and wanted me. But I'd been deluding myself. I was nothing to him, no more than a stranger showing up on his doorstep, like a missionary asking for a donation, offering him a copy of *Watchtower*.

The next day he called.

"Janice is not OK with you living with us."

"OK," I said.

"Good-bye," he said.

"Good-bye."

That was our entire conversation. Maybe if I'd feigned some affection for him, I thought, some love, things would have gone differently. But I knew this wasn't true, that I was just fooling myself. I couldn't pretend. He felt my simmering rage. Yet even as I acknowledged my bad attitude, I couldn't let him off the hook so easily. Wasn't it a father's job to take care of his child, even if she was bitter? I seethed over Janice, wondering what sort of evil stepmother kicks her husband's kid to the curb. But I blamed Dad more. I wasn't Janice's child. I was his. She was a young mother, inexplicably married to an old bald guy. Even if he was telling me the truth, it was his job to stand up to her.

I was unwanted by my father, and my mother was in the loony bin. I had never felt more alone. It was tempting to wallow in self-pity. So I did. I wallowed for a few hours, sprawled on my lavender bed in my purple room. Then, finally snapping awake, I remembered I had to find somewhere to live before the authorities tracked me down.

I was too humiliated to ask my school friends for help. None besides Monica knew how bad things had become. Anyway, I couldn't imagine my school friends' families would want to take on another teenager. I also worried some misguided busybody might report me to Child Protective Services.

Logically, I knew should've been even more depressed than I'd been earlier. But something had shifted inside me after I hung up with Dad that afternoon. After my wallow, I became energized by anger. *To hell with all of them! I am going to survive, and have a good life, and they will all be sorry!*

I packed my shoulder bag full of underwear, jeans, and T-shirts and grabbed my heavy jacket. I checked my jeans pockets and counted my cash. I had $46 and no idea where I was going.

Floating Alone

I took the bus to the wharf and wandered around the Cannery and Ghirardelli Square, as Monica and I had seven years earlier, when we were eight years old. I befriended a group of musicians and street artists who crashed where they could. I slept on someone's floor. I slept on someone's couch, fleeing that apartment when I awoke to the sensation of a fly on my skin that was in fact a strange man caressing my breasts.

I continued to ride the bus to school each day, never sharing the desperation of my nights with my classmates. It was June, there were only a few days left in the school year, and I promised myself I would keep on going.

At the bus stop, a man dressed like Super Fly asked me to come work for him. He said I was sitting on a gold mine. I told him no thank you.

The cash in my pocket lasted ten days.

I was at Hunt's Donuts, skimming the classified ads in a *Chronicle* someone had tossed aside. "Models Wanted." I wasn't a model but I was fifteen, homeless, and down to my last three dollars; maybe I could be a model. He told me to come to his apartment that evening, a couple of blocks north of the Tenderloin. I knew how stupid it was, how dangerous.

"Don't be nervous," he'd said before hanging up. He said he was an artist and his wife would be there the whole time. I didn't ask what sort of pictures he would take, or how much he would pay me. I didn't think I had the right.

I rang the doorbell, and the rusty metal gate buzzed open. He was thirtyish, balding and thin. His loose T-shirt was stained with something brown, an earthy smell came from his jeans. Or maybe the earthy smell was coming from me. I hadn't bathed since leaving the breast molester's apartment. A woman, twenty-ish and pretty, poked her head out of the kitchen and nodded but did not smile. I walked into the front room, where a camera hovered over a tripod.

"So first, I'll get some headshots," he said. And he did.

I needed to ask him about money, about being paid, but I couldn't make the words come.

"Would you take your top off?" he asked. And I did. I was cold, my nipples hardened beneath my bra. *What am I doing?*

"Would you take your bra off?" This time I hesitated. I had never been topless in front of a man before. Or a boy. Or any stranger. Yet here I was, slowly unhooking my bra. Hadn't I agreed to all this by answering his ad? Like I'd crashed his party. Like I owed him something.

As I stood half naked before his lurking camera, I knew with certainty I deserved this. I'd been a fool answering the ad. Where would this end? What else would I do?

Then, as if waking from a spell, I suddenly grabbed my bra and T-shirt and ran down the hallway, pulling my shirt over my head as I fled the building.

I need help. That's what I was thinking as I picked up the pay phone to call Jim. Yes, though I hadn't seen him in months, Jim saved me again. Now he was selling used furniture in a ware-house on Valencia Street. The head shop business had dried up as the 1970s disco scene replaced the flower children's moment on the world stage. To save on rent, he lived in some rooms above the store. It was essentially a crash pad, mattresses scattered on the floor. He took in transients who camped there until they moved on to the next spot.

I told Jim about Mom, and about Dave, though I couldn't bring myself to tell him the humiliating modeling story. He moved me into the warehouse that same day. We returned to Bonita Street in Jim's grey Chevy pickup and packed what was left. The apartment had been ransacked while it was vacant, so there wasn't much left to pack. We drove away, and I never looked back.

I crashed on a mattress on Jim's warehouse floor and finished out the school year. Jim always made me feel welcome, never an imposition. We took our showers at his ex-wife Sheila's house, cooked our meals on a hot plate in a large communal pot— franks and beans, spaghetti, stew. I settled into life at the warehouse and would have been happy to stay there for the remainder of high school. But Jim's used-furniture business was failing, and he had little choice but to give up on it. Mom remained hospitalized, and Jim decided that if he returned to working as a printer at the *Chronicle*, he'd be able to afford an apartment close to my high school.

Jim stepped in as my sole, if illegal, guardian. I was fifteen, and even at that age, I understood his generosity and the risk he was taking. I'd had a small taste of life as a homeless teen, and I was certain if not for Jim, I would have been in serious trouble. So we began our search for an apartment. Jim told the landlords he was my stepfather in order to explain our different last names. An occasional building owner would raise his eyebrows, as if we were Lolita and Humbert Humbert. But it only took a few weeks to find an affordable one-bedroom in the Inner Sunset.

Just as we'd settled into the new apartment and I'd started the new school year, Mom called from the hospital. I hadn't visited her the entire time she'd been in Napa, though we'd spoken on the phone a few times.

"Hi, Karen. They're letting me out of this hellhole in a couple of days. The social worker found me a studio on Ellis Street."

"How are you feeling?" I asked, as if her illness were physical. I could think of no diplomatic way to ask if she still heard voices telling her I required exorcism.

"I'm fine. I just want to get the hell out of here. What are you doing?" I hesitated, worried about what she would do when she realized I had no intention of ever living with her again.

"Jim found us an apartment on Twelfth Avenue. It's closer to Lowell. I think I should stay here." My chest ached as I told her I was choosing Jim, not her.

"Well, I guess I get no say in the matter. Do whatever you want." She was civil—cold, but civil.

Living with Jim gave me the opportunity to have normal high school friendships. I felt free of the burden of taking care of Mom for the first time, though I was plagued with guilt for wanting to free myself.

On weekends I rode the bus downtown to visit her in the Tenderloin. She lived in a closet-like studio, with just enough room for a bed, a chair, and a reading lamp. I couldn't imagine where she would have put me, even if I'd wanted to live with her. The cramped space gave us both an easy excuse to avoid the issue.

After I knocked, I heard her creep toward the door—the Thorazine Shuffle. The shuffling was a sign she was taking her meds. A Marlboro simmered in an ashtray like malodorous incense, an Agatha Christie paperback was open on the seat of her chair. I snatched it up before she sat on it.

"How's it going?" I balanced on the edge of her twin mattress and handed her the box of peanut brittle I'd brought as a peace offering. Mom's fingers were stained a deep brownish yellow. I'd seen paint that color, hipster coffee houses painted Nicotine. I wondered how many cartons of cigarettes it took to stain human skin that color.

"I'm OK. The guy down the hall has been helping me out. Some days I can hardly get to the corner store for a can of soup. Martin walks down for me."

Now I felt terrible for bringing only candy. But two weeks earlier when I had brought a bag of groceries, she'd screamed at me and called me Lady Bountiful, insisting she was not my charity case. She'd then gone on a tirade against Jim, accusing him of making me his sex slave. Her rant hurt me, mostly because of her unfairness toward Jim, who had never laid a hand on me. But on the bus ride home, I was overwhelmed with sadness for Mom, feeling like the worst daughter in the world for abandoning her, the sole survivor of an unnamed holocaust.

Jim and I settled into a routine. I cooked dinner before he left for his night shift at the newspaper. The lobster shift, he called it. In the old days in some town somewhere, printers ate lobster after working the night shift. Was it in Maine? I always wanted to contribute to my keep, feeling guilty for burdening him with a child he'd never asked for. But he always refused to let me pay for rent or groceries and told me to save my salary from my weekend job at the health food store.

Jim liked to brag that he hadn't set foot in a doctor's office since his induction into the army at age eighteen. This worried me because he had a terrible smoker's hack that got worse with each passing year. Mom, an armchair medic, had diagnosed him with emphysema. I never knew why he avoided doctors; if it was some sort of phobia, he never let on. But then, he came from a generation of men who were not allowed to show fear.

He began asking me to cut his hair to save money. I was really nervous at the idea, having had no training as a barber.

"What if I make a mistake? What if I miss a spot, or take too much off?"

"One thing about hair, it always grows back," he would say. And, freed of the fear of being judged for making a mistake, I became a somewhat competent barber.

And finally, I was able to hug Jim, and express my gratitude

Junior year, I fell in love with Etienne, a high school classmate who was one year ahead of me. He was a gifted long-distance runner, handsome and Mediterranean looking. His family virtually adopted me, and his sister became my best friend. Though Etienne and his sister couldn't believe I thought so, to me they seemed like the perfect family. They had dinner together every Sunday, always including me. Then everyone played an insanely complicated French card game that I never even tried to learn. By watching his mother, I learned how to cook and how to give a party. She worked a demanding job and also managed to take excellent care of her family.

Then, with the predictability of the changing of the seasons, Mom was arrested again. This time she was held at San Francisco General Hospital Psychiatric Ward. Etienne had met Mom a few times when she was on her medication. But when he offered to come to the hospital with me, I refused to let him and boarded the bus alone. I wasn't ready for him to see Mom like this. I feared he might believe the terrifying aphorism that girls become their mothers, that if he met Mom when her illness was in full force, he would see my future and run away screaming.

A patient shouted from his window, welcoming me as I approached the hospital door: "Patty Hearst, Patty Hearst!"

It was 1974, and the kidnapping was in the news daily. Maybe I wore my hair in a similar style to Patty's, but I could see no other resemblance. But the man's greeting made me even more wary to go inside the hospital.

This psych ward was terrifying, nothing like the hospital in England. It felt like a prison. Upon entering, I was pat-searched. An orderly secured a heavy metal door behind me with one of dozens of keys hanging from a chain on his belt. The raving of patients resonated from every direction. My heart was racing and I was short of breath. It was all I could do to stay long enough to find Mom and deliver the cigarettes and candy she'd asked for.

She was seated in the recreation room at a card table with three catatonic patients staring vacantly at the wall. A television boomed in the background. I sat down, and she focused her zombie eyes on me. Behind her, a large, angry man rose from his seat in the television room and motored toward me, muttering obscenities. Two orderlies grabbed him just as he lunged forward and led him away.

"Get me out of here," Mom said, but there was no oomph to it. I gave her the candy and cigarettes and a cursory hug.

"I'll try," I said, not meaning it.

As I signed out, I looked at the nurse's face. Her eyes were as glazed as her patients', as if she'd medicated herself to make it through her shift. Mom had been telling me to be a nurse for so long, I'd assumed someday I would be one. But now I wondered if I could stand working in a place like this.

The next year Etienne was accepted at UC Berkeley. He encouraged me to apply for the following year and taught me about scholarships. In our argument about college, Mom had never mentioned the possibility of a scholarship. It had never even occurred to me that I might be eligible for one. As I filled out applications for financial aid, I read some small print explaining the meaning of *emancipated minor status*. I learned that since no one had declared me as a dependent for income-tax purposes, and I didn't live with a legal guardian, I was eligible for financial aid I never would have received otherwise. Mom's illness and Dad's failure to care for me had miraculously paved my way to college.

After high school I followed Etienne to Cal, and we moved in together. Berkeley did not offer a nursing program, so my plan was to study there for two years, then apply to nursing school at UCSF. It seemed straightforward enough, but I grossly underestimated how much time, study, and effort would be required to achieve even mediocre grades in the science classes.

When Mom had suggested nursing, it seemed plausible. I'd been a *M*A*S*H* fan as a child, imagining myself as the nurse who raced to the chopper ahead of all the others to save the wounded soldiers. I would save them! I cared the most! By high school, I pictured myself riding through the Appalachians on a white motorcycle wearing an all-white leather jumpsuit. On my back, emblazoned in red cursive embroidery, were the words "Angel of Mercy." My long, dark hair floated in the wind behind me. (I wore no helmet in this fantasy.) Driving from shanty to shanty, I would inoculate impoverished children. People would be so happy to see me. "She's here! She's here!" the children would shout as I passed out nutritious snacks. I never noticed that my fantasies revealed no desire to be a nurse, only a longing to heroically rescue people and to be loved and admired.

Meanwhile, I searched for another part-time college job. The state was covering my tuition, but I needed at least twenty hours a week of minimum wage to pay my half of the rent. A local pharmacy was advertising for clerks, so I applied, thinking pharmacy experience might look good on my nursing-school application.

Don Papadopolus, the owner of Will's Drugs, was a redwood tree of a man, approximately nine feet tall, maybe forty-five years old, with a black moustache the size of a young ferret. He was handsome, in a terrifying way. He would have made a decent Dracula, though he was beefier than the average vampire. His shellacked ebony hair glimmered in the store's high-wattage fluorescent lighting. Ten minutes into my interview, he proudly revealed the Colt .45 he wore on his hip beneath his white phar- macist's coat. I wasn't sure what sort of reaction he expected, but I sensed he wanted me to be impressed. I hoped my facial expres- sion conveyed admiration, not terror. In just a couple of years, a gun would be as familiar to me as a tube of lipstick, but at that point I'd never seen any gun up close. Mr. Papadopolus was the most intimidating person I'd ever met. Well, there was Mom to consider in any such contest, but even so, Papadopolus might have won. Nonetheless, I was relieved, even elated, when he hired me. I had moved into a new apartment, without Etienne, and my rent was almost due.

Etienne and I had just broken up after nearly four years together. I had been holding on to him for dear life because I loved his family so much, and I couldn't stand the thought of losing them all. But we both knew our relationship was over. Not having a clue what a healthy relationship looked like, I had perpetually picked fights, imitating Mom's relationship techniques. Eventually he left me for someone else, and I couldn't even say I blamed him.

I was working the Will's Drugs post office register, in the far corner of the store, staring at my reflection in the window and obsessing over Etienne when a gruff male voice interrupted my thoughts.

"Gimme the money!" I turned to face the muzzle of a gun.

The robber's deep voice didn't match his boyish face. I'd have guessed he was younger than me, nineteen or so. His blue Adidas jogging suit, I later learned, was the standard uniform for armed robbers. He lifted his gun higher and pointed it at my nose. Though it was probably half the size of Papadopolus', looking down the barrel made it seem enormous. A hot surge of adrenaline rushed through me. His hand was shaking like he'd never held a gun before, and I suddenly and unhelpfully recalled reading somewhere that shaky-handed robbers were the most dangerous.

As I opened the register and began packing bills into a brown paper bag, I glanced over my left shoulder toward the elevated pharmacy counter where Mr. Papadopolus was counting pills into bottles. Couldn't he see what was happening? But then I thought, *No! Don't notice, Papadopolus!* I didn't even know if he was a good shot, and the robber stood mere inches from me. I pictured Papadopolus whipping out his gun like some town sheriff in a western saloon, bullets ricocheting off the L'Oreal and Revlon displays I'd spent hours arranging. *Don't look this way, Papadopolus! Just let me give this guy the money and get him out of here.*

Malibu Matt, the surfer kid from Ventura who worked with me in the store, was on the other side of the room with his back to me, dusting off a showcase and admiring his sun-kissed reflection. *Hey, Dude! I'm about to get killed, and you're polishing furniture?* I thought about the gold necklace Matt always wore: "Live, Laugh, Love." I had been baffled the first time I saw his pendant, disbelieving that people really lived that way, as if living, laughing, and loving were a simple matter of choice. *Were they?*

"I want some things from this case over here too," the robber squeaked. He'd given up the manly-voice charade. He pointed to a display case on the other side of the room, by the window.

"I'll need to get the key." I pointed to the drawer. He nodded, and I opened the register to remove the long keychain. I inched around the counter. He pointed to the showcase and followed close behind as I walked over, unlocking the sliding glass cabinet door.

"I want that." He pointed to a backgammon set. I wouldn't have taken him for the backgammon type, but it didn't seem like a good time to mention it. He picked out a few more indiscriminate items—a lava lamp, a box of dominos, a fake scrimshaw whale tooth, like he was on a television game show where contestants had mere seconds to grab random merchandise. I glanced up at the pharmacy counter where Papadopolus continued counting pills, sliding them into bottles.

Finally the robber said, "Thank you for your cooperation," and fled out the door. I dashed to the pharmacy counter, which sat a few steps above the main floor.

"Mr. Papadopolus! I just got robbed!"

"What! What register? Why didn't you call out to me?" Papadopolus hopped off his stool and drew his weapon. "Why do you think I wear this gun?" His face became the exact shade of the Cherries in the Snow lipstick tester. He ran out of the store, pointing his gun skyward. I followed him from the window as he crossed to the IHOP parking lot where Berkeley police officers often parked. He was brandishing his firearm like a madman and screaming something at the cops, his pharmacy uniform the only clue he was a crime victim, not a random, gun-wielding lunatic. He pounded on the patrol car door, like he was insisting on getting inside. It occurred to me that he had not asked me to describe the robber, and he might need that information. But what did I know? This was my first armed robbery. Papadopolus, on the other hand, seemed to be used to it.

A few minutes later an officer came into the store and took my statement. He repeated my description into his radio, then tipped his head, listening to the mike on his shoulder.

"Some officers have stopped a man, and they want you to come take a look."

"Will he see me?"

"No. You'll be in a dark patrol car. He won't be able to see you."

I followed him outside and got into the backseat. My last ride in a police car had been in England, the day the cops picked me up at school. Kippers and Georgie Best popped to mind.

"Now, just because they've stopped someone doesn't mean he's the guy, OK?"

"OK." I slouched down in my seat, as low as I could.

The cops drove a half mile, then stopped abruptly. I prairie-dogged and spotted two officers standing on the sidewalk next to some homeless-looking guy who was easily twenty years older than my robber. I shook my head.

"Not him."

"Are you sure?" said the officer.

His question made me wonder. *Was I wrong? Maybe this was the guy?*

"I think it's not him. Is it him? Does he have the merchandise on him?" Had he been older? Maybe I'd imagined the blue jogging suit. Did the robber have time to disguise himself as a homeless man to throw us off the track?

"We can't tell you anything," the officer said.

"OK, well, I don't think that's him."

"Are you sure?"

"I don't know. Is it him? Did you find the backgammon set on him?"

"We can't say anything to you."

"OK, well, I don't think it's him."

"Don't think, or you know?"

"Well, maybe it's him. Does he have a lava lamp?"

"We can't tell you that."

"I guess it's probably not him, then."

"Probably not?"

"Well how about dominos? Are there any dominos?"

"I can't answer any of your questions. You have to tell us if this is the man who robbed you or not," he said, a bit impatiently, I thought.

"Well, I guess it's not."

"Guess or know?" said the officer.

"Yes."

"Yes what?"

"Yes, I guess I know it's not him."

Both cops sighed in exasperation. The officers drove me back to the drug store. I vaguely noted that all of the officers I met that night were white men. In fact, I realized, in all the encounters I'd had with police, all were white males. But I didn't give the subject much more thought that night.

Later, when I became a cop, I learned the viewing of a suspect by a victim is called a *cold show*. Whenever I did one on the street, I would remember how I felt in the back of that police car, and how tempted I'd been to pick the wrong guy just to make the cops happy.

When I returned to the store, Mr. Papadopolus was in a horrible mood.

"So, I'm just wondering if you might know this guy who robbed me?" he asked.

"What?" I was indignant. Did he think I had masterminded this? How dare he think so little of me! OK, I hadn't been employee of the month, drinking Irish coffee with the girls during our lunch break, pocketing the occasional lipstick tester, but accessory to a robbery? Come on! Why was he even thinking that? Had I mistakenly told the cops to let the real thief go?

"No, I did not know him!" I insisted, too loudly. But Papadopolus wasn't quite through with his inquisition.

"Well, I just wonder why he chose your register, not one of the others?"

"Is that a rhetorical question? Because I do not know the answer to that." I wasn't in the mood for his guessing game.

"Maybe he chose the one closest to the door. Or the one furthest from me," he theorized. "Or maybe he saw there were two registers at your counter, and thought he'd get more cash."

"Mr. Papadopolus, I have no idea why he picked me." I sighed. All of a sudden, the energy seeped from me, and I slumped down onto the pharmacist's chair. And then Papadopolus must have noticed I was shivering.

"OK, then. Would you like a Valium?"

"Sure."

Wench

Not long after the robbery, Mom called me.

"Guess what, Karen?" She was flying high. I'd learned to differentiate from her voice between manic high and slurred, drunken high. This sounded like drunken high.

"What?"

"You're never going to believe this one, Karen! I met a guy named John this weekend, and we fell in love!"

"That's great, Mom." Running late for physiology class, I tried to cut her off.

"And that's not all! We got married!" A chill ran through me. *Uh-oh.*

"Don't worry. We're like soul brothers or kindred spirits or something. We don't even notice bad smells on each other!"

I tried not to think about what that might mean. Then she lowered her voice to a whisper.

"And he's rich! But don't get any big ideas about getting your grubby little hands on his money."

Mom told me John had made his fortune in the newspaper business in Southern California and had been a lonely widower for several years before meeting her. Mom quickly moved from her government-subsidized studio in the Tenderloin into John's roomy house atop Twin Peaks, and the two of them took off to see the world. She had the same wanderlust she'd had when I was a child, but now she was traveling first class. It appeared Mom had suddenly overcome her lifelong disdain for the bourgeoisie.

Graduation loomed before me, just months ahead, and it was looking very unlikely that any nursing school would be accepting me. I'd even investigated Mom's suggestion of joining the army. But that proved to be a dead-end street. The army only wanted enlistees who had already been accepted to nursing school.

I expected it was merely a matter of time before the pharmacy was robbed again, and I wasn't willing to risk my life for minimum wage—though in just a few years I would be willing to risk it for a few dollars more. College friends were telling me that great money could be made working as a cocktail waitress. Ben Jonson's Olde English Taverne was advertising for cocktail waitresses, so I tarted myself up with too much makeup and headed to the bar to apply.

When I met Mike, the manager, I lied about my age. I wasn't quite twenty-one, and I exaggerated my previous experience, but he must have been desperate, because he hired me on the spot. Mike had worked as a San Francisco police officer and had been forced to retire early. He wasn't even forty, but he walked with a pronounced limp. Though we became friends during the time I worked there, I never asked him how he'd been injured.

The serving-wench job was extremely lucrative; the combination of low-cut corsets and $1.25 happy-hour drinks equaled big tips for the waitresses. Unfortunately, the cheap drinks combined with a free all-you-can-eat Henry VIII hors d'oeuvres buffet had not proven to be a profitable business plan. Just as I bonded with my faux-Renaissance co-worker family, I had to face the reality that Lowry's was about to close us down.

That was when I had my police car sighting at Vesuvio. The

next day, I came into the bar as usual and immediately bumped into Mike.

"Hi, Karen."

"Mike, can I ask you a question?" I was afraid he would break out laughing at me.

"Of course. Shoot." I ignored the irony of the word.

"I've noticed the city is recruiting women police officers, and I was thinking of applying." I waited for his guffaw.

"I think you'd be great at it," he replied without sarcasm.

The next day, without my even asking him, Mike brought in the application card.

Two weeks before my academy class was to start I called Mom, knowing I could no longer avoid telling her.

"Mom, I have some good news."

"Let me guess: you're getting married," she said, without enthusiasm. Married? Where had that come from? I wasn't even dating anyone.

"Well, no," I worked to keep my tone upbeat. "I've decided to join the San Francisco Police Department. They're doing a big hiring drive and opening the doors to women."

"Are you out of your mind?" she shrieked. "How could you even think of joining them after everything they've done to me? They've been persecuting me for decades! I knew you hated me, but this is the worst thing you've ever done to me! Why not just drive a stake through my heart?"

I took a deep breath.

"Mom, this is not about you. It's just something I have to do."

"Well, isn't that the world's greatest news! My daughter's becoming a fucking Nazi!" She slammed down the receiver without saying good-bye.

PART TWO

Day One

I was hoping Mom and John would miraculously disappear on another one of their European adventures before I started the academy, but no such luck. Though Mom had never learned to drive and probably wouldn't be able to find the police academy, I still worried she might show up drunk and create trouble. She'd been calling me daily as my hiring date approached.

"Jesus, Karen. Even that ridiculous wench job was better than this idiotic police thing. At least Ben Jonson's had a decent happy hour." Mom and John had enjoyed the complementary hot hors d'oeuvres at the bar, the Merlin's Meatballs and Ann Bo-links.

I got up at 6:00 a.m., giving myself plenty of extra time to get ready. After I dressed, I checked and rechecked my purse fourteen times for my driver's license. I grabbed the ream of paperwork and scanned it one last time: *Bring valid driver's license* had been highlighted in bold print. I hopped into my blue Ford Falcon, a rusted heap that threatened to die each time I started it, and headed downtown. I was nagged with thoughts that if I made one small mistake, lost my paperwork, or got stuck in traffic, my entire career would be over before it began. But mostly I was excited as I looked forward to being sworn into my academy class. This would be my fresh start, my chance to be part of that happy family I'd longed for. I was almost delusional with joy that this exclusive men's club was considering me for membership.

The letter told us to meet in the assembly room of the Hall of Justice, a dilapidated building with a décor apparently inspired by the color of bile. I soon learned the police and attorneys who worked there called it the "Hole of Justice."

"Take a seat, people! I am Sergeant Meyer, the leader of your academy staff." Sergeant Meyer was a basso-voiced, mustachioed linebacker of a man. He wore his glossy, black hair slicked back; his broad chest strained the polyester of his white polo shirt. "I, along with these other officers, have been assigned the tedious and thankless job of training you for the duration of the police academy, starting right now. From now on, you answer to me, and to these officers." He waved dismissively at the four men standing beside him, all wearing matching blue slacks and white polo shirts bearing the academy emblem.

Sergeant Meyer's speech seemed well rehearsed. His canned gestures and facial expressions made me think he'd watched every movie ever made about boot camp drill sergeants and stolen all the lines.

"Look left, then right. Take a good, long, hard look."

Following his order, all forty-seven of us turned to meet the eyes of the recruits beside us. The guy next to me was Marty. He had introduced himself when I sat down, and I liked him immediately. I counted only three other women in the room. I felt conspicuous being in such a small minority, but also a little proud, as if I was making some sort of crucial feminist statement merely by showing up.

"One out of the three of you will not graduate from this academy," Meyer announced bleakly. His announcement alarmed me. We'd all gone through loads of testing and had waited on the hiring list for months. While I'd assumed some recruits would not graduate, I had never anticipated losing a third of our class. Maybe this academy would be harder than I thought.

"Right now, you people are losers. For the next nineteen weeks the academy staff will work to mold you into police officers. Most of you will never have what it takes. Few of you will ever be real cops. Think about this carefully. There is no disgrace in walking out the door right now. If you leave now, you may save yourself further embarrassment down the road. This job is not for everyone." Meyer looked us over, dubiously, as if we were the sorriest recruit class ever. "Some of you should probably leave right now and go apply for a job driving a bread truck." This would be the first of many occasions when Sergeant Meyer would suggest the bread truck driving job as our only alternate career path, as if law enforcement and delivering baked goods were simply different branches of the same line of work.

Though we were not being sworn in as actual police officers, we raised our right hands and pledged to protect and to serve the City and County of San Francisco anyway.

"You are not allowed to do any police work. You will not be a police officer until Chief Murphy pins that star on your chest. You have no police powers!" He said *police powers* as if they were superhero powers. "Don't go out there playing the Hardy Boys. Do you understand me?" We all nodded, but his instructions were annoying me. It was vaguely insulting to be told not to do something I had no idea how to do in the first place.

"I said, '*Do you understand me?!*'" The walls reverberated with his bellow.

"Yes, sir!" responded someone behind me. We all followed suit. "Yes, sir!"

"You are members of a paramilitary unit now. The next time you dimwits forget to say 'sir,' you will regret it! This organization is all about discipline. Our discipline equals our strength." My palms began to sweat. Up until now, my life had been completely discipline-less.

"Betcha he says something about the weakest link," Marty whispered.

"We're only as strong as our weakest link!" Meyer bellowed, right on cue. I stared at Marty as if he were psychic. He smiled proudly.

The sergeant then issued each of us a requisition for uniform shoes.

"Report to Butler's on Market Street and get fitted for your shoes. Then report to the academy with them by one o'clock."

The academy was on the other side of the city. It was 12:15 p.m. when he distributed the vouchers. It seemed unlikely that a group of nearly fifty people would be able to accomplish the shoe-purchasing task in the allotted time, and I sensed there would be repercussions if we failed. I imagined myself scrubbing a toilet with a toothbrush or washing the academy windows with my underwear while my classmates jeered.

Some already seemed to have inside information about how things worked. I learned, by eavesdropping, that a few recruits had been through the academy before. They were known as *recycles*. One of the recycles was yelling at us.

"Get your asses moving fast, people! We'll be in deep shit if we're late!" He was tall, older than most, sporting a gray buzz cut. I sensed he was former military. Someone call him Ed.

Boot camp anxiety had begun. We would soon learn that when one of us failed at a task, we would all pay the price. If we wanted to avoid mass punishment, we would learn to ferret out and eliminate any recruit who held us back. It was Darwinian. Learn to kill and eat the weak to save yourself.

We formed impromptu shoe-shopping teams. I searched for a group quickly, afraid of being the last one chosen. Of the other three women, I found myself most drawn to Molly, a spunky, curly-haired-blonde with a smattering of freckles. We were both relatively big and strong, and I sensed a determination in her. I attached myself to Molly, who I learned was the single mother of two young girls. A handsome young Chinese American named Keith was our driver, and Mark, an extremely attractive blond Irishman, rode shotgun. We set off for the shoe store like kids heading out for a scavenger hunt. We sprinted to Keith's car and sped to Market Street, noting with satisfaction that we were the first team to arrive. We were quickly fitted and were paying with our vouchers as recruits continued to stream into the store. We dashed back to Keith's car, clutching shoeboxes to our chests like winning lottery tickets.

It was 12:45 p.m. when we left the store. The Silver Avenue academy was a sixteen-minute drive. Lunch was out of the question—not that I had much desire to eat anyway. With my stomach anxiously roiling, it was probably best to avoid food. Keith raced to the academy.

"Yay! Record time! We won! First team back!" I cheered and high-fived Keith as we ran through the cyclone gate into the concrete schoolyard.

Sergeant Meyer was leaning against a rusty cyclone fence, arms crossed. He looked bored, not even a little impressed by the amazing time we'd made.

"You're a minute late. You get to wait for everyone else, show-offs."

We huddled as our remaining forty-three classmates trickled in.

"Let's tell each other how we ended up at the academy," said Molly. "You first, Keith."

"OK. Well, let's just say it wasn't pretty. My family owns a food company. My parents always expected me to someday run the business with my brothers. Maybe if this doesn't work out, I will. But I always dreamed of being a cop, ever since I was a little kid." He turned to me. "How about you?"

I remembered that strange afternoon. Should I tell him the story? *I saw myself driving a police car on Columbus Avenue and took it as a sign from the universe.* Would he think I was a nut? I decided to play it safe.

"I guess it was like a calling. I felt like I was meant to do it." I checked his face but found no indication that my answer was too strange.

By 1:45 p.m., all our classmates had found their way to the academy. Most of them, empty-handed and defeated, hadn't had enough time to claim their shoes.

"OK, recruits, listen up! Because so many of you dawdled at the shoe store, I'm going to teach you a lesson about punctuality," Sergeant Meyer shouted. "Get down and give me fifty burpees right now!"

We looked around with confusion. The letter the police department sent us specifically stated we were to wear business attire. I was proud that I'd finally learned what business attire should look like and thought I'd made a sensible choice. To make a good impression on the first day, I'd worn the new suit I'd finally purchased—eggshell white, skirt hem two inches above the knee—and sensible high heels. Molly wore a black skirt and heels, and the men wore suits or sport coats and ties.

We'd been told that Day One would be our swearing in, nothing more. No one mentioned we'd be doing physical training. But a burpee, we soon learned, was an acrobatic version of a push-up (probably invented by a sadistic police academy drill sergeant) in which we started from a standing position, fell down into push-up, then jumped back up and into the air with our hands over our heads. Had I known we'd be doing burpees,

I would have worn pants. I felt foolish in my suit. It occurred to me, not for the first time, that I had really had no idea what I was signing up for when I put in my application.

We counted repetitions: "One, sir. Two, sir." My classmates in the back row were being treated to a no-doubt unappetizing view of my panty-hosed, stuffed-like-sausage booty as my skirt crept higher with each backward leg thrust. Luckily, everyone seemed distracted with other clothing challenges. Some of the guys were cramming their neckties down their shirts to keep from tripping on them, and I heard an occasional seam ripping.

I scrutinized the competition as we waited for Sergeant Meyer's next order. If two out of three would quit or be fired, who would they be? Almost everyone was in decent shape, and a few even looked like former athletes. And then it dawned on me. Me! It was me! I realized with some despair—there was no question about it—I had an excellent chance of being among those eliminated.

"That was just a taste of how things work here. When I say, 'jump,' you say, 'how high?' Got it?"

I rolled my eyes at Molly.

"What movie is that line from?" she asked.

"*I said, 'Got it?' dimwits!*"

"Yes, sir!" We replied—but too late.

"Get down and give me a hundred!"

Sergeant Meyer and his cohorts had a full afternoon of physical fitness planned for us, the 145th San Francisco Police Academy class. Although I discarded my shoes early on, running foot races in shredded, panty-hosed feet was not at all how I'd imagined spending my first day. Then again, I hadn't really been able to imagine much of anything. I had no idea what went on in a police academy. It would be years before the satirical movies depicting academy life would hit the movie theatres. The police world was still a secret brotherhood, a mystery to most civilians.

"Left, left, left, right, left," we chanted as we marched in formation. Turning while marching presented a challenge for our group. There were many collisions and much stepping on other's feet as we mastered left face and right face. Our civilian attire gave the whole afternoon a surreal effect, as if an evil genius had kidnapped a bunch of stockbrokers and forced us to march around for his amusement.

Then the 143rd class strutted obnoxiously into the yard with their training staff. Molly and I gasped as they fell into pristine platoon formation. They were to graduate in just a few weeks and they marched in obscenely perfect unison. It was impossible to imagine our mangy group ever resembling them.

As he excused us for the day, Sergeant Meyer shouted, "Report here tomorrow at 0700! Full uniform! By the flagpole!" It was four o'clock. The shoe store closed at five o' clock. I began to feel anxious for those who might appear the next day without correct footwear. And then, remembering we were all for one and one for all, I felt anxious for us all. Anxiety, my childhood companion, would be my default emotional state for the duration of the academy.

George Davis, a scrawny recruit with a face like a weasel, introduced himself before we left for the day. "Hi. You can call me Golden Gloves." He offered his hand, and I instantly regretted shaking it. "I have it on good authority that three out of the four women in this class are dykes. Which one are you?"

"You'll never know." I walked away from him quickly.

Before leaving for the day, we were told to purchase our uniforms: pants and shirts the color of cigarette ash adorned with cheap black clip-on ties. Previous recruits had dubbed it the Maytag repairman uniform. The outfit reflected the dismal gray theme of the building we inhabited. It was a nondescript Halloween costume, a Greyhound bus-driver's uniform.

We would wear the Maytag until the last four weeks, when we would finally trade it for a genuine blue police jumpsuit. Sergeant Meyer told us we could purchase a brand-new Maytag or choose one from the recycle rack. I briefly wondered if buying a secondhand uniform might be bad luck, but I'd always loved shopping thrift stores. While rummaging through dozens of extra-large uniforms, I met a knee-bucklingly handsome recruit with golden-brown eyes named Art. It dawned on me that I was single and surrounded by attractive, single young men. I'd been so obsessed with proving I would be a great cop, and so desperate to show Mom my choice had been right, the prospect of also finding a relationship at the academy had never crossed my mind. I was stuck at the lowest rung of the pyramid of human needs, focused only on providing myself food and shelter. A relationship had seemed like a luxury, or a distraction.

Then I considered the consequences of dating a classmate. Not only would it complicate things but the skewed ratio of men to women might also be cause for resentment. And what if the relationship ended badly and we were trapped here together? No. Best to abstain.

On the other hand, going through months of self-imposed celibacy could also prove challenging. Temptation was everywhere. I wondered about the best way to treat these men. Clearly, some of them did not approve of women police. I'd already overheard a few conversations: "The girls aren't strong enough." "The girls will wimp out when the going gets tough." Was there some way to win them over? What if I pretended they were the brothers I'd always longed for?

I sized up a few pairs of pants and rejected each of them while chatting with Art. He was almost thirty, a senior citizen by the standards of our class.

"I was teaching high schoolers at a seminary, but this police idea just wouldn't go away. It reached the point where I could no longer ignore it." Art was well educated and clearly possessed marketable skills, yet he felt his true calling was police work. *Calling* was a word so many classmates echoed that I began to feel the job had some mysterious spiritual facet. With rare exceptions, my classmates were idealistic and had chosen their profession driven by the desire to help people.

By the end of week, Father Art as he quickly came to be known, would become a reassuring figure to the entire class. He had a gift for listening with rapt attention, making everyone feel they were fascinating. And his years of teaching experience made him the perfect den father for our sophomoric class.

I finally found and paid for my uniform, relieved that I'd made it through the first day without a Mom appearance. But I shuddered at the thought of getting through nineteen weeks with the constant expectation she might appear any moment.

I said good night to Art, and headed home with my ill-fitting, recycled Maytag. The uniforms, made for men, provided little accommodation for female curves. I got home, tried my "new" outfit on, and took a look in my bathroom mirror. The boxy cut of the shirt flattened my breasts as if I'd wrapped them in Ace bandages. Where I was once curvy, I was now matronly. Examining myself sideways, I had the appearance of a barrel-chested, but not wholly unattractive, man. My requisite short haircut and the fact that we were allowed no earrings or makeup further accentuated my manliness. On the bright side, I would most likely no longer have to worry about my classmates dueling for a chance to date me. My evening was spent laundering, ironing, and studying the reams of department general orders for the next day's test.

Survivor

It was a restless night. I woke up every half hour to check the time, certain I would sleep through the alarm. When I finally fell into a deep sleep, Mom woke me with a 5:00 a.m. phone call.

"John tried to kill me last night. I thought you should know, not that you care." She was doing her bombed Bette Davis impersonation, full of sighs and loud puffing of smoke.

"Mom, I have to leave for the academy in an hour. I can't help you now."

"No, of course you can't! You'll help the world, but won't lift a finger for your own mother." She pronounced *muthaaa* with emphasis. "Just go to your fascist storm trooper job! I suppose those assholes are turning you against me now. Thanks for nothing!" She slammed down the phone.

In the next scripted scene I was supposed to call her back and come to her rescue. I knew this act by heart. Over the years, we'd performed our show on four continents. The audiences were usually captive; train bar car customers, ocean liner passengers, and mental hospital patients. I dressed quickly and fled the apartment before she could call again.

When Sergeant Meyer said that a third of us would quit or be fired, he overestimated the tenacity of our class. By the second week, five recruits had already quit.

"Who will it be this morning?" asked Keith, before we fell in.

"Five bucks on Breathstank!" wagered Marty Desmond. Marty and I had become fast friends. I felt an instant affection for him, maybe because we were both half Jewish in a mainly Irish club, or maybe because he always made me laugh.

"No way, I say it'll be Shade Monitor, five bucks on Monitor, who's in?" bet Blockhead, a burly young Irishman. Cash flew out of gray pockets.

We'd all acquired nicknames by the third day. Some were dubbed according to physical characteristics, like Blockhead, a muscular jock with a head like a cube of concrete. Some needed no explanation, like Breathstank, a recruit who had the misfortune of reeking as if rotting from the inside out. For once, I'd skated. My moniker was just K. I was glad the guys had given me a nickname. It made me feel like I had a chance at being accepted by them. Most classmates were open to the idea of women at least getting a chance to do the job. While few supported affirmative action, most were reasonable enough to say they believed if a woman was capable she should be given a chance.

I looked down at my shoes to examine their shine, then glanced over my shoulder at the front gate, as had become my habit. Good. No sign of Mom. Monitor and Breathstank finally arrived and hustled to get into formation. Disappointed, Blockhead and Marty returned their fivers to their pockets.

The relentless attrition gave those who remained the illusion we somehow had improved our odds of graduating. We couldn't believe the academy would risk losing a whole class of recruits. Think of the expense! Wouldn't they at least try to hang on to a few of us? We discussed this daily. Had reality television existed, we would have dubbed our class *Survivor: Small Abandoned Elementary School in the Bayview District of San Francisco Edition*.

The campus location made it difficult to take our training

seriously. There was none of the authoritative feel I would have expected from a law enforcement academy. Several years earlier, the city had found this school in need of seismic retrofitting and deemed it unfit for San Francisco children. Yet they decided the building was an acceptable habitat for barely postadolescent police cadets. The new academy, in Diamond Heights, would not open for years; so, like it or not, this would be our home. Our Lilliputian desks and toilets mere inches above the ground would prove challenging for the beefier recruits. But that was the least of our concerns.

We kept these complaints to ourselves. The job market was dismal and wasn't expected to get better anytime soon. The city was offering us $24,000 a year and health insurance, more than many of us had ever expected to make. Getting this job would mean financial security, and we were willing to forfeit our physical security for it.

Truthfully, most of us hadn't yet grasped that the job could be life threatening. With the average recruit's age a mere twenty-two, our mortality was still an abstraction. We knew nothing of the dangers police faced daily. I believed the uniform acted as a shield and that no one would be stupid enough to hurt a cop. I would soon learn I was more naive than I had ever imagined.

Molly and I bonded quickly after Officer Devlin, our tall, blond, and creepy physical-training instructor, cornered us in the hallway during the first week.

"What are you two doing here?" he asked with a smirk. "Girls have no business in police work." We stood in front of him, speechless. Though I had expected some resistance to the idea of female cops, I hadn't expected a training officer to be so outspoken about his opinions. He turned and left us staring at each other in the hallway.

Molly had grown up in the mostly Irish Catholic Sunset district of the city, along with many other future police officers. We made each other laugh, and though we were plagued with self-doubt, we never let the guys see our lack of confidence. We spent a lot of energy acting as if we were certain we could do everything required of us, though we honestly had no idea what that might be.

Although not all the recruits were particularly likeable, Molly and I invited everyone when we went out dancing on the weekends. We chose our nightclubs by their location, outside the city, in case one of us did something stupid, got too drunk, or got in a bar fight. When we went out to the clubs on the Peninsula, Molly and I made sure we danced with everyone. We figured we needed the guys in our corner and sensed our best defense against the likes of Devlin was to become accepted as part of the team. Our classmates would probably have no power to save us from termination, if that was how our careers played out. But it seemed like a good idea to have the guys on our side anyway. Plus, for the most part, we were really growing to like them.

When the DJ played my favorite Blondie song, *The Tide Is High*, I hurried to the far side of the table to grab a partner.

"Come on, Breathstank! Let's dance!" I took the hand of the skinny recruit and led him to the dance floor, hoping he wouldn't notice I was holding my breath. Breathstank came along willingly. After our dance, I worked my way around the table, making sure to dance with each classmate, including Diane and Molly. Sylvia, the fourth female recruit, never joined us on our field trips. She kept to herself, and we never saw her outside of class.

The Shining

Being a police officer had never seriously crossed my mind until that day I saw the woman cop from the window of Vesuvio. Oh sure, I'd watched *Charlie's Angels* and thought Jaclyn Smith looked cool in her police uniform, but it hadn't occurred to me that police work was a possible career choice for a woman.

In 1979 the San Francisco Police Department was forced by court order to begin hiring women and minorities. Many of the older policemen were outspoken in their opposition to this development. There even seemed to be an unofficial caste system for those of us hired under the consent decree. Among the newly hired recruits, the black men seemed to get the most respect. As a group, they were resented the least, unless they were outspoken or radical. I sometimes overheard the old-school cops say things like, "At least the black guys are strong enough to do the job."

The Asian and Latin men, by my estimation, were in the next caste. A member of the old guard might say, "Hell, sometimes we need a translator, so the city might as well hire a few of them."

The next rung of the ladder held the butchy-lesbian-type women. "Some of these broads are as tough as the guys, and although it's pretty unlikely, it's possible one or two of them might be able to do the job. And at least the old ball and chain won't be breaking our balls about working with a woman, if she's a dyke. Ha ha ha!" The men might say.

Then came the caste of feminine women. "Let's face it, some of them look OK in the uniform, but they are just not strong enough to do the job. Well, if we got to have broads, let's keep the ones that aren't so hard on the old eyes. Some of them are real double baggers, and who the hell wants to look at that all day? Geez, I can look at that at home."

But the group that had it the hardest was undoubtedly the gay men. A guy might be buff, heroic, strong, and brave, but if he was rumored to be gay, he was in a caste of untouchables and was treated like a leper. So, understandably, few newly hired officers were openly gay.

On academy day three, as I passed Scot's desk, he sang, "I really need this job, please, God, I need this job." I stopped to join him in soprano harmony.

"*A Chorus Line* is my all-time favorite show!" I told him, never expecting to find a kindred musical-theater fan in this unlikely place.

"Me too!" Scot replied.

"A man who knows musical theater is my kind of guy!" I got the sense Scot might "play for the other team," as my classmates said. Still, he claimed to have a girlfriend. He was originally from the East Coast and was muscular and handsome. His dad was retired from the New York City Police Department, and Scot seemed to understand police work by osmosis.

Growing up in San Francisco, my gay friends had mostly been open about their sexuality. But I was learning that even in San Francisco, there were places where being openly gay was unsafe. The police culture was clearly different from the rest of the city, and I was just beginning to realize how much so. If Scot was gay, I thought he was smart to play it safe. We were all trying to conform and be accepted by the group. As the weeks passed and we grew to trust each other, Scot admitted the "girlfriend" had been a beard. He proudly showed me a photo of his true heart-throb, a buffed, naked Adonis.

"Yep, my dad used to say, 'I have three children . . . one of each.'" He'd recently done a few stand-up comedy gigs at the Holy City Zoo and was trying out his new material on me. The chorus "Please, God, I need this job" became our daily punch line to every torture and obstacle we met.

The platoon, as they called our class, was divided into four squads. My squad leader was Ed, the recruit who'd been mysteri-ously recycled from an earlier class. The rumor was that Ed had been hospitalized under a psychiatric hold after having a violent argument with his girlfriend. From experience with Mom, I knew a psychiatric hold could only be placed on a citizen when officers have determined the person is a danger to himself or others. After Ed's brief confinement, the academy staff decided it would be best for him to leave his last class. Most of us wondered why he had been allowed back in with our class. He was univer-sally viewed as odd. The reason the staff had decided to appoint him our squad leader was even more of a mystery.

Our academy day began at precisely 0700 hours military time. Each morning, we assembled in formation by the flagpole. Then the sergeant inspected us, paying particular attention to our shoes.

"Your shoes pass inspection when I can see my reflection in them! They should look like patent leather! This is known as a spit shine," announced Sergeant Meyer. Somehow, I had never heard of spit shining, not even in the boot-camp movies. Having grown up with people who wore Birkenstocks and flip-flops, it had never occurred to me that shoes could be shinier than they were when you first removed them from the box. My first week of the academy, and already I was failing. My shoes had not passed muster. *Muster* was not a word I'd used much, if ever, before, but I was learning that muster was a big deal in the academy. Whatever muster was, I would frequently not pass it. My punishment for failing would predictably be fifty burpees and a 1,000-word essay. During each inspection, I prayed my squad mates would not be punished because of me. I would rather do thousands of burpees and write encyclopedias of essays than be the cause of my classmates' punishment. I couldn't risk them turning on me and identifying me as the weakest link.

Ed was the only member of my squad who reliably passed shoe inspection. Ed, I remembered, was also the only veteran. Clearly, spit shining was a skill one acquired in a military setting. If I was ever going to pass, I was going to have to learn his shoe-polishing secrets. I used our lunch break to befriend Ed. After complimenting him excessively about his masterful shoe-shining skills, I asked him if he would teach us how to shine our shoes. Ed took his duty as squad leader quite seriously, and I watched in amazement as he unloaded an inordinate amount of supplies from his backpack. Then he demonstrated how he painstakingly polished his shoes, using cotton balls, matches, wax shoe polish, Q-tips, and cloth diapers. And as it turned out, disgustingly, actual spit was also required for the job.

"To do a true spit shine, you will have to invest some hours." Ed said. "You can't do a half-assed job at this. As the shine builds, it'll take a little less time. But the first few times you do it, plan to polish at least two or three hours."

During my time at the academy, I will spend approximately 417 hours ineffectually polishing my shoes. I will try various shortcuts to avoid the shoe-shining task, and will fruitlessly search the city for a shoe repair shop where they might do it for me. I will purchase an aerosol can of black goo that promises to give my shoes a mirror-like finish. This product will actually work for two weeks, until the hard, glassy shoe top cracks into a thousand obsidian arrowheads, ruining the leather and destroying the mediocre base I spent hours building. No matter how long I rub, the secret of the spit shine will elude me. I will do burpees virtually every day because of my inadequate shoe-shining skills. After failing inspection thirty times, I will consider offering Ed money, or even sexual favors, to polish my shoes. For the next five months, these shoes will be the bane of my academy existence.

Shin Splints

I fought to keep my eyes open through our hypnotically dull morning classes, all about laws we would hypothetically enforce one day. Much to our disappointment, we would not handle a firearm or drive a police car until the final weeks. But whenever I found myself drifting off, I could always snap myself awake by imagining Mom popping into the classroom. It concerned me that there was absolutely no security at the academy. Anyone could walk through undeterred. Of course, Mom was the only terrorist I truly feared. Her capacity to humiliate me was so great, I'd almost rather be shot at my desk than have Mom barge in and insult my classmates.

In the afternoon, we had physical training (PT), a source of dread for all but the most fit recruits. I regretted I hadn't worked out more during the previous year. Even jogging a couple of miles daily would have been helpful. By the end of the first week, we learned to skip lunch on PT days. One classmate had already acquired the unfortunate and unimaginative moniker Barf-Boy after vomiting four days in a row during the run. Devlin had then browbeaten him into quitting. I felt bad for Barf-Boy. He would have been a good cop, but Devlin had no sympathy for anyone he perceived as weak.

Devlin was a repulsive sadist, and Molly and I grew to despise him. After our first encounter in the hallway, he called me into his office on a weekly basis. The conversations were predictable: Devlin berated me, and I said nothing.

"What the hell are you still doing here, Nassberg?" he asked, not bothering to wait for an answer. "You'll never be a cop. Why don't you look into social work? That seems like a good job for you." He dismissed me before I could thank him for his career counseling.

This game felt very familiar. Devlin, like Mom, insulted me; I stood there and took it. The more he berated me, the more angry I became, and the more certain that I would graduate the academy. It felt no different from Mom telling me I wouldn't go to college. I had played Devlin's game many times, with a woman who was much more intimidating than he was.

On Monday in the middle of the night, I awoke to an insistent ringing of my doorbell. As I climbed down the ladder from my sleeping loft, I heard Mom pounding on my door, screaming.

"Karen, it's an emergency!"

Even though I seriously doubted it was an emergency, I opened the door. She was standing on my doorstep, suitcase in hand.

"I'm leaving that bastard! I'll stay here until I can find my own place."

She was already shoving her way into my front room. In a few hours, I would need to be in class. If I didn't get out the door by 6:15 a.m., I'd be risking an all-day burpee session. But I worried if I left her in my apartment alone she might set the place on fire and kill my neighbors.

"Oh! And guess what that halfwit said about you! He said you wear too much makeup. You look like a whore." She let the line land, gazing into my eyes, waiting for my reaction. It stung. It was true I had been overcompensating during my off-duty hours by wearing extra makeup. But the comment sounded more like Mom than John. She had complained about my use of cosmetics for years and was no doubt trying to pull me on board her "let's all hate John" wagon.

"OK, we'll talk about this when I get home. I have to get dressed." I was leaving two hours early, but I wasn't in the mood to stay and be insulted. She plopped onto the couch and lit a cigarette. I found a small bowl for her to use as an ashtray, and passed it to her on my way out the door.

"Sure, go ahead! The world awaits you, Lady Bountiful." She knew I hated when she called me that. As I fled, I began obsessing about what sort of trouble Mom might conjure up while I was gone.

Our class ran in formation as a platoon through the Bayview district several times a week. The asphalt was unforgiving. We loped past the neighborhood homes chanting jodies, annoying rhyming songs, in cadence to our step. The neighborhood was dodgy, and the residents heckled us as we passed. Some made oinking sounds; others made remarks about bacon.

"We are peedee, mighty, mighty peedee. Here we go, all the way, up the hill. What hill? No hill," Ed shouted, and we all echoed, with the staff encouraging us to be louder. "Everywhere we goooohhh, people wanna know who we are. So we tell them. We are peedee. Mighty mighty peedee. Here we go, all the way." On, and on, and on. No one would have blamed the neighbors for shooting us. Play a tape of our horrible singing and any jury would have acquitted them. These residents had innocently moved into a neighborhood near a grammar school, not a military academy.

I soon learned running in formation was unlike running alone, or even with a partner. The men in front set the pace for the group. We lined up four abreast, the fittest men in front, the rest of us queued behind them by height. As we ran out the parking lot gate, we stayed in tight formation. I usually ran between Mark and Keith because we were close in height. For the first few blocks, staying with the platoon was easy enough. The pace was manageable, and the hostility of neighborhood onlookers served as an impetus to keep moving. No one wanted to be the straggler. No one wanted to break off from the herd. Although a staff member followed in a patrol car, if you broke from formation the car was likely to pass you and leave you to be cooked and eaten by the unfriendly citizens on dicey Palou Avenue, or wherever you happened to fall out. At least that's what I told myself to keep going.

We all suffered from bleeding, pus-filled blisters caused by our brand-new running shoes. But the discomfort of blisters was minor compared to the pain of shin splints. I tried every conceivable remedy for the aching shin splints that plagued me every day. When conventional treatments failed, I turned to a chemical everyone was using called dimethyl sulfoxide (DMSO).

"Try it, K!" said Eduardo one day after PT. "The wrestling team at my high school used it all the time. It stinks, but it kills the pain." He handed me his bottle. I had no idea what this chemical was, or where it came from, but I was desperate, so what the hell? It smelled like garlic, but it didn't hurt or sting when I applied it. I used it every day for months, although it did nothing to relieve the gnawing pain. The potential consequences of using a mystery chemical stew for body lotion didn't even cross my mind.

I ran along, reeking of garlic, trying to keep pace with the platoon. By the time we crossed San Bruno Avenue, I was losing steam, and Mark, who I had developed a crush on, could see I was about to fall out. Mark grasped my hand and pulled me along, as usual. The first time he grabbed my hand during one of our early runs, I was so touched by the gesture, I promised myself I would never fall out. I would never let him down.

"You are not a quitter!" he said.

I wanted to hang in. If I fell back, I'd end up with the slug squad, the stragglers who always ended up a block or two behind the platoon and ran endless penalty laps. The slug squad was comprised of the women, three smokers, and three guys who had lost a hundred pounds each to make it into the academy.

I wanted Mark to like and admire me as much as I liked him. I wanted to be as good as the guys, dammit! This desire kept me running with the platoon for another two blocks, but ultimately, I was a quitter.

"Yes, I am," I muttered to myself, ashamed, as I escaped his firm grip and fell back with the slugs. Maybe Devlin was right. Maybe I didn't belong here.

When I got home that afternoon, miraculously, Mom was gone. She'd left no note, but that wasn't unusual. She popped in and out, materializing like a witch from a television sitcom. I emptied her makeshift ashtray and sighed with relief. Did I really want to call John to see if she'd made it home? I wrestled with myself for a while, then I dialed Mom's number. She surprised me by picking up on the second ring.

"Oh, you made it home."

"Of course I did. Where the hell else would I go? You had nothing to eat, and I ran out of cigarettes."

"OK, bye." I kicked myself for the hundredth time for renting a house within walking distance of Mom's place.

Street Smart

Molly and I had fallen into a routine of studying at her place after school, then heading to one of the bars to hang out with the guys. Academically, neither one of us was finding the homework overly taxing, so we had ample time to drink and dance. Cops have a saying: you're either book-smart or street-smart. I had recently learned that in cop world, book-smart was not considered a good thing. I decided it would be best to pass the tests but not bring undue attention to myself by studying too hard, thereby increasing my chances of being perceived as street-smart.

We were plodding our way through a bunch of department general orders, quizzing each other on officer-involved shooting procedures, prisoner booking procedures, and crowd control, all written in torturously dry language.

"Let's head out, Mol. I can't take much more, I'm falling asleep."

We found the guys shooting pool in the backroom of our regular bar. As soon as we walked in, Scot waved me over. I followed him to a quiet corner.

"What? Why so mysterious, Scot?"

"It's Devlin. Watch your back."

Scot looked over his shoulder as if Devlin might suddenly appear. "The rumor is he's planning to get rid of all the women in this class. He's getting ready to retire, and he wants his last class to be all male—like the good old days."

"But he can't just fire us for no reason? Right?" Or could he? I had no idea what he could do.

"I think he needs to have just cause. But be careful. Tell Molly, too. Oh, by the way, did you hear about Diane?" Diane, one of the other women recruits, was around my age, and we had grown to be friends, but I hadn't seen her all that day.

"No, what?"

"She quit this afternoon. The staff told her she was failing. They brought her into the office and let her choose between quitting or being fired."

"What?" I was stunned. She had seemed to be doing well.

"Just a heads up, K."

I bought a couple of beers and waved Molly over to the bar to fill her in.

"Well, they're not getting rid of us that easy!" she said.

"Damn straight!" We clinked bottles and took a swig. But I wasn't feeling the same confidence as Molly.

During one of our afternoon breaks, I bumped into Rich in the academy hallway. He was a beat cop I'd known during my serving wench days. I hadn't seen him since he and his partner Joe had patrolled Fisherman's Wharf. They had occasionally dropped into Ben Jonson's for a cup of coffee and, no doubt, to check out the wenches. When I began the department testing process, they checked in with me for updates on my progress. They were always encouraging, and if they believed women shouldn't be cops, they kept that opinion to themselves.

"Hey, Karen! I heard you finally made it in. How's it going? How are they treating you?"

"So far, so good, I guess." I wasn't sure how to answer. In some ways the academy was going well. Many of the disagreeable guys had quit. The recruits who remained mostly got along well, almost like the brothers I had envisioned. But I was still on edge because of Scot's revelation about Devlin. I worried he would find some way to fire me. "Devlin's an interesting person," I said in a near whisper. I was fishing, not sure if Rich was his friend, though it seemed unlikely Devlin had any friends. I had really tried to find some redeeming quality about the man, but it was hopeless. Devlin was what my high school English teacher would have called a flat character, a walking caricature of himself.

"Devlin's such a dick, he'd arrest his own mother. Just hang in there, and watch your back." *Great, more back-watching advice.*

As we chatted, a tall woman in street clothes with long, wavy, dark hair approached, and I felt a glimmer of recognition.

"Hi, Rich! They caught up with you, too, I see. Advanced Officer Training, what a thrill. The only thing worse than going through the academy the first time is having to come back for in-service training." She looked at both of us and laughed.

"You don't by any chance work in North Beach, do you?" I asked.

"Sure do! Central Four car."

And that was how I met Gina Tarantino, the woman who had unwittingly convinced me I belonged in a patrol car. Gina had been in one of the first academy classes that admitted women a few years earlier. By all accounts, those women had been hazed relentlessly. Gina had taken it upon herself to support the new female recruits. She gave me her number, and we agreed to meet for a drink later that night.

"That woman's a hero," said Rich, as she walked away. "She shot a guy who almost killed her partner. She saved his life."

"Wow." I had never heard any of the men speak about a woman cop with that sort of respect. It gave me a glimmer of hope.

Golden Gloves

Although he did not have the stink of those destined to be academy flunkouts, George Davis, a.k.a. Golden Gloves, exuded a creepiness that over time caused even the most affable recruits to shun him. From the beginning of the academy, George had bragged constantly about his prowess in the boxing ring. He claimed to be a Golden Gloves champion, featherweight by the looks of him, and he spoke of little else. I'd disliked him from the moment he rudely introduced himself the first day. During PT, I avoided being paired with him by standing near Mark or Keith. George was prematurely bald, but instead of sporting a buzz cut like the other young guys, he'd chosen to grow out one side of his hair then comb it over, like someone's ancient uncle.

Normally, if a recruit's hair touched the neckline of his T-shirt, he was sentenced to one hundred burpees and required to write an essay explaining why he'd failed to comply with academy rules. We were not allowed to wear any pins, clips, or bands in our hair. The staff told us this rule was for safety reasons during wrestling and other physical activities, but the women believed it was just another tactic to discourage females from applying for the job. Since not complying with rules was grounds for dismissal, the women had no choice but to cut their hair extremely short.

I didn't object to George's hairstyle simply because it was unbecoming, I objected because when George's hair unraveled, it was ridiculously long. It seemed inherently unfair that he was allowed to have foot-long hair, but I was not. I wondered if I'd pass inspection if I imitated George's comb-over style, though it seemed silly to wear such an ugly hairstyle just to make some vague feminist statement.

Boxing was a required part of physical training. These were the days before women's kickboxing classes, years before Laila Ali, Mohammed Ali's daughter, would hit the ring. Boxing at the academy was supposed to scare the girls away.

Molly and I had mastered the art of appearing to hit each other hard without causing undue pain. Devlin's mouth watered as we threw punches at each other. Though he couldn't require us to mud wrestle, this was almost as good. My college stage training finally became useful. I grunted in exaggerated pain and doubled over, grimacing when one of Molly's punches made contact, and she did the same when I landed a blow. With our grotesque mouthpieces and near buzz cuts, we were a terrifying sight. So far Devlin had only paired girls with other girls, but at some point Molly and I expected he might make us box with one of the bigger guys. I suspected Devlin might pair me with George. Though I had twenty pounds on him, if he was, in fact, a great boxer, he could probably break my nose, or make me really ugly, before I passed out.

By week six the whole class had grown irritated with George and his tiresome Golden Gloves stories. He claimed to have knocked out dozens of opponents and he told anyone who would listen that he was the baddest ass in the Sunset District. By week eight, even the PT staff had grown tired of George's bragging.

To my relief, when it was George's turn, Devlin paired him with Father Art. Although I was relieved to be spared, I feared for Art's well-chiseled features. I worried that as a former seminarian, Art might turn the other cheek, allowing himself to be pummeled to death in the name of Jesus. We all circled the ring and sat down as Devlin and Sergeant Carry tied on the boxing gloves.

The pair approached the ring: Art an aquiline Greek god, George a monkey-faced buffoon. Devlin blew his whistle. They hopped from side to side for a few seconds, George's spindly legs propelling him quickly around the ring. Then, with supersonic speed, Father Art punched George in the face so hard, his mouthpiece went flying across the gym, and he hit the deck howling. The punch was so loud and unexpected, and George so universally disliked, that the class erupted in spontaneous cheers. George curled into a ball, covering his face with his gloves. Devlin hovered over him, gleaming with delight. A few seconds later, George stumbled to his feet and danced around a bit more. But he was unable to land a single punch. Art bopped at him a few more times, but his heart was no longer in it. He'd made his point.

That afternoon, Father Art told us he had taught boxing at the seminary. While the academy staff had been privy to this information, Art, in his humble way, had never mentioned his skill to his classmates.

We'd heard the last of George's bragging.

Balls

When we were not wrestling or boxing, the PT staff engaged us in a variety of sadistic games that bore little, if any, relevance to police training. My least favorite was medicine ball. I had never been much of a fan of dodgeball as a child. Dodgeball had always struck me as organized bullying, tacitly sanctioned by grade school PE teachers. At what other time do the physically fit have the opportunity to injure the less fortunate and be cheered on by their teachers?

Medicine ball is exponentially more painful and humiliating than even the most mean-spirited dodgeball game. The contestants stand in a circle, shoulder to shoulder. Each player takes a turn standing in the middle, while his classmates relentlessly pummel him with a medieval torture device. The ball feels like a lead weight, but covered in leather, it has the deceptively harmless appearance of a basketball. While dodgeball affords players the option of actually dodging the ball and escaping pain, in medicine ball, players must stand perfectly still, turn to face their assailant, and allow themselves to be struck repeatedly in the solar plexus—the center of the stomach. As the inner circle victim is not allowed to cushion the blows by attempting to catch the ball, the breath is continually knocked from him until he either collapses or survives long enough to be replaced by another victim. The player then moves to the outer circle, where he can avenge the pain inflicted upon him. No one ever wins.

During the first PT sessions, I had yet to learn the secret to surviving medicine ball. With dread I headed to the center of the ring. Marty threw the ball at me, first with a gentle toss. Then Scot threw it a bit harder, as he saw Devlin approaching.

"Harder!" Devlin shouted.

Breathstank thrust the ball with all his might, striking me hard in the navel. Now that Devlin was watching, the game was moving faster. After eight or nine hits, I felt like I was being pulverized. I envisioned my liver dissolving. *Didn't Houdini die doing something like this?* Then Shade Monitor hit me mid-breast. My eyes filled. Devlin looked like he was going to have an orgasm whenever I got hit in the chest. He leered at me, waiting, perhaps hoping I would start sobbing. Few of my classmates wanted to intentionally hurt me, but the game moved fast, and boobs were collateral damage.

"You're going easy on her!" Devlin complained. He grabbed the ball himself to give it a try. Leaning in, he used all his body weight and hit me square in the diaphragm. He knocked the wind out of me, and I doubled over. When I looked up, he was on the other side of the room, getting his licks in with Molly.

I was learning in the police academy there was little that could not be mastered once the recruit learned the insider secrets. Once the code was cracked, the recruit became invincible. There had to be some sort of trick to this game. I thought back to the wall. There was always more than one way. Blockhead took me aside in the gym on the second day of medicine ball.

"Tense your abdominal muscles so hard they almost cramp. If you do that, the ball will bounce right off of you, like Teflon." Blockhead's advice was good. On the next round, I contracted my abdominal muscles before each impact, and my internal organs were mostly spared.

Nineteen weeks of physical training was not enough time to

master a martial art form, so Sergeant Carry, a thick fireplug of a man, taught us a variety of painful holds we practiced on each other endlessly. The most dreaded of these takedowns was the chokehold, also known as the carotid artery restraint. Devlin taught this particular technique himself, refusing to allow his minions to steal his pleasure. We'd heard tales from survivors of previous classes that Devlin would choose a few recruits as demonstration models for the carotid. He described the procedure to us for the millionth time in his shrill tenor.

"To perform this hold, the officer places his arm around the neck of the suspect. His hand extends to the far shoulder of the suspect and his elbow points forward, parallel to, but not touching, the larynx. The officer then crosses his other hand behind the suspect's head and places his hand on his own shoulder. When he applies squeezing pressure to the sides of the neck by flexing his bicep and pressing with his forearm, the blood flow to the brain from the carotid artery is momentarily stopped, and the suspect passes out. While passing out, the suspect will sometimes appear to be having a seizure. He may urinate or defecate. This is called 'doing the chicken.'" Devlin always smirked when he said this. "The chicken" appeared to delight him beyond belief. He seemed excited by the thought of one of us doing it. As recruits, he told us, we were not allowed to actually put the full restraint on each other. He, however, might apply the carotid to anyone he chose, at any time.

We all lived in fear of being Devlin's test dummy. It was not the fear of discomfort or passing out that terrified us; it was the fear of shitting oneself in front of one's classmates. That sort of humiliation would have made Barf-Boy's torment seem trivial. We'd already spent two days practicing the hold, and Devlin had not yet put anyone out. He was letting the suspense build. With anguished speculation, we theorized about who it would be. Would he choose the weakest of us? Or would it be one of the bigger guys in an effort to prove his strength? We analyzed the man like a team of Viennese psychiatrists. I was certain I'd be one of his victims. I imagined he would want to put the hold on a woman, just to demonstrate his fairness, and there were only three women left. Sylvia was so tiny I couldn't imagine him picking her, and Molly was a mother. He would no doubt think I would be the most expendable. We parsed this out during class breaks.

"I know it will be me, Molly. He hates me so much. You've got two little kids. He can't kill you."

"Are you nuts? He hates me even more. He'll probably decide to kill me first since I've lived longer."

"That makes no sense. You're stronger than me. He'll want to kill the weakest first."

"I bet Devlin's going to try to pick us off one by one. First he made Diane quit, next it will be Sylvia, then us," said Molly. We worked ourselves into near panic, then put on our game faces and returned to the gym.

We waited on the sweaty blue rubber mats as Devlin browsed, shopping for poultry. *Who would it be?* I examined the other recruits curiously. Maybe I could send Devlin a telepathic message. *Yes, look at Golden Gloves! Wouldn't he be a good choice? He's just right. Pick George! Pick George!* I used all my mental power to telepathically send Devlin the picture of George.

"Mahoney!" Devlin barked. "Front and center."

He pointed to the space on the mat before him. Blockhead was the last recruit I'd expected him to choose. He was one of the more burly guys. Blockhead had an unusually large neck, perhaps making him more attractive for this exercise. I hadn't even considered neck size as a potential factor in how Devlin might make his selection. *Am I out of the woods?* As a female, my neck must be relatively small. A picture of Ann Boleyn climbing the scaffold flashed into my mind.

The class sat in a circle, cross-legged, Devlin center stage, enjoying his moment. When Blockhead stood, we all knew exactly what was going to happen. Devlin had been yammering about doing the chicken for days now. We could almost taste his excitement. Blockhead strolled calmly to the middle of the circle. Really, what else could he do? We'd been through weeks of training, and although there would be more tortures ahead, no one could really walk out that easily. *Could they?*

"Sit here!"

He obediently followed instructions. Devlin got down on his knees behind him. Then he spent another five minutes recapping how the chokehold was applied: "The officer places his arm around the neck of the suspect . . ." His arm was firmly around Blockhead's neck as he spoke, but he was not yet applying any pressure. By now everyone could do this hold blindfolded, so Devlin's only motive for blathering was to prolong his victim's agony.

"His hand extends to the far shoulder of the suspect," he droned on. He would be ecstatically happy if one of us were to cry, scream, piss, or otherwise embarrass ourselves. Blockhead was maintaining his composure admirably. I wondered to myself if I'd have been able to do the same. Then I had a horrible thought. If only I had known how to do this hold when we'd been on that train in Cheyenne! Of course, I immediately felt guilty for the thought.

Abruptly, Devlin applied a full-force chokehold. I began silently praying Blockhead would not die or pee. He was a well-liked classmate; no one wanted him to be humiliated. Suddenly, Blockhead was doing a full chicken. His eyes rolled back, and his head lolled onto his shoulder. His body writhed in waves of convulsions. He drooled a little down his class T-shirt, and then he was dead asleep. With relief, I noticed his pants remained dry. We sat silently, waiting for him to regain consciousness. It seemed to be taking forever. He was still breathing, but I wondered if Devlin had put him into some kind of coma. Minutes later, Blockhead awoke, slightly disoriented, but seeming no worse for the experience.

"What happened?" He wobbled to his feet. We prayed Devlin had gotten his fill of chicken as we broke for lunch. It was a foodless lunch break for all, except Blockie. Everyone agreed that it was safe for Blockie to eat. Even Devlin would not be cruel enough to put out the same guy twice in one day. They'd already told us the hold could cause brain damage, and I doubted he would risk turning one of us into a vegetable. *Vegetables, ugh, I am so hungry.*

Huddled around the cafeteria tables, class discussion revolved around whether it was worth the risk to eat or drink. Most of us decided fasting would be prudent. It would lessen the risk of involuntarily evacuating our bowels or bladder in the event Devlin continued his chicken feast.

"So, Blockhead, what did it feel like?" I wanted as many details as possible, to be mentally prepared in case Devlin chose me.

"It didn't really hurt. It was like going to sleep. I don't remember a thing." He took a bite of his turkey and cheese sandwich. I was not finding his testimony convincing. The way he'd thrashed around before passing out belied the tranquil nap he described. "Want some?" he offered, holding out the other half of his sandwich. It smelled really good, but I couldn't take the risk. The academy cafeteria food was notoriously gastro-disastrous. The consequence of doing the chicken during a bout of intestinal cramping was too gruesome to contemplate.

When we returned to the mats, Devlin focused his demonic

grin on me. I doubted he played much poker. His grin was an uncontrollable tic that preceded all his moves.

"Nasssssberg! Over here!" he hissed, pointing to the mat. As I rose from my spot, I considered dashing for the door. But if I left now, I could never return. I'd forever be branded a coward and would never be a police officer. I'd be a disgrace to my gender. I felt legions of future women cops slowly pushing me toward Devlin. I took a deep breath and thought, Devlin can either scare me out of the gym or he could scare me into becoming a cop.

I took my place in his hellish inner circle, and he secured his ropy forearm around my neck. I imagined Mom bursting into the room shouting, "See? I told you those Nazi bastards would kill you!" Devlin was jibber-jabbering to the class, but I wasn't listening. I was taking a trip outside my body. "The officer places his hand . . ." and I closed my eyes, traveling to a beautiful sun-flower field in Japan. He held me in this position, almost gently, as he repeated the instructions.

I returned to my body. My throat tightened. *Why was this taking so long? When would it happen? When would I start the convulsions? How horrible would my face look? Would I drool as much as Blockie had? Damn, why didn't I use the restroom one more time during our last break?* Then I felt pressure on both sides of my neck and thought, *OK, this is it! Don't pee!! Don't pee!*

Without a word, Devlin suddenly released me. As he let me go, I could have sworn he softly stroked the back of my neck.

"Go back to your spot on the mat, Nassberg. It's your lucky day." I was stunned and confused. Why didn't he put me out? I wondered if he released me because I was a girl. No, he'd never been the chivalrous type before. And what was with the little caress? Or had I imagined that?

Smirking, Devlin rose and left the gym. Thank God, our chicken days appeared to be over.

Wrestling

Wrestling was winding down because the majority of our PT time was devoted to mastering what was known as the Baton Dance. The Baton Dance did not involve leading a marching band through a parade route, but it did require memorizing a series of choreographed steps. None of this so-called dance was accompanied by music. It was a joyless dance.

Mark and I had been wrestling partners for weeks. We had all the moves down and knew how to do them without actually hurting each other. Rolling around on mats with really cute guys was a job benefit I had not anticipated. We took turns pinning and putting half nelsons on each other every day. For weeks I let myself believe I was as strong as Mark. Then one day, after our usual bout, Mark deadlifted me off the floor and held me over his head like a human barbell. Although I was not resisting, this feat seemed incredible. I was 145 pounds, and Mark didn't weigh much more than me.

The reality of the superiority of male strength hit me like a slap. Years of feminist indoctrination fizzled before this display of pure force. I wondered if I was wrong to think women could do the job. Would some criminal lift me over his head as Mark had? Mark put me down, and we both laughed. But the incident humbled me. Maybe there were good reasons few women wanted this job. Maybe I was making a horrible mistake and my overblown pride was keeping me from realizing the truth.

For my last wrestling match, Devlin paired me with Donut, an easygoing teddy bear of a man. With his chocolate-brown skin and soft hair, he even resembled a bear, or maybe a bear claw—some sort of soft, brown pastry. He was large and squishy, a Donut. Devlin was grinning, never a good sign.

"In the unlikely event you ever make it to the street, Nassssssss-berg, you're not going to get to pick and choose who you have to take down. This guy is half the size of the ex-cons who are going to kick your ass if you somehow get out on patrol." I did some quick mental math. By Devlin's estimation, I could expect the average ex-con to weigh over 500 pounds. He took Donut aside and whispered something. He knew Donut and I were friends. No doubt he was telling him if he went easy on me, he would be cleaning toilets in his underwear.

We assumed our positions on the mats. Many teams were wrestling at once, but I felt the eyes of every member of the staff on Donut and me. Sergeant Meyer stationed himself in a folding chair beside us. Devlin blew his whistle, indicating the bout was to begin. In less than ten seconds, Donut had me pinned. All 250 pounds of him paralyzed my upper body and shoulders; it was like being crushed under a small, brown bus.

I could think of only one thing to do, but not only did I not want to hurt Donut, I wasn't sure I wanted to raise our intimacy to the next level. If Sergeant Meyer were to see this move, my academy career might come to a quick end. But I had to do something. I couldn't just lie there and give up! I tried squirming my right arm down between our bellies. Such a tight squeeze. All his weight squashed my arm. Finally, my hand shimmied between his legs, and quickly, I grasped Donut's balls and twisted as hard as I could.

This was not any kind of hold the staff had taught us, and I figured I would pay the price for it later. But instantly, Donut propelled himself off me. Up on his feet, he was bending over and cussing, his hands protecting his scrotum from further assault. I rolled to my feet and peeked over at Sergeant Meyer, expecting he would rage at me. But Meyer was laughing and shaking his head saying, "Now, *that's* what I'm talkin' about!"

Unbelievably, my desperate action seemed to have won me new respect from the training staff. A few of them even smiled at me as we filed out of the gym. For a moment, I allowed myself to believe I might actually graduate.

Later that night, I met Gina at Amelia's in the Mission District. It was still early, so we had the bar to ourselves. I was excruciatingly nervous, as if I were meeting my favorite movie star. She was a hero cop, and I was an FNG, a fucking new guy. It was an honor to be allowed in her presence. I slid onto the barstool beside her, and Gina passed me a bottle of Bud.

"The first thing you need to know is the academy is the hardest part of the job. If you make it through, you'll do fine on the street. Don't let those guys tell you we can't do the job. There are dozens of women out there working patrol, and most of them are really good cops. Women were working as patrol officers in New York for years before San Francisco opened the doors." She took a sip from her bottle. I tried to think of something intelligent to say, afraid I might blurt out *I'm your biggest fan!* or something even sillier.

"Before 1975, there was a rank called *police woman*. But those women never worked street patrol. The men never considered them real cops, though a lot of them were pretty damn tough. They were mostly stuck working Juvenile Division," said Gina.

"That sounds like a boring job."

"Mostly paper shuffling. It was a dead-end street with no possibility of promotion—ever. Most of the men in the department are Irish Catholic, sons or grandsons of other cops, and they'd like to keep it that way."

"When did the first women street cops come in?" I asked.

"After the black officers sued the city in 1973, the women, Asians, and Latinos joined the suit. They started letting in some women in 1975, but the recruitment drive didn't really happen until after they won the lawsuit in 1979."

I toasted Gina. "Thanks for paving the way."

"You're welcome. But don't think it's going to be Easy Street. There are some guys who are trying to drive the women out by making their lives miserable." Yep, I'd already met a couple of those.

"When did you know you wanted to be a cop?" I asked.

"I can't remember ever not wanting to be one. It's like I was born to do this job. There is nothing else in the world I would rather do. They'll have to force me to retire when I'm an old, gray-haired hag." I laughed. "Just hang in there. Don't quit, no matter what they say or do." She took a long swig of her beer. "So how is it being one of the only girls in your class? You only had four? It must be strange."

"Actually, I'm kind of used to being the oddball. When I was a kid, I always ended up being the token something. I was the only Caucasian kid in my elementary school class. And for some reason, I feel comfortable being one of the guys. I guess I'm strange that way."

"All women cops are strange," she said. We laughed and toasted to that.

Dark o'Clock

The next afternoon our municipal law instructor called in sick, so we were released an hour early. Blockhead rounded up the troops to celebrate.

"I'm heading to Grandma's for a beer! Who's in?"

It was an unusually warm San Francisco day. Most of the guys chimed in.

"See you there, team!" Blockhead shouted.

"You're not coming?" Molly asked. Normally, I'd be first to belly up to the bar, but today I was beat, and also I'd made a dinner date with Jim in North Beach. The daily workouts and constant anxiety of shoe, hair, nail, and uniform muster were wearing me down. Despite daily nail and hair trimmings, I'd failed so many inspections that every time we lined up, Scot sang "Maybe this time, I'll be lucky" from *Cabaret*, eliciting a weak smile and an elbow in the ribs from me.

The inspections occurred before PT, where we wore our class T-shirt: white, with our class emblem stamped on it. We'd voted on the emblem the second day of the academy, choosing between three designs created by classmates. We'd finally settled on Shade Monitor's, a cross displaying words on the horizontal and numbers on the vertical, *145, One for Life*. It was an optimistic aspiration, implying we would be a team of friends forever, connected until death through long careers of police work. Given our attrition rate, the motto became increasingly pathetic. As our numbers dwindled from forty-seven to twenty-five, the likelihood of our team staying connected for life was minuscule. Marty disliked the slogan from the beginning. He thought it sounded overzealous and found the cross disturbing. "It makes us sound like a bunch of Moonies or born-agains!" he said.

I'd actually voted for Monitor's slogan, preferring it to two even cornier alternatives. But since Marty had made that comment, I could see his point and felt slightly embarrassed I'd helped choose it. During that first week, I'd wanted so badly to keep our strange tribe together, imagining these men would become my new family. I'd envisioned most of us making it through, working at stations for twenty or more years, bonded by the nostalgia of our academy days. I pictured summer barbecues and camping trips, never imagining half these guys would leave, never to be seen again.

Most of my inspection failures were hair related. My long hair had always been my favorite feature, and I had hated to lose it. I was certain I was trimming it short enough, yet I'd flunked hair inspection three times in a row. Although my skill at burpees had improved considerably, I did not enjoy doing them any more than I had that first day. I had also run out of ideas for my hair essays. I'd written about the history of hairstyling, male pattern baldness, and the amazing studies proving hair continues to grow after death! It was clear my essays went unread. I'd written drivel, and no one had even bothered to make me do extra burpees. Finally, I found a barber willing to give me a virtual buzz cut. My vanity had been replaced with a stronger drive—survival.

So when they released us early, all I could think of was a nap. A few hours would be so refreshing, and then I could meet Jim for dinner, go home, and crack the books to study for tomorrow's case law test.

"Maybe I'll catch you there later, Mol. I'm beat."

Donut and I ran to my car and I sped down Silver Avenue. We'd been carpooling for weeks because he and his wife owned just one car. He was a good sport, and harbored no bad feelings about my illegal wrestling move. I dropped him at his wife's office and headed straight to my apartment on Saturn Street. I was asleep on my futon, still fully clothed, minutes later. I had a wonderful sex dream featuring Harrison Ford as Indiana Jones. He'd left his hat on.

I awoke in a panic. It was six thirty! *How did I sleep through the alarm? What was I wearing?* Good, I was still in my wrinkled gray Maytag. But I had less than half an hour to get across the city! I jumped into my blue jalopy, praying it would not choose today to die, and raced to the academy. *Shit, I didn't even have time to spit shine my shoes!* I found a great parking place, right in front of school. *Wow! I made really good time!* Rushing into the yard, I headed straight for formation by the flagpole. Two minutes before seven, and I was the only one there.

How odd. Usually by 6:45 a.m. half the class was milling around, the anxiety of being late was so universal. Then I noticed the sun wasn't rising, it was setting. I'd arrived twelve hours early.

"Dinner! Shit! I'm late!" I ran back to my car, putting on my jacket to disguise my ugly uniform and pulling off my clip-on tie. I sped toward North Beach praying I wouldn't get pulled over. Real cops loved nothing more than citing wannabes, especially those still wearing Maytags.

I hadn't planned on wearing my Maytag to dinner, but Jim would get a good laugh out of my story. We met at the Green Valley. Jim was waiting patiently at the bar. The hostess seated us in at a corner table, and we ordered. I'd loved their pasta al pesto since childhood. The steaming noodles arrived topped with a decadent dollop of butter atop neon-green sauce. I sprinkled on the Parmesan generously.

"Cute outfit. How's the academy going?" he asked.

"Jim, I'm beginning to get the feeling this women's recruitment thing is a bunch of crap. I think the academy staff wants the girls to fail or quit." I took a sip of the wine he'd ordered.

In spite of Jim's lack of affection for police, he had been supportive of my decision. For the last few years, he'd spent every holiday with Barb, Steve, and me, often including me in family gatherings at his ex-wife Sheila's house. We all loved the way Jim wrapped our Christmas presents in the Sunday comics. He made a point of spending the same amount on gifts for each of us on Christmas and birthdays. He must have told me about his gift budget because he worried I would feel somehow less loved than his biological children. Having been adopted himself, he was sensitive to that.

I had never felt entitled to Jim's generosity. He hadn't known he would inherit a child when he met Mom. But he had chosen me, just as his own adoptive mother had told him that she had chosen him. And with an incredible degree of generosity, Jim's children always treated me as their sister. If they had any resentment toward me about sharing their father, they never gave me the smallest hint.

"Don't quit. Give them a run for their money. What are your classmates like?"

"Mostly, they're great. They're the funniest guys on earth. Each one tries to outdo the other, like they're in a stand-up competition. It's like a night at the Improv all day long. A few guys are jerks, but the good guys torture them. How are things with you?" I rolled a forkful of noodles into a spoon, pretending to be Italian.

"Not so hot. They're changing everything at the paper."

"What do you mean? How are they changing?"

"Typesetting is going to be a thing of the past. Everything is going to paste-make-up," he said.

"What does that mean?"

"It means instead of setting the type down, the way we have for decades, we paste together a bunch of Linotyped words, and then everything is printed. It means my trade is dead. I'm a dinosaur."

"That sounds bad." I put down my fork, losing my appetite.

"It could be worse. At least they aren't going to fire the guys who've been there a while, so I still have a job. It just means there will be no future generations of printers."

"I'm sorry, Jim." He had always been so proud of his trade.

"Hey, good news, though! Steve's doing great at UC San Diego, and Barb got an apprenticeship with a carpenter. Have you heard from Ann lately?"

"Yup, same old routine. Still fighting with John. At least they have each other to make miserable, though. I've been avoiding her as much as possible since starting the academy."

"Well, do what you need to do to take care of yourself. Your mom somehow always lands on her feet. Hey, have I told you lately how proud I am of you?"

I gave him a long hug before I left, then raced home to polish my shoes. The next morning, as we mustered by the flagpole, I kept the story of my early arrival to myself.

The Gas Chamber

Of course, I'd done the exact thing the instructor told us not to do, and that was why I was now dying. Stinging needles penetrated the pores of my face, neck, scalp, and hands. Every atom of skin not covered by my blue jumpsuit was being suffocated. This invader would kill me, I was certain. My body was in primal panic mode, unwilling to accept an early death at twenty-two. Every molecule of my being was fighting to survive. I had fought for my life with my Mom seven years earlier using only my bare hands, but against this attacker, I was defenseless.

It was week sixteen, and we were in a Quonset hut at Santa Rita Prison being bombarded with tear gas so we would know how it felt. The logic of the exercise seemed iffy. I just hoped they wouldn't require us to actually shoot each other during firearms training.

Recruits perceived the gassing as a rite of passage separating the men from the boys. As the usual stream of rumors from previous academy classes filtered down to us during the weeks preceding the gassing, the stories became more horrific. According to the stories, the anxiety built to such a point that some recruits from earlier classes had resigned right before gas training. Like heretics in the Tudor court, simply being shown the instruments of our torture was enough to get us to confess anything.

During the morning lecture, Sergeant White told us we would enter the hut wearing gas masks. After the canisters were thrown into the hut, White would give us the signal to remove our masks. We were then expected to sit still—it wasn't clear for how long—and then calmly walk out in "column of files," police-speak for single file.

"Do not breathe in the gas!" Sergeant White warned. "If you do so, you will feel like you are going to die! You will not die! Do you copy that? You will not die! But your body will believe it is going to die. The effect is worse for people with light skin and light-colored eyes."

All morning I tried to prevent myself from flashing back to the volumes of information Mom had shared on the inner workings of Nazi war camps. As a child I'd often imagined life in the concentration camps, and now the horrific scenes flashed into my mind uninvited.

As the hands-on portion of our training began, I moved from generalized *about to get on a scary roller coaster* trepidation to specific *no one's getting out of here alive* panic. Once again, pride kept me from running out screaming. I told myself to think about the women cops who would follow me. I told myself that submitting to this pointless torture was an act of feminist heroism.

They issued us gas masks that appeared to be WWII relics. The rubber was cracked and the plastic eye coverings were scratched to the point that seeing while wearing one was not an option. We practiced putting the masks on and taking them off over and over. The staff always trained us as if we were kinder-gartners, incapable of learning anything on the first try. OK, well . . . maybe they were right to do that.

Then Sergeant White said, "Some of these masks may leak. You may feel gas leaking into the mask. Do not panic! You will want to take the mask off. That will make it worse. I repeat: Do not panic and take off the mask until I give you the signal! Do not breathe in the gas. Hold your breath until you are outside the hut."

I wondered how long we would actually be in the hut without masks. Gina had told me we'd be ordered to sing the "Star-Spangled Banner" before being freed. *How long can I hold my breath?* I'd never really timed myself. *Can't those Japanese pearl divers hold their breath for twenty minutes or something?* We put our leaky masks on for the last time and filed into the hut. We squeezed in tightly, as instructed. I jockeyed for the best spot. But what was the best spot? Should I get behind everyone and try to hide from the gas? Or did I want to be in front, so I could get out first when the door opened?

There was no time to decide because Sergeant White suddenly herded us into the corner. There we simmered like meat in a roasting pan, anticipating the torture. I willed myself to stay calm, silently counting to one thousand.

The door swung open, and two grenade-like cylinders flew to the center of the hut. The canisters steamed and hopped, bouncing off the floor like small metal predators. We jumped up and down, blindly trying to avoid them, the air thick with smoke. Sharp needles stabbed insistently into my uncovered neck. The gas, not surprisingly, was leaking under the cracks in the rubber. I held my breath, but I was no pearl diver. I would need to breathe before they released us.

We were supposed to wait for the sergeant to give the designated signal to remove the masks. But in the thick fog, I could see nothing. Suddenly, I felt recruits around me pulling off masks. So I pulled at mine, urgently, as if this would provide relief. Instead, I was staggered by a body blow of more burning pins poking the newly exposed pores on my face. The gas mask had provided a small barrier against the attack. But once removed, the full power of the gas hit me, and I gasped. A gasp, I learned that instant, is a very deep breath. Drowning in poison, my internal organs sent my brain an unmistakable message: *I am dying. I am dying.* There would be no anthem-singing today, no column of recruits calmly filing out.

Other recruits pushed me forcefully toward what I hoped was the exit. I imagined being trampled by my classmates, suffocating in this rickety metal coffin. I imagined my lifeless body being discovered hours later, sprawled beside an empty gas canister. Stumbling outside, I took in a breath of sweet, fresh air as my brain slowly began getting the message I was not dying. I'd never appreciated the simple sweetness of air before. When I could finally stand up straight and open my eyes, Mark was standing beside me, coughing.

"You OK?" he wheezed. I nodded, and then saw Molly several feet away, sprawled face-up on the concrete. Blond haired, blue eyed, virtually albino, she, of course, would be the most sensitive to this. *Is she dead? What will I tell her daughters? What a pointless way to die. . . .* No, she was moving! Some of the guys were fanning gas off her with cardboard. Eduardo was throwing water on her face. Wait! Didn't Sergeant White say not to pour on the water after being gassed because it would make it worse?

"Stop! Eduardo, no water!" I croaked, staggering toward them.

When Molly finally could stand, we found Sergeant White and thrust his disgusting masks at him without a word. We trudged to the parking lot and climbed into Keith's truck in stony silence. Keith sped away from Santa Rita Prison as if Molly and I were jailbreaking and he was our getaway driver. I didn't bother looking back. I felt exactly the way I felt the day Jim drove me away from Bonita Street.

It was a long while before any of us could speak. When we

were halfway home, I asked them, "If I gave you one million dollars, right now, to go back and do that again, would you do it?"

"No fucking way!" They shouted at once.

We all agreed there was no amount of money that would ever tempt us to return to Santa Rita.

Not at Home on the Range

The class was looking forward to firearms training. This meant we'd be away from the dreary academy for an entire week, training instead at the Lake Merced police range. We were excited that carrying a gun would take us one step closer to being real cops or, if nothing else, armed losers.

Our service revolvers were six-shooters, Smith & Wesson .357 caliber handguns that looked like guns from an old John Wayne cowboy movie. The first morning we mounted paper targets on hooks, donned protective glasses and sound suppressors, and dry-fired our guns. It turned out we would have to wait until after lunch to fire live ammunition. For hours we aimed empty guns at human-shaped paper silhouette targets and pretended to shoot.

Scot soon became bored with the snail's pace of the day. "Enough already with the dry-firing!" he muttered. He was already an excellent marksman and was looking forward to proving it.

"Maybe they want to make sure Ed's on his medication before they give us bullets," suggested Molly. Sergeant Grant overheard her and looked away, smirking.

"At least the range guys have a sense of humor," I said. They weren't like the staff on campus, who constantly reminded us of our loser status and the importance of submitting our bread-truck driving applications. The range master, Sergeant Inglenook, might howl at us like a grumpy uncle served a cold cup of coffee, but he never got crazy- mad or made us do burpees.

Sergeant Inglenook had given me a nickname he found hilarious.

"OK, Noosbomb, I want you to line up your sights like this and close your left eye. Noooooosbommmmmmb. It's always you, Noooosbomb! You are always my problem child. I said squeeeeeeze the trigger, not yank it, Noooooosbomb. You're not following directions, Nooosbomb!"

I didn't mind the range master riding me. He reminded me of Fred Flintstone—a funny old guy, close to retirement and enjoying his job. I figured maybe Sergeant Inglenook had been teased about his name, too, so when he called me Noosbomb, I took it as a term of endearment.

The only thing close to hazing at the range was the gun-cleaning ritual. At the end of each day, Sergeant Grant inspected our guns, and if they were not clean enough, we had to strip them back down and clean them again. Dismantling a gun takes time and skill, and most of us were not yet adept. We quickly learned to clean our guns meticulously to avoid repeating the procedure.

"Davis, this is sub-par. Do it again!" Sergeant Grant returned George's gun to him for the third time. Each time George was sent back to the gun cleaning room, Scot and Marty pelted him with a pile of cleaning rags. Everyone laughed, but we also kept polishing.

That afternoon, Sergeant Grant issued us each two boxes of fifty reloads. We lined up at the ten-yard line, in front of our targets.

"Good luck, K," Keith said. He saw the worried look on my face. *What if it turns out I have horrible aim and fail qualification?* Obviously, shooting was a necessary skill for a police officer. This was a make-it-or-break-it week for all of us.

"Thanks, Keith."

The firing line could accommodate only half the platoon, so while one group fired pistols, another trained with shotguns. Shooting didn't come naturally to any of the women in the class. As a group, we seemed to be having more trouble hitting the target than our male classmates. Our ineptitude was embarrassing. It was hard to argue women could do the job when the three of us couldn't hit an elephant with a bazooka from the one-yard line.

On the other extreme, there were some recruits who shot as if they had already spent years on the SWAT team. Once again, Ed was proving to have benefited from his time in the military. The man could shoot, but as strange as he was, knowing he was a good shot was little comfort.

Sergeant Inglenook was becoming irritated with Shade Monitor. Surprisingly, Monitor, the nerdiest guy in our class, appeared to be an expert marksman. But he'd brought with him a collection of shooting habits that were proving hard to break. He refused to use the cup-and-saucer hand position our instructors required, and insisted on using a stance he called the Weasel, or was it the Weaver? The instructors weren't happy with the way he stood with legs sprawled and hands covering both sides of the weapon. But the instructors disliked his know-it-all attitude even more. The sergeant had told us earlier he would prefer to train a novice than to have to retrain a recruit who had an ingrained bad habit. When Sergeant Inglenook shared that sentiment, Molly and I high-fived each other, glad the training staff was finally appreciating the advantages of our inexperience.

Though we were not likely to be recruited for the SWAT team anytime soon, Molly and I improved with each round of fire. I didn't care that I would never be a sharpshooter. Actually, I hoped to be one of the many cops who go through an entire career never having to shoot anyone. While I had been impressed with the story of Gina's marksmanship and heroics and hoped that when it came down to it, I would do the same, I was at heart a pacifist and planned to use my gun only as a last resort. I even liked the fact that in the penal code, police officers were officially referred to as "peace officers." I viewed my job as keeping the peace, something I was pretty sure I already knew how to do. My fear of shooting an innocent person far outweighed my fear of being shot. But my responsibility to keep my partner safe was the duty I took most seriously.

Still, I had to acknowledge there was something compelling about carrying a gun. I hadn't considered this idea when I first applied to the department, but if I was truly honest about it, maybe there was some part of me that wanted a gun for protection. This latent desire to carry a gun was coming from somewhere, and I couldn't help but suspect it had something to do with Mom. Everything in my life had something to do with Mom.

A veteran cop, Officer Brosnan, had given a lecture the week before about the traumatic effects of being involved in a police shooting. He recalled a sunny afternoon when he had been talking to a couple of small-time drug dealers in the Tenderloin. Suddenly, one of them pulled out a gun. Officer Brosnan managed to draw his weapon and shoot the suspect. Although it was a justified shooting that had very likely saved him from being shot, it was still the worst experience of his life. The interviews with Internal Affairs and Homicide were bad enough, but the nightmares were even worse.

"I wish I'd never stopped my car that day. Don't ever wish to be in a shooting. It's not exciting or heroic. It's nothing like what you see on TV," he said. After listening to this burly Irishman tell his story, nearly in tears, the class had been subdued for the remainder of the day.

By afternoon, Molly and I were gaining confidence in our shooting ability and becoming a little full of ourselves.

"Hey, Mol! We're the bomb!" We high-fived, danced, and celebrated our newfound skills.

Sylvia had always kept to herself and never socialized with the other women in the class. Now she was having a hard time with the pistol. She was petite, and her hands were so small she did not have the strength in her index finger to manage the trigger pull. The instructors were kind and patient, and even let her use her middle finger. But after shooting hundreds of rounds, she still had not passed qualification, and the staff encouraged her to resign rather than be fired. I wasn't upset about losing her. She had never shown any interest in connecting with the rest of us.

The next day, Inglenook spent some time demonstrating how to load and unload dummy rounds into the shotgun. He got a kick out of saying "dummy" over and over to Molly and me. Then we worked on combat loading—putting rounds in through the ejection port and pumping them into the chamber. Finally, we took turns shooting. I lifted the shotgun to my shoulder and fired. The kick was tremendous. We began with lighter birdshot, but I was still having a hard time controlling the gun. Then Sergeant Inglenook surprised me by slipping a double-ought buck round into my four-shot mix, and the kick almost knocked me over. When I'd watched the guys shooting earlier, none of them had much trouble. I expected there might be a secret to this shotgun thing that Molly and I didn't yet know. I needed to ask someone about it as soon as I had a chance. *Where the heck was Ed? He knew all this G.I. Joe stuff.*

Sergeant Inglenook handed me four more rounds of double-ought buck. With four rounds of this heavy ammo, I figured I'd be on my ass by round three. I pumped a round, and took my first shot. Even with sound suppressors, the concussion was ear piercing. The shotgun tried jumping from my hands to escape my wimpy grip. By the second shot, the gun was all over the place, the butt swinging dangerously toward my jaw. Molly laughed in the background.

"You look like Barney Fife," she yelled.

Sergeant Inglenook liked that line, and the two of them yukked it up. The gun shot the remaining rounds by itself, popping in and out of my hands and hitting the target once. I looked over my shoulder as I finished, hoping no one had seen me. No, thank goodness; just Molly and Sergeant Inglenook, watching and laughing.

Molly had an equally hard time. She flailed the gun, sometimes shooting the sky, sometimes shooting the target. Hopping from foot to foot, she wasn't really shooting the gun. The gun was shooting her.

"Ha! Go for it, hotshot! Who's Barney Fife now?" I heckled. Sergeant Inglenook laughed. This was our only hope. If we kept him laughing, maybe he'd want to stick with us and help us pass qualification.

"If we don't get this, we're toast, finished," Molly said. We spent the lunch break worrying.

"Mol, there's gotta be some kind of trick. Monitor can do it, and I'm pretty sure we're as strong as he is."

Sergeant Inglenook stayed late, spending two extra hours with us, showing us how to brace the gun in the crook of our shoulder and lean our weight forward. His kindness made me think back to a time in high school when Jim had helped me learn how to reassemble my puzzle ring. The ring had come without instructions, and he spent hours playing with it until he had figured it out, then patiently taught me how to do it myself.

By the end of the day, we had finally learned to put our whole body weight into the butt of the gun, and amazingly, we were reliably hitting the target. As we were leaving, long after the other recruits, our shoulders and chests sore, dreading returning the next day for more bruising punishment, I noticed Ed on the far side of the parking lot leaning against his car. *Why is he still here?*

"Hey, K, come over here," he called.

I shrugged at Molly. "Hang out for a minute, Mol, OK?" I walked over, trying to remember what I'd wanted to ask him earlier.

"Let me tell you something," he whispered, like it was top secret. "Go get a box of sanitary napkins."

"What the hell, Ed!" I reflexively checked my jumpsuit crotch. *Geez, why did I think this nut could help us?*

"No, K," he said. "No! I mean go buy a box for the guys. You tape them on your shoulder so the shotgun kick doesn't hurt as much. Bring them tomorrow and I'll bring in some bandage tape."

Oh, now I was catching his drift. Maybe he wasn't totally nuts. OK, Kotex might be an embarrassing item for a guy to pick up at the drug store. And his idea sounded plausible. This wasn't Ed's first time at the rodeo.

The next day, I brought the Kotex, and Ed brought the tape. We shared with any recruit who wanted them—on the down-low, so the range masters wouldn't accuse us of being wimps. In the restroom stalls, we taped the pads into our armpits and over our shoulders, concealing them with our T-shirts and jumpsuits. Then we commenced surprisingly painless shotgun training.

It was Friday, and range week was finally over. We felt we'd been living there for months. We'd lost Sylvia and three others who never got the hang of shooting. Molly and I had, much to our relief, passed range qualification. I thought about what Mom would say if I called her with the news. *"Hooray! You're now a full-fledged, gun-toting Nazi."* So instead, I called Gina.

"That's terrific, Karen. You're in the home stretch now. Last five miles of the marathon."

That last afternoon the entire class met up with the range masters at the Boat House bar. Sergeant Inglenook and Sergeant Grant were relaxed and happy.

"Hey, Nussbaum! You had me worried there for a little while with that shotgun. I thought you were trying for a free nose job on the city," said Sergeant Inglenook. The whole bar laughed.

"Wow, I didn't think of that! Would the city foot the bill for that kind of plastic surgery?" asked Molly.

"Pipe down there, Blondie!" said Inglenook. "You probably took down half the native goose population! The EPA is coming after us for disrupting migration." Everyone laughed, relieved the range was now an amusing memory. We all took turns buying the sergeants rounds, which added to their good humor. They were treating us like we were part of the team now, part of the police family.

"I think we might be home free now, Mol."

"Yep. I think they'll want to hang on to us after spending all that money on extra ammunition!" We laughed, clinking beer bottles, carefree.

The rest of the academy would be a piece of cake. We were almost real cops now. They'd want to keep us on the team. That's what we kept telling each other.

Code Three

I had never been a great driver as a teen. Growing up without a car, I learned to drive in high school when students still received driver's training as part of a public-school education. The training was free, but each student was rationed only a few hours behind the wheel, hardly enough time to become proficient. The only vehicle available to me for practice had been Jim's old Chevy pickup, with a manual transmission on the dash and no power steering. It looked like something the Beverly Hillbillies might have driven before they struck oil. But it wasn't the truck's lack of cosmetic appeal that deterred me. The rattletrap perpetually stalled, and as kids, Barb, Steve, and I often ran behind pushing while Jim tried to jump-start it. This involved choking, clutching, and other painful-sounding procedures. I refused to even try driving it, fearing that if I actually did get the thing moving, it would die on me in the middle of nowhere.

I did eventually buy myself the blue jalopy, but at twenty-two I was still an overly cautious driver, never breaking the speed limit. Now I would have to hide my anxiety and master Code Three driving at the academy. If I revealed any self-doubt, the training staff would certainly flunk me. I figured I'd use the Stanislavski Method I'd learned in drama class, where you embody what it would feel like to be whoever it is you're portraying. I closed my eyes briefly and channeled my inner race-car driver.

The first phase of emergency vehicle operations class (EVOC) tested skills such as parking a patrol car and backing up a paddy wagon. After demonstrating our basic driving proficiency, we spent a day experiencing the skidpan: a slippery course designed to teach us counter-steering skills. Then the final phase arrived, the one I was dreading: Code Three driving and high-speed pursuit. Most of the guys couldn't wait to try their hands at race-car driving. I felt like I was the only one worried about my skill.

The EVOC trainer shrieked, "Nassberg!" I wiped my sweaty palms along my blue jumpsuit and ran to the patrol car. Officer Warren, frizzy haired and grizzled, jumped into the old car's shredded passenger seat. I squirmed in the driver's seat, compulsively adjusting and readjusting the mirrors.

"Put on your seatbelt, recruit!" he howled. "What's the matter with you?"

I fastened the seat belt and turned on the ignition. Fearing my lack of experience would be obvious to all, I'd hardly slept the night before. This training officer was no Inglenook—he found nothing about me amusing or charming.

The course was arranged in an abandoned Treasure Island parking lot, a circular maze the size of a football field. The view of the city of San Francisco from the island was spectacular, and it was a crystal-clear day, but I wasn't paying attention to any of that. I focused on the mock traffic lanes. Every few feet an orange cone marked a spot where drivers were supposed to turn or avoid an obstacle.

"Drive!" Officer Warren snarled.

I began slowly building speed. They'd told us the exercise was supposed to simulate regular city driving, so I thought it best to observe the speed limit. Seconds later Officer Warren was shouting, "Faster! Faster! One of your partners is calling for help in the Tenderloin. Get your ass moving Code Three! Light it up!"

I fumbled below the console to activate the lights and siren, nervous about removing a hand from the ten o'clock and two o'clock position. Afraid to take my eyes off the road, I blindly searched for the switch with my right hand, unintentionally stroking Officer Warren's knee. He grabbed my hand and threw it back with violent disgust, then activated the system himself. The high-pitched whine of the siren only increased my panic.

"Faster! Faster, recruit! People are being killed in the Tenderloin and you're dicking around here!" His voice was hitting soprano: "Faster!" *Was he kidding?* My heart was pounding in some bizarre arrhythmia. I was already having trouble navigating the cones. *Wouldn't it be crazy to go this fast on city streets?* We had hopped straight into a Code Three response exercise without being told the parameters. Or maybe I had fallen asleep during the monotonous morning lecture part of the class. I wasn't even sure how fast cops were allowed to go on city streets. Had anyone told us?

Although I was now way out of my comfort zone, I increased speed, swerving between cones that now appeared much more closely spaced than I'd originally perceived them.

"Faster, faster!" *What were those thumping sounds?* "You just killed another kid, Nassberg!"

What the hell was he talking about? "Should I stop and help him?"

"No, he's dead. It's too late, you should have thought about that before you killed him. Go help the cops in the Tenderloin."

We'd made one complete loop around the course. As we started loop two, my rearview mirror reflected a trail of flattened cones. Oh.

"Don't bother looking, Nassberg. The damage is done. You've killed hundreds. Just keep going. They're still calling for additional officers."

As we came speeding around the last turn I clung tightly to

the steering wheel, trying to stay in my seat as centrifugal force pulled me toward Officer Warren.

"*Stop!* You're there. Get out!"

I stumbled a little as I exited the car, queasy, as if I'd just hopped off the Tilt-a-Whirl at the county fair. I staggered to the bench and watched the next victim, Keith, get behind the wheel of the car. No doubt he'd have to contend with some pejorative Asian driver remarks. But at least he was following me, an orange cone serial killer.

Ed was leaning against the concrete hangar wall, fidgeting as if he was jonesing for a smoke.

"What's the deal here, Ed? Am I going to flunk?"

"Listen, K, they're going to try to stress you out, make you melt down and give up. No matter how fast you go, it won't be fast enough. Mario Andretti couldn't make those turns without hitting cones." Ed shook his head like this was all such bullshit. "So here's the deal. Ignore the instructors when they yell to go faster. Drive at a speed where you can navigate the turns. They won't fire you because you're not the fastest, but they might fire you if you run over too many cones."

"Thanks, Ed, that helps a lot." Ed was becoming a treasure trove of helpful tips.

My Code Three driving skill improved with each run of the course, especially when Officer Warren wasn't my passenger. Our last exercise was hot pursuit. This time we would simulate a chase on city streets. The suspect vehicle was a rusty marked patrol car, and Officer Warren would play the part of the bad-guy driver.

Warren could make this exercise hell. To pass it, I assumed it would be necessary to actually catch him. He would never let me. *This was it. Devlin would finally get his wish.* I could picture the glint in his eyes as Officer Warren bragged to him that he'd flunked out another woman.

My new passenger was Officer Matteo, a handsome Italian. Molly and I had schoolgirl crushes on him, and we'd nicknamed him The Hand because of his beautifully sculpted, unusually large hands. We admired him and giggled when he taught our street patrol classes. Molly winked at me theatrically as I got inside the car with him. My crush on Officer Matteo was only adding to my anxiety.

The chase started slowly—no chase at all, really, just an officer out on a lovely day following some car in front of her—no big deal. Then Officer Warren abruptly floored it. I hit the gas and tried to keep up as he whizzed around cones at an outrageous speed, not hitting even one. Minimally increasing my speed, I heeded Ed's advice. Better to let him escape than to kill more innocent cones.

"What's the plate on the car?" Officer Matteo asked calmly. "Tell dispatch."

"Three Adam David Sam four two six," I picked up the disconnected radio transmitter and used the phonetic alphabet we'd memorized.

"Good," said Officer Matteo. But as I took the last high-speed turn, my seatbelt suddenly popped from the latch, and centripetal force pulled me toward Matteo. My hands remained glued to the steering wheel, but my ass was nearly on his lap. *How the hell did that happen?*

Officer Warren was miles ahead now. I pulled myself back into my seat, scarcely having time to be embarrassed, and continued the pursuit, knowing there would be no way I would ever get close enough to pull him over.

Abruptly, he stopped. The exercise was over. I got out of the car and shuffled back to the bench. Officer Matteo was laughing as he took a seat beside me. "Thanks for the lap dance!" he said, elbowing me in the ribs. I smiled anemically. "What's up, K?" he asked.

"Well, I flunked, right? I wasn't close to catching him."

"Hell, no," said Matteo. "No one catches Warren. You didn't kill any cones and you put out the plate to dispatch. You passed."

Unbelievable! I'd survived Code Three driving.

An Offer You Can't Refuse

When Molly and I returned from EVOC training with the rest of the class, Devlin took one look at us, closed his eyes, and shook his head. Just the night before, our class had spent several hours near Lake Merced doing simulations—responding to pretend calls for service and critical incidents. After jogging around sand dunes for hours, Molly and I had lost some steam. Officer Lemon, a visiting training officer, saw us lagging as we trudged up the dunes.

"Get your fat asses up the hill!" he yelled.

I imagined the entire class turning to inspect our fat asses. I wanted to sprint back to Lemon and pummel him. I wanted to put the whole weight of my fat ass on his chest. Lemon's insults echoed one of Mom's old favorites, and that only increased my rage. Because of Mom's remarks, I had come to believe that my somewhat larger than average behind was enormous. She had convinced me I was huge, when in fact, at five foot seven and 145 pounds, I was a fairly average size.

Lemon continued heckling us as we ascended the hill. "What makes you broads think you'll be able to do this job? Who's gonna want a partner like either of you two? No one's ever gonna work with you."

After seventeen weeks of working out every day, we were solid and muscular. We had come a long way from our early workouts, when we barely eked out ten pushups. Molly and I locked eyes.

Lemon was old and wimpy. It would have required little effort to squish him like an ant, and the temptation was killing me.

"Let it go, let it go, just two more weeks," muttered Molly.

If we reacted, even verbally, he could bring us up on charges. Of course, when Lemon said no one would work with us, we couldn't help but wonder if he was right. But Molly and I had already solved that; as soon as we were done with field training, we would ask to be partners. That was our plan.

Devlin called only the two of us into his office and ordered us to sit against the wall. It was clear he was playing a new card, but we had no clue what it might be. Then he left the room. Fearing he was crazy enough to plant a recording device, we didn't dare speak. I looked around trying to guess what he might have planned. His shelves were cluttered with trophies from martial arts tournaments. The walls were decorated with weight charts and posters depicting the proper position for push-ups. He loved sentencing us to supplemental exercise, but normally he wouldn't have bothered calling us into his office for something that mundane.

Suddenly, he stormed back in and shouted, "You two girls are obese!" He waved his arms and pointed at the weight chart. "You will never graduate because you are obese!" I almost burst out laughing. OK, maybe I had a fat ass, but obese? He seemed near hysteria, chanting the same phrase again and again. The word *obese* was the chorus to his tuneless refrain: "You will never be police officers—obese! You will never be police officers—obese!"

Then I realized he was serious. This was a new one. He'd never mentioned our weight before. He must not have anticipated our return from EVOC training. He'd been banking on our failure. I stared at him, aghast, and frankly, insulted. Seventeen weeks, and he was just now accusing us of being overweight? *Hey, and how about Donut? Donut made the two of us look anorexic! Why wasn't he in here?* Devlin had been weighing the class weekly, and Molly and I weighed less now than the first week. All three of us knew he was lying. We were not, in fact, over the weight limit. But we didn't dare respond.

His tone became soft and condescending. "OK, there is something you can do. There is a way you can get another chance." He closed his eyes pensively and nodded, impressed with the generosity of the offer he was about to make. "It would behoove you to do exactly as I say."

Behoove us? He had our full attention. He had all the cards. We would do whatever he asked—starve ourselves if necessary. What did he have in mind? An all-spinach diet? Running a marathon?

"If you resign today, you may be eligible to return in a future class. If you don't resign, you will be terminated for being obese."

Molly and I stared at each other, flabbergasted. *This was his deal? Quit or be fired?* The height and weight limits were posted all around the gym. Sure, I was close to the upper range. Maybe five pounds below the maximum. I didn't know Molly's weight, but she definitely did not look obese. She looked solid. We both did.

He said we had twenty-four hours to accept his offer. We returned to our desks just inches apart in the back of the classroom. During the remainder of the afternoon, we whispered and passed notes as instructors droned in the background. *What should we do? Can they really fire us? Couldn't we just get weighed before a jury of our peers and destroy his argument?* The possibility that he would allow us to return with some future class seemed far-fetched.

By late afternoon, I'd convinced myself Devlin was bluffing. In any case, with only two weeks to go, there was no way I was going through this academy again. And I remembered Gina's advice. *Don't quit no matter what.* Before we left for the day, I was certain Molly had reached the same conclusion.

The next morning, when she arrived in uniform, I was relieved Molly had not fallen for Devlin's stunt. We fell in for inspection as usual. We did some burpees because Golden Gloves had misplaced his cap again, then we marched into class. When she took her seat beside me, her eyes were red.

"Today is my last day," she whispered. Her eyes filled with tears.

"What! No! Don't let him do this! He's bluffing. Don't go!"

"No. I talked to Dad last night, and he thinks it's best. He says they'll let me back into the next class after I lose a few pounds." Molly's dad was a fire department chief and had some understanding of the inner workings of civil service. There was no question she was in a tough position. A single mom with two young daughters, she couldn't afford to gamble with her future. If Devlin fired us, no government agency would ever employ us again. Resigning would at least keep the doors open.

I was infinitely sad, but I did not try to dissuade her. I had no way of knowing if Devlin would be successful with his plan. I only knew I could not go through all this again. At the end of the day, we hugged good-bye, promising to see each other in a few days.

Devlin's Dance

"I'm surprised you're still here, *Nasssssssberg*," hissed Devlin the Monday after Molly left. "I figured you'd leave with your chubby little buddy."

"No, sir." It killed me to feign respect for him. His smirk led me to suspect he had come up with another plan to rid himself of me. I was the only woman left in my class. I tried to feel some pride in that thought, but I knew the truth. I was no better than Molly. We had been in exactly the same boat, and she had as much right to be here as I did. Anyway, I still had a couple of weeks to go, and who knew what Devlin had in store.

Over the weekend, I'd called Gina for counseling and learned a few things. She'd told me that to fire a recruit, the staff had to establish just cause. The terminated trainee was entitled to what was known as a Scully Hearing. A recruit could be fired only for failing an essential skill: firearms training, emergency vehicle operation, or written tests on laws and procedures, or for being over the weight limits. All of these requirements were objectively measurable. The baton dance was the only exception.

Devlin himself bragged he had invented the dance and had made it a requirement for graduation. The San Francisco Police Academy was the only one in the world that even taught Devlin's dance. Passing it was based on subjective evaluation by the PT staff. The State of California did not care about the baton dance, probably because it had absolutely no practical application in police work.

The routine itself was not complicated. It consisted of nine choreographed steps and maneuvers. The officer stepped forward, drew the baton from the ring, performed a series of strikes and pivots, then a back thrust with the butt of the baton, and returned to starting position, placing the baton back in the ring. When performed properly, the dance was an elegant display of martial art. We practiced the routine daily, and there was not one of us who ever missed a step. We were the Rockettes of baton dance. It had been hammered into us so insistently that even the terminally clumsy could not help but learn it.

The rumor was that when Devlin wanted to get rid of someone and nothing else worked, he had the staff continually fail her on the baton dance. The class had all been talking about a terminated recruit who was in the process of suing the city. She had actually performed her dance before a jury and hired her own baton dance expert to prove her case. The plaintiff was alleging that the staff repeatedly failed her because she was a woman. The former recruit's trial dragged on as I repeatedly failed the test, and I prayed she would win her lawsuit.

I was beginning to imagine that I would also be demonstrating my baton skills to a jury of my peers, and I feared I might soon be calling around for that expert's name. I'd taken and failed the test nine times. The instructor would never tell me what my mistake was, because I was making no mistakes. For hours, I practiced before the mirror. Still, it seemed like I would never pass.

Each afternoon the staff watched me go through my steps, barely looking up as they wrote notes on their clipboards. Then they handed me yet another form documenting my failure. I returned to the classroom and plodded on through case law, first aid, community relations, and domestic-violence classes, wondering if I would ever have an opportunity to use all this training.

Mark, Keith, Marty, and Scot had spent hours watching me perform the dance, trying to help me pass, but not seeing anything wrong. "What's his problem?" asked Keith. "You're doing it the same way everyone else does. You've passed every single post requirement. He's just a jerk. I can't see why he would keep flunking you."

"Remember what the old-timers told us? 'Devlin's such a dick, he'd arrest his own mother!'" said Marty. "Karen, I hope you don't end up having to sue the city like what's-her-bucket."

I doubted I'd sue the city. Begging for this job before a jury would be beyond humiliating. I pictured myself in gym shorts and my "One for Life" class T-shirt, dancing around a courtroom, brandishing a stick, and I imagined a jury hooting with laughter. No, it was make it or break it. Fire me and I walk away. *But then what? In this economy, what jobs are even out there? Oh yeah, the bread truck.*

After our run, calisthenics, burpees, and baton practice, PT was over for the day. Officer Hamilton called my name and told me to see him at the back of the gym. The class filed out, but my friends stayed near the door, sending me moral support. Everyone knew what was coming. This had become a daily routine. Shade Monitor and Golden Gloves had failed multiple times, but even they'd passed by now. I was the last one.

"Today, I will be testing you on the baton dance," said Officer Hamilton, as if this were my first time taking it. I looked around the gym. Devlin was missing. Probably with the Police Athletic League kids again. Devlin had one redeeming trait: he volunteered his time teaching underprivileged children martial arts. But that wasn't enough to make me like him.

"OK, Nassberg, show me your dance." Had I not cared so desperately about passing and graduating, I might have spontaneously performed a comic ballet—an ode to spring or something—just to get a laugh from my friends. But I'd lost my sense of humor. This was the final card in Devlin's hand, and I was certain he would not stop playing it until he won.

I stepped forward and assumed the bladed stance position. I drew my baton crisply from the ring; step forward; forward thrust; swing; pivot; back thrust; pivot; swing; downward thrust. The same way I always did. I replaced the baton in the ring on my gun belt and returned to at ease position.

"OK. Here, Nassberg," Officer Hamilton handed the evaluation sheet to me. "Congratulations, you passed." He cracked a micro smile. I looked closely at the paper. Each box was checked: "Pass, pass, pass." Nine passes checked off!

"Thank you, sir!" I ran to the door, ecstatic, and leaped with joy. Keith, Mark, and Scot group-hugged me. It was the Friday before our final week.

On Monday, Devlin was seething, clearly regretting having taken Friday off. "So, you're still here, Nassberg. Well, don't get your hopes up. You'll never cut it as a cop. If some training officer lets you slip through, you'll get your ass kicked or killed. Don't worry."

Our last day ended with a long run around the parking lot. We wore our full regalia; jumpsuits, gun belts, helmets, and body armor. Carrying our thirty-six-inch batons in port-arms position, we ran as a platoon. Over the weeks, we had lost nearly half the recruits we'd started with. Twenty-two were gone. Twenty-five remained.

We ran in perfect unison. After running together for months, we now ran as onc body, as if our shoulders were stitched together with invisible thread. There were no annoying cadence songs sung on this day. We ran in proud silence.

The staff stood along the cyclone fence, just as we recruits had on Day One. Devlin, again, was absent. They watched as we ran twenty laps, and they beamed with pride, all signs of derision absent from their faces. They had turned a group of adolescent misfits into a cohesive police unit—we were a real platoon.

Mark slid his hand off his baton and took my hand in his for the last time. "See, I told you, you weren't a quitter," he said, smiling. I looked into his bright blue eyes, then turned away as tears began rolling down my face. During the entire nineteen weeks, I had not allowed myself to cry, and now here, on the last day, I could not stop. I had never thought I'd be the only woman graduating from my class. I felt a flicker of pride, chased by something like survivor's guilt.

I ran, crying silently, not just for Molly, but for the whole crazy thing, everything we'd all been through together. I felt a budding nostalgia for this time and place. The academy had given me a sense of belonging like nothing I'd ever known before. I didn't know it then, but I would never see many of my classmates after graduation. We would never again share this sense of us-against-them pride and unity. The police academy was a once-in-a-lifetime experience, and I missed it already.

Don't Hesitate, Terminate

Things had predictably soured between Mom and John. Not surprisingly, they were consuming massive quantities of liquor. I arrived just as the owner of the Seventeenth Street corner store delivered a case to their door. Mom reacted to our simultaneous appearance with mild embarrassment.

"Oh, come in, Abraham. Just leave it there, thanks." He put down the box, and Mom handed him a check without making eye contact. "I know, Karen. It's just unbelievable how much John drinks! He's a raving lush. We're getting these deliveries every week now!" Alcohol wafted from her breath. Inside the carton, I recognized the familiar silhouette of Cutty Sark bottles. Half the dozen bottles were Cutty, half some other brown liquor. "He just sits on his throne drinking! But guess what? He's taking me to my ancestral home! We leave for the Hebrides in two weeks. I'll finally get to see Barra!"

"That's great, Mom." *Maybe you'll decide to stay in Scotland!* I handed her a shopping bag containing the two blouses she'd requested. Her shopping aversion had only become greater over the years. She'd once relied on Jim to buy her clothing, but now I'd taken over the thankless chore. I waited for her to berate me, as usual, for my choice of department stores. But she took the bag without comment, distracted by the booze delivery.

"Oh, thanks. Do you want to come in?" she said. *Ugh.* I never wanted to come in. The house had a panoramic view overlooking

Twin Peaks. Though the walls and carpets were showing signs of neglect, it was the nicest place Mom had ever lived. I went in cautiously, as if entering a crime scene. John, seated on his leather throne, looked up from his highball glass and grunted, rattling the ice as a greeting.

"Karen, come here." Mom waved me into the kitchen. "I finally figured out why I hate the way this place is laid out!" she said in a stage whisper. "Linda was left-handed!" I stared at her blankly, wondering what John's first wife had to do with anything. She looked at me as if I had a learning disability. "Left-handed, Karen! I'm right-handed!" She enunciated each syllable deliberately, so I could follow her. "Everything in this kitchen is laid out for a left-handed woman. See!" She opened cutlery drawers and dramatically gestured to utensils like Vanna White. The arrangement appeared unremarkable. *Was I missing something?* Then she opened a cabinet, displaying glasses and cups lined in rows. "See!" She crossed her arms with a nod and gazed at me, wide-eyed. More cups and glasses than Mom had owned in her entire life.

"Oh, yeah, I see."

"Oh, you don't see! You're full of it! Do you have any idea what it's like to live in a house in which another woman's presence is everywhere?"

"No, I can't say I do."

"Well, that bitch is everywhere. John's perfect dead wife!" She was intentionally increasing her volume now so he could hear her from the front room.

"She was perfect," he replied. "Compared to you!"

"Maybe we should call a clairvoyant and have her spirit called back! Then you can be with your beloved Saint Linda. Anyway, you'll see her soon enough when they plant you next to her, in your tacky Catholic his-and-hers cemetery plots."

"Thank God I won't have to go through eternity with you, Ann."

Mom had finally found a man willing to banter. But I'd retired from my career as Mom's couple's counselor and had no intention of picking up John as a new client.

"Bye, Mom. Bye, John. Gotta go!"

The graduation ceremony took place a few days later in the auditorium of A.P. Giannini Middle School in the Sunset District. The October fog blanket gave the evening a vaguely sinister aura. Or maybe it was just the anxiety of Mom appearing that was causing me the sense of dread. Just hours before, I'd called and as soon as she answered, the alcohol-induced nastiness began.

"Oh, so tonight's your big night. Well, big fucking deal! You know what I think about cops. How the hell could you join those fascists after everything they've done to me?" She sounded like she was winding up for a long rant.

John took the phone from her, somewhat less inebriated. "Don't worry, I'll get her there on time," he slurred.

"No!" I interrupted. "No! John, please don't bring her! I am begging you, please."

"I'll try," he said. He hung up, and I felt my heart rate escalate.

Thankfully, Mom still hadn't learned to drive. I doubted she'd ride the bus so far across town. She could, of course, still call a cab.

The audience was overflowing with family and friends of the soon-to-be new officers. The police chief and the police commissioners sat together in the front row.

I had spoken to Jim on the phone a couple of hours earlier. "Are you sure you still want to come? I'm hoping Mom and John won't show up, but you never know."

"Of course I'm coming. Unless you don't want me there?"

"Of course I want you there!"

"I'll see you afterwards and I'll take you to dinner. You pick," he said.

The new cops waited backstage until they told us to file out to our chairs on stage. Scot watched me pace back and forth nervously. The excitement of finally receiving my star, the talisman of all we had worked for, was tainted by the possibility of Mom appearing. If she walked in I was sure she'd embarrass me, yelling obscenities or berating my classmates.

At every major event of my life—every graduation and school performance—I'd lived with the dread of being publicly humiliated. She'd actually been fine during my high school graduation, attending with Jim and on her best behavior. But I hadn't even bothered to attend my college graduation. Since I hadn't made it into nursing school, I'd already felt like a failure, and the ceremony seemed meaningless. The possibility of Mom showing up drunk had been just another reason to skip it.

"Still worried Miss Crazy will show up?" said Scot.

"Yup. I'm trying to convince myself she won't come. But I can't imagine she'd give up a chance to publicly humiliate me." I peeked around the stage curtain to check the audience once more. *Good, still not here.*

There was a way in which Mom had made me street-smart. Not street-smart as in knowing the criminals on the street, but street-smart in other ways, like being able to read people and knowing how to calm people. For a second, I felt a glimmer of affection for Mom.

"Scot, I had a strange thought this morning. If I hadn't grown up with my crazy mother, I wouldn't have become a cop. I don't know if I would thank her for it, but in a way, Mom made me a cop."

"Wow. If I give her the yarn, will she make me one, too? Ba-daboom!" Scot said. We laughed at his dumb joke and he put out his arms for a hug, but they suddenly called us out onto the stage.

"Ugh, now I can't erase the picture of you playing with your yarn cop."

Scot put his arm around my shoulder and sang me a little Mama Rose as we filed out, "You'll be swell. You'll be great! Gonna have the whole world on a plate!"

Scanning the room, I watched as Chief Murphy pinned the seven-pointed stars on my classmates. Sergeant Meyer had told us each point of the star represented one of the seven gifts of the Holy Spirit—wisdom, understanding, counsel, fortitude, knowledge, piety, and fear of the Lord. Our stars would serve as daily mementos of the legions of Irish Catholic men who'd patrolled the streets of San Francisco for more than a century before us.

I rose when I heard my name called. After pinning more than a dozen men, the chief hesitated as I approached. He stared at my chest with some confusion, appearing uncertain of the protocol for pinning a police star on a woman. *Hadn't he done this before?* The chief poked the pin into my uniform shirt, avoiding eye contact, his face ruddy with embarrassment. The auditorium went uncomfortably silent. The pinning seemed to be taking an excruciatingly long time. I finally reached up to help, and smiled at him. The audience laughed and clapped. I wondered if the chief would ever get used to pinning a star on a woman's breast.

I simultaneously monitored the rear door of the auditorium and watched the chief pin Scot and Marty. Then, once we were all wearing stars, we raised our right hands and swore to protect and serve our city. Magically, the stars had made us real police.

As the chief swore us in I made a silent vow to never be the kind of cop who talks about what she's having for dinner while someone is suffering in her patrol car. I would treat people with kindness and respect—especially children and teenagers—

always remembering how it felt to ride in the back seat, power-less. I promised myself I would never again smoke marijuana or break any other laws. I would not be a hypocrite. I promised when I could give someone a break for something trivial, I would do it. I'd never arrest a kid with a clean record for something minor, like smoking a joint.

And then the ceremony was over. Mom had not shown up, and with relief I found Jim in the crowd.

"You did it!" he said, as we hugged in the lobby. "That was hilarious when the chief fumbled around with your star!" We laughed. I excused myself to say good-bye to my classmates. The shoe store alliance had made it, sadly without Molly, who never did return to the police academy. A month after she left, she accepted a position as a parking control officer. We did not see each other again for years. For Molly, I was a reminder of what she had worked so hard for and lost. And for my part, when I thought of Molly, I blamed myself for not making her fight harder, for not calling Devlin's bluff.

But Keith and Mark had graduated, as had Marty, Scot, Blockie, Eduardo, Art, Donut, Ed, and even George. We didn't know we would lose more recruits during the next phase, when we would work as real police officers and face daily evaluation. In the crowded lobby, I found as many classmates as I could. We hugged and congratulated each other.

Ed stood alone, away from the group. Had no one come to see him graduate?

"You were a great squad leader, Ed. You're the reason I made it."

"Aw, that's bull, K. You were always gonna make it. I had faith in you."

"Thanks for everything, Ed." We hugged, and I walked over to the group. As I reached Scot, we broke into spontaneous song.

"Kiss today good-bye, the sweetness and the sorrow. Wish me

luck, the same to you, but I can't forget . . ." Marty and Mark howled in with an off-key chorus, "What I did for love! What I did for love."

Walking back to Jim, I bit my cheeks hard to hold back the tears.

The 145th Academy class donned our official police costumes and hit the streets on Halloween. The irony of the timing wasn't lost on us. The three training stations in San Francisco were Mission, Northern, and Central. When Sergeant Meyer told us our class would train at Central, North Beach station, a chill went through me. Just as I'd imagined, I would soon patrol Columbus Avenue in a black-and-white. I'd be working at the same station as my heroine, Gina. That scene in Vesuvio now took on an eerily prescient quality.

But we were still far from being full-fledged police officers. Perhaps we were no longer the losers Sergeant Meyer had once dubbed us, but no veteran cop considered a rookie in the Field Training Program a real cop. Every academy class lost recruits during field training, so the veterans didn't bother to get too attached to us.

Our future careers would now depend on the training officers we were assigned. Past graduates had filled us in on the various reputations of the field training officers (FTOs). We already knew which of them preferred to terminate their recruits and which were easygoing. Some of the trainers boasted about the number of recruits they had fired, and many, big surprise, were not fans of female police recruitment.

On Sunday I snuck in through the station's back door. The women's locker room was a utility closet adjacent to the garage, filled with boxes of dusty station logbooks dating back to the 1950s. The room could accommodate no more than three women at once and seemed to send the tacit message *we don't want you here, and you won't be here long.* The city wouldn't build a real women's locker room at Central until 1989.

I found a vacant locker for the tons of equipment I'd been issued: my uniform, body armor, batons, gun belts, boots, riot helmet, hats, and tag books. In addition to this, I had purchased additional "luxury items": a heavy-duty Streamlight flashlight, clipboard, and an extra pair of handcuffs.

When I reported for duty the next day, I entered through the back door again. I suspected that my presence as the lone female survivor of the 145th might generate curiosity, or maybe something worse. Having learned from my wench-costume-donning days, I'd given myself a generous two-hour cushion before my first lineup, arriving at 6:00 a.m., though lineup wasn't until 8:00 a.m. Not having done a rehearsal, I had no idea how long dressing would actually take. It took nearly an hour just to figure out the equipment placement. *Where do I position the Mace canister on the gun belt? Hmmmm, the cuff case? The baton ring?* Before long, I would be pulling the stuff on in minutes, but that first day, the simple process of dressing seemed overwhelming.

The vest weighed five pounds, and when the belt was fully loaded with gun, extra ammo, two sets of handcuffs, baton, key ring, flashlight, and Mace, it weighed more than twenty. My generous hips were proving useful—the gun belt rested comfortably above my hipbones, and I didn't have to worry about it sliding down to my knees as some of the skinnier guys did. They'd purchased special leather keepers to hook their gun belts to their trouser belts. During the academy, we'd spent plenty of hours running with pretend gun belts, so now I hardly noticed the extra weight. I checked the scratchy mirror and admired myself. I looked like a real cop: a little severe, a little scary, but at the same time, curvy and fiercely female.

At 7:45 a.m., I emerged fully dressed and worked my way upstairs to the assembly room. Our FTOs—the dozen men assigned as our training officers—had removed their uniform shirts so the rookies could read the message emblazoned across their black T-shirts in huge white letters: DON'T HESITATE, TERMINATE.

The shirts were meant to intimidate and demoralize the new recruits. They were advertising their burning desire to fire us for any possible reason. Officer Warren stood in the center of the room, holding court, while a couple of other trainers stood around him, laughing.

My eyes traveled to the wall. Mounted in pride of place was a large poster version of a recruitment ad. Four uniformed female cops: one Asian, one black, one Latina, and one white. A couple of the faces were familiar to me. Two of the officers taught classes at the academy. Over the women's faces in black Sharpie scrawl were the words *we're unwanted*. The graffiti cancelled out the ad's message: "Join the SFPD." I pretended it was just an innocuous wall hanging, but the hostile graffiti shook my confidence. Why did I insist on staying where I was unwanted? *Had years of dealing with Mom taught me to confuse being berated with being loved?*

There were six other women officers at the North Beach station. I wondered how they felt about the poster, but looking around the assembly room, I was the only woman assigned to work that morning watch. My classmates and I barely acknowledged each other, already in camouflage mode. Perhaps Gina was wrong. Maybe the Field Training Program would be more difficult than the academy. There'd be no more alliances and no more team spirit. For the next few months we'd all jockey for position, distancing ourselves from other rookies in case they were failing, masquerading among the real cops to gain acceptance.

My primary FTO was Brian. He was rumored to be easygoing, not one of the famous terminators, though he wore the T-shirt along with the rest. He was a tall Clint Eastwood type and was known as a good training officer with a great sense of humor. He genuinely liked women and believed us capable of doing the job.

Standing for my first lineup in the assembly room, I fantasized I was on the cop show *Hill Street Blues*. After the sergeant called roll and read bulletins from the clipboard, I hoped he'd say, "Be careful out there," but disappointingly, he simply said, "That's all."

Brian looked over at me, and grabbed the hat off my head. "First thing you need to do is lose the grommet." I looked at Brian's hat, a squishy thing without the stiff structure of mine. His looked like someone had thrown it into a mosh pit and hundreds of dancers had stomped on it for hours. He removed the hard plastic ring from the inside of my hat, flinging it into the trashcan, and handed the hat back to me. Now mine looked old timey, like a newsboy's cap—or a bread truck driver's hat.

"Thanks."

Day watch was the slowest shift, and our days flowed by without major incident. It was unusual for a serious crime to occur during day watch, so it was a good place for a rookie to get her feet wet. Brian taught me the basics of routine patrol. We spent a lot of time in the Financial District taking burglary reports. Writing reports hours or even days after the crime had occurred was a necessary part of the job, but it wasn't the sort of exciting police work we rookies longed for.

When a robbery or other serious crime happened, every available car in the district responded. The banks had recently been outfitted with devices known as RAT (radio-assisted tracking) packs, and each downtown station ran a few cars outfitted with tracking devices. If a bank robber took a RAT pack from a teller, the police could track the thief for as long as he held it. The RAT packs would explode after a short while, covering the robber in blue dye. The gadget in the patrol car was a compass-like gizmo, and using it was fun, like playing a kid's game of "hot and cold."

On a slow Wednesday morning during my second week, dispatch put out a bank robbery call.

"We have a 211 in progress, Market and Powell, Hibernia Bank, RAT pack taken. Suspect is a white male, twenty-five years old, six feet tall, medium build. Units to respond." Ten units came up on the air at once, everyone wanting to respond. Our car was RAT equipped, so I raced toward the scene. As I reached Turk and Mason, the needle on the device swung sharply to the right, emitting a faint whine.

"We've got it! We've got it!" I turned onto Turk. Brian handled the radio.

"Three Adam Two to headquarters, we have the signal at Turk and Mason."

Seconds later, the needle swung sharply left, indicating the device was now behind us. Another unit advised dispatch they'd also picked up the signal at Market and Sixth. My heart raced. *We might actually catch a bank robber!*

I sped toward Market and Sixth. As we pulled up, we saw an abandoned patrol car blocking a traffic lane with both doors open. Two officers raced along the sidewalk in foot pursuit, tackling the robber just as we drove alongside. We ditched our car and ran over to the man. I pulled out my handcuffs and snapped them on.

"Code four," Brian told dispatch. "Suspect in custody." Although we hadn't actually made the arrest ourselves, I finally felt like I was part of a team that was doing something important.

A half hour later, the station keeper called us back to Central Station. "Three Adam Two, 902." As I headed in, I worried. *Did*

I do something wrong? Return-to-station calls had an ominous feel, like being called to the principal's office.

Officer Grant was sitting at the station keeper's desk, a concerned look on his face. "Karen, your mom's on the phone. She says she there's an emergency at home and she needs you right away. She said she would just stay on the line because she didn't know the pay-phone number."

"Thanks, Tom." He handed me the phone.

"Mom?" I turned my back to Tom, who seemed overly anxious to come to Mom's rescue.

"Karen, that bastard threw me out! I crashed his precious car into the washing machine in the garage!"

"But you don't know how to drive," I said without thinking.

"Don't be an asshole. It didn't seem all that difficult. And John is a horrible driver. He drives like a snail with that idiotic old-man golf cap! I couldn't stand his driving another minute! I thought the stick thing was in reverse but it wasn't. I need to stay with you."

"Where are you?"

"I'll wait for you at the Twin Peaks."

"I don't get off for another hour." I felt the energy draining from me. After another hour of drinking at the Twin Peaks, I didn't even want to think about what sort of shape she'd be in. "I'll be there when I can." I had already forgotten how happy I'd been minutes before. Mom had a superpower, some sort of Karen-happiness detector that activated and reminded her to interrupt my life whenever I felt good.

When I finally got to the bar, to my relief, she was nowhere to be found.

"The one thing you can never do is criticize your partner about his driving," Brian said, as we drank coffee the next morning. "Or her driving." Brian often offered me advice not directly related to police work, but valuable nonetheless. "Everyone thinks they're a good driver. Have you ever heard someone admit to being a bad driver? If your partner is a bad driver, you just have to keep your mouth shut." I was receiving his subliminal message that my driving sucked. *Maybe I had been a little reckless on the way to the robbery?*

Living with Mom had given me insight into the subtlety of nonverbal communication. I'd learned to protect myself by reading Mom's moods and predicting her behavior. Now I was finding I was good at predicting the behavior of people I encountered on the streets too. If I sensed a suspect was ready to run, or was thinking of hitting me, I often had him in handcuffs before he finished his thought.

But I was facing a new dread. I kept imagining being sent to a call and arriving on scene only to find that the troublemaker was Mom. Unbelievably, I'd never even considered this. I began having a premonition of a mortifying scene where she'd curse at my partner and reveal I was her daughter while I cuffed her. I'd deny her like Judas. *No, I do not know this crazy woman!*

But despite my worries, those first four weeks with Brian were smooth sailing. There were some sophomoric antics. Some comedian ordered me subscriptions to knitting and cooking magazines. They arrived in my station mailbox every few weeks, but this was harmless enough. I chose to view the magazines as a gift rather than a reminder that my place was at home.

Hazing

Joanie was one of four female training officers at Central. She was a great cop, agile and boyish, and reminded me of Peter Pan. I was relieved my luck was holding out: I'd been assigned two good trainers in a row. Each rookie rotated through three. After Joanie, I'd have one final FTO, then return to Brian, my primary. But Joanie had scheduled a day off during my first week on swing shift, so I would be assigned to a substitute.

It turned out I was working with Officer Warren on Joanie's day off, Sunday. When I'd seen Officer Warren in the assembly room that very first day, my stomach had dropped, but I hadn't panicked. We'd been given the names of our FTOs, and Officer Warren was not on my list. I was grateful for this, because seeing him flaunt his intimidating DON'T HESITATE, TERMINATE shirt had nauseated me.

All day Saturday I obsessed about training with Warren. He had taken such an immediate dislike to me during the driver's training, I couldn't imagine spending eight hours in a car with him. Then I thought I was being ridiculous. *What's the worst that could happen in just one night?* Maybe he disliked women, but it seemed more likely he just enjoyed having power over rookies in general. He was notorious for treating his recruits horribly, terminating the majority and causing many of the remainder to resign. We'd all sympathized with the classmate who ended up stuck with him as a primary trainer. That recruit had already resigned.

But Warren wasn't my only concern that weekend. My phone rang at 2:10 Sunday morning. I stared at it, debating with myself. This was before the creation of caller ID. I wasn't due to work until three that afternoon. I considered the possibility that there was a city emergency and they were calling everyone in. Then I decided it was probably Mom with some crisis. But what if it was the station and I failed to respond? By the sixth ring, I decided I'd better pick up.

"Karen?" *Damn!*

"Yes, Mom." I made my voice sound feeble and exhausted, hoping she'd take the hint.

"That simpleton left me stranded in the Castro! I wanted to sing at a piano bar, and he abandoned me without any damn cab fare! Now he won't answer the goddamned phone to come get me." Of course, it was that time of night when the bars announced last call. *I should have figured it was Mom.* It was tempting to tell her to walk home. After smoking so many years, the climb up the Seventeenth Street hill might kill her. As usual, I felt terrible for having this thought.

"Come get me! What are you waiting for? I could get raped and killed out here!"

"Mom. No one's going to rape you in the Castro."

"No! No one would ever rape an ugly old woman like me! God, Karen! What sort of ignoramus are you?"

"I don't know what sort, what are the choices?" She ignored this.

"Don't you know rape has nothing to do with sex? It's a crime of violence, and gay men are just as violent as straight men!"

Now I had no choice but to pick her up. If anything happened to her, it would be my fault. "Where are you?"

"Eighteenth and Castro. And hurry up! It's freezing out here. I lost my jacket in Moby Dick."

"You lost your wool jacket in a leather bar?" She hung up on me.

When I got there, she was on the corner, chatting with two transvestites who were in desperate need of a shave.

"Can you give these girls a ride over the hill, Karen?"

"Sure." They were drunk, but pleasant. I dropped them on Haight, then took Mom home.

Mom pounded on her front door with both fists. If John was inside, there was no indication. Of course, her keys had been in the pocket of the lost jacket.

"I guess I'm staying with you," she said. "I know you're thrilled about that."

"Hold on a second. Let me see if I can get in." I'd do anything to avoid her coming home with me. I climbed around the side of the house and shimmied up the back deck of the in-law apartment, then pulled myself to the upper deck. I hopped over the railing and rattled the sliding glass door. John was passed out on his leather throne and didn't budge as I rapped loudly on the glass.

Defeated, I drove Mom up the hill to my place.

She was out of breath after climbing the two flights to my apartment. "Do you have any scotch?" she wheezed. "I could use a nightcap."

"No, Mom. I don't have any booze. I need to sleep. I have the night shift tomorrow."

"You and that goddamned job! You take care of the world and you just leave me alone to suffer with that bastard. He'll probably murder me one day, and you'll have to investigate the case. How would you like that?"

"I wouldn't like that."

She continued her monologue, showing no interest in going to bed. "I bet you would just love it if he killed me! Maybe you'd even find some way to get your greedy little hands on John's millions once he was put away."

She carried on until she passed out on the couch. I dressed quietly and went to a ridiculously early breakfast at Church Street Station. There was no point in trying to sleep. The anxiety over working with Warren was now compounded with anxiety over leaving Mom alone in my house. A greasy plate of eggs, I hoped, might be an effective sedative. Maybe I could nap later in my car.

We stood in two rows for lineup. I took a place beside Officer Warren and said hello. He didn't look up or bother to grunt. After lineup, he threw the car keys at me without making eye contact, grumbling to himself.

Before getting in the car, I made a show of checking the shotgun, unloading and reloading it. The passenger usually checked the shotgun, but I thought it best to play it safe so Officer Warren wouldn't fail me on equipment inspection. He ignored me as I circled the car, checking for damage and marking the vehicle inspection log.

I headed toward our sector south of the station, hoping a call would come over the air to save me from the silence. Patrolling Geary Street, I looked for suspicious activity and monitored both radios, the low-band station, and another channel on my handheld radio. It had taken me a couple of weeks to learn to decipher all the air traffic. When you added driving, looking for criminals, and answering your training officer's pop quizzes, police work felt like the Olympic decathlon of multitasking.

I waited for Warren to play the game the other trainers liked, where they'd call out some obscure alley name and tell the recruit to get there immediately, but he said nothing, giving me no hint of how he liked to work. The passenger-side window reflected his contemptuous grimace. His distaste for me rode between us like a third partner. This would be a long, uncomfortable night if he planned to continue his silent treatment.

"Go to the TL," he finally snarled. The Tenderloin, which was the highest crime neighborhood in our district, was not our assigned sector.

"OK. Anywhere in particular?"

"Turk and Taylor," he snapped, shaking his head at my stupidity.

"Park," he ordered as we approached the intersection. I followed his lead as he hopped out of the car and walked straight to one of the homeless winos camped out on the corner. "Get up, Bobby." Officer Warren then bent down and whispered something into his ear. Immediately Bobby, a drunk who looked over fifty but was in his thirties, staggered to his feet and swung wildly. Officer Warren seemed to expect this because he showed no surprise. Bobby tried a couple more careless punches, missing Warren each time. As I moved in closer, grabbing Bobby's arm, Warren hopped away to the curb and left me alone with the swinging drunk.

Pulling my handcuffs from their case, I rushed him, ducking as his fist narrowly missed my cheek. He reeked of Night Train or some other cheap wine. Wrestling his arm behind him, I managed to get one cuff on. Then I pushed him against the wall of Frenchie's Adult Superstore, trying to force his other arm behind his back. But Bobby was feeling no pain. I didn't know what we were arresting him for, but I knew if someone tried to hit your partner, he had to go to jail. Warren watched me struggle, doing nothing. Using a wristlock, I finally got both cuffs on and led him to the car. Leaning him against the trunk, I performed a meticulous search, knowing Warren would deduct points if I didn't check every filthy crevice. Bobby's crotch was disturbingly wet. After putting him in the back seat, I drove back to Central.

At the booking counter it would be my responsibility, as the rookie, to search Bobby again, remove his property, and escort him to the holding cell. Officer Warren would sit safely on the opposite side of the booking counter, a metal grate protecting him as he typed the booking card and took inventory of the prisoner's personal property.

Bobby wasn't 500 pounds, as Devlin had once predicted my arrestees would be, but he was pissed off. Whatever Warren had said to him earlier really set him off. Officer Warren removed the handcuffs and took his seat behind the typewriter. Leaning him against the counter, I removed Bobby's belt, the change in his pockets, and his soggy cigarettes. Officer Warren itemized the property onto the booking card. When it was time for Bobby to sign the card, he turned and began swinging again. I bobbed and weaved, avoiding his fists, and pulled out my handcuffs.

"No cuffs!" ordered Warren. He stayed seated on the stool, motionless. Bobby had a nice full head of hair. As I grabbed a handful of hair, I kicked the back of his knees and pulled him down. He continued kicking and swinging as I dragged him toward the cell. A couple of cops standing behind Officer Warren saw the commotion and moved quickly toward the booking cell door.

"Don't!" Warren told them. They backed off.

Central had a creepy, ancient cell, pitch-dark and full of colossal cockroaches. It was a dungeon, really, two phone-booth-sized cubicles facing each other. The booking officer had to unbolt the lock with a huge, antique key, then slide open the heavy, metal door while keeping control of the prisoner.

Officer Warren could no longer see us from where he was seated, but he had to have heard us thumping around, wrestling. It was virtually impossible for one officer to keep control of a resisting suspect and unlock the cell door simultaneously. If I let go of Bobby, he'd get a punch in. If I didn't free up a hand, I would not be able to unlock the door. I needed more hands. Finally giving up on unlocking the cell door, I pushed Bobby into the tiny space between the two cells, backed out, and locked the heavy steel outer door.

I was furious. Not with Bobby—he was just a wino. But what Officer Warren had done was unforgivable. Letting your recruit subdue a resistor was one thing—all rookies expected we would have to prove we were capable. But he had wanted me to get hurt. He hadn't even moved off his chair to see if Bobby had gotten the upper hand and locked me in the cell. I could think of no other training officer who would have done something like that. He pretended to type as I stood beside him, waiting.

"I couldn't get him in the cell, so he's locked in the space between," I finally said. He continued his two-fingered typing, not looking up. "Why didn't you help me?" *Isn't that what a partner is supposed to do?*

"All you had to do was ask," he said, still fixated on the type-writer. Tears welled in my eyes and I tilted my head, willing them back into my tear ducts. I turned away and without hesitation marched into the lieutenant's office. I pulled my gun from the holster and placed it on his desk, then fumbled to unpin my star.

"I quit."

Ask

Lieutenant Frost was startled when I pulled my gun out of the holster. Then, as I placed it on his desk, he looked puzzled.

"Why? What happened?" Frost was a kind, fatherly boss. Everyone loved him. "You've been doing so well in the program."

"Warren happened. He jacked up a resistor and left me to clean up the mess. He wanted me to get my ass kicked and wouldn't let anyone help me. I couldn't get the key into the cell door and control the resistor. I needed more hands. I'm done."

Frost sighed and shook his head. "Karen, listen to me." His body language said, *Here we go again.* "Once you're done with the training program, nothing like this will ever happen again." The lieutenant spoke in a matter-of-fact way that had a calming effect. "When you call for help in the future, cops will come from everywhere. Officer Warren is an odd duck. Don't quit. You're good at this job."

I am? Lieutenant Frost's statement was news to me. *A real cop, a lieutenant no less, thinks I am good at this?* I took a breath and looked behind me. The guys at the assembly room table had stopped writing reports and were looking through the office windows expectantly. I felt the impulse to re-create one of Mom's tirades: *"What are you assholes looking at?"* Maybe even break into song. But I wasn't Mom.

Lieutenant Frost waited. I considered the men behind me, then gazed down at my shoes. Was I really ready to give up everything I'd worked for? Was I just being dramatic? Overreacting because of lack of sleep? Then I saw the ridiculousness of this moment: putting my gun on the lieutenant's desk and turning in my star, like a scene from a Dirty Harry movie. *Have I gone through six months of training to quit now? And won't Devlin just love getting the news that Warren had made me quit! And Mom!* No, I wouldn't let any of them have the satisfaction of seeing me quit.

"OK." Grateful the lieutenant had stopped me, I sheepishly put my gun back in the holster and pinned my star back onto my shirt.

"Do you want to put in a card for the rest of the night? Joanie's back tomorrow. You won't have to work with Warren again."

"No thanks, Lieut. I'll finish the shift."

Officer Warren was like my mother telling me I'd never go to college. Like Devlin saying I'd never be a cop. I walked toward him with the most severe look I could conjure, attempting to burn holes into his skull with my eyes. He was still on the stool with his back to the typewriter, but now he was leaning back, arms crossed, talking to a few other old-timers and laughing boisterously.

"Are you ready to go back out?" I asked, a little too loudly.

He looked up, startled. Since we'd come in with Bobby, the entire station had been watching our little drama unfold. I could imagine the older cops thinking Warren had won another hand in his favorite game—terminate the broads. They looked surprised that this broad had hung around. Somewhere, I'd found the voice that had eluded me for twenty-four hours, the voice I wished I'd found when Mom had called the night before. Officer Warren seemed surprised I'd come out of the lieutenant's office and surprised I was still speaking to him. He nodded, and we headed back to the car, continuing the rest of the night in silence. But this time his silence was more like stunned silence.

Officer Warren may have been a jerk, but he was right, I'd never asked for help. I had assumed it was obvious I needed help, but the fact was, I had never uttered one request for help. Somewhere along the line, I'd stopped asking for the things I needed. Pride, or fear of showing just how vulnerable I was, had stopped me. Aunt Connie's words came back to me: *Karen, you must always ask for what you need.* She'd recognized my weakness years before I had, an overblown sense of pride that had only grown worse after Dad's rejection.

When I got home that night, Mom was camped on the couch watching *The Tonight Show.* "Hi, honey," she said, "how was your night?"

Kindness. *Bad sign.* She clearly intended to stay for a while and did not want to wear out her welcome too quickly. She was sober, benignly perched on the couch, ashtray balanced on her chest. She'd probably slept the whole time I'd been gone. Her craziness from the night before had been alcohol-induced, not a manic episode. I supposed this was good news, but her usual pattern was to go on a "toot," as she called her two-day drinking sprees, which then set off a manic phase. I felt like I was waiting for the next nut to drop.

"It was OK, sort of." It was tempting to unburden my Officer Warren saga to her, but that would open the door to a big "I told you so," followed by a lecture about fascists. "How are you?" I wanted to ask if she had any intention of going home, but that would undoubtedly start another fight as well as a scolding about my use of the word *home.*

"I'm not going back to that bastard, if that's what you're asking!"

"Is he that awful?"

"Karen, he's a monster! He sits all day long, guzzling whiskey. Yesterday he actually defecated on himself in the chair and didn't bother to move. He's a tyrant!"

I probably wouldn't have described a man who spent his days drinking in a giant chair as tyrannical, but Mom no doubt resented having to clean up after him. In spite of her professed youthful aspiration to become a nurse, Mom had no stomach for the more gruesome aspects of caretaking.

Of course, the last thing I wanted was for her to stay with me. But even with my recent epiphany, I couldn't bring myself to tell her to go. If I kicked her out, she might start off in a bar and end up in jail or dead, and I would never forgive myself.

"Well, you can stay here until you figure it out. Actually, you could do me a big favor. The used appliance store is supposed to deliver the refrigerator tomorrow while I'm in court. I was going to ask Monica to come let them in, but if you could do that it would save her the trip."

"Of course I can do that! What time are they coming?"

"Between 9:00 a.m. and noon. Please make sure they put it where the old one was, in that space next to the oven."

"I'm not stupid, Karen. I know how to receive an appliance delivery!"

"I wasn't implying you were stupid." *Oh, why am I bothering? It's exhausting.* "OK, thanks. Are you OK on the couch?"

"Sure, you know me and my insomnia. I'll be up all night watching television anyway. Good night."

"Good night, Mom."

The next day, I left the preliminary hearing for the bank robbery and headed straight to Central for my swing shift. If Joanie had heard about the incident the night before, she didn't let on. We started our shift with an 802, police code for a dead body. It wasn't the first dead body I'd seen. I'd dissected cadavers in college anatomy and wasn't squeamish. But the college cadavers hadn't really seemed like people anymore; they'd looked like dried jerky and reeked of formaldehyde. This was my first dead-body call as a police officer.

A dark-haired man in his forties waited in front of a house on Valparaiso Street in North Beach. He held a handkerchief over his face. When we got out of the car I was overcome with the stench of decay and realized the handkerchief was his futile effort to mask the odor.

"It's my father," he said. "He's been in there for more than two weeks."

Joanie stepped back and signaled for me to follow her lead.

"Take the collar of your turtleneck and pull it up over your nose. I usually spray mine with perfume," she whispered. I'd worn a T-shirt under my uniform that night, the fall weather just beginning to chill. I pulled my perfume-less T-shirt over my nose as we inched into the hallway.

Heat swirled around us, radiating from the kitchen stove at the end of the hallway. An older man's body lay on the linoleum below the stove, steeped in a pool of gooey, black liquid. The rank odor intensified as we neared. It was as if someone had left the stinkiest Camembert cheese in the world out on a warm countertop for months. As I looked more closely, I noticed the body was white and pulsating. I thought back to the academy class about death investigations. The instructor had shown us photographs and told us that those moving grains of rice were swarms of maggots. I could handle the visual, but the stench was unbearable, as if all the oxygen molecules in the room had been sucked out and replaced with some heavy, rancid fluid. Joanie's turtleneck-T-shirt tip was doing nothing to make breathing easier.

"OK, we've seen enough. Come on, Karen." She signaled me

to follow her out just as I was afraid I was about to lose it and throw up.

While we waited for the medical examiner, I took a statement from the son.

"I haven't seen him for weeks. I live in San Mateo and visit him about once a month. He hasn't been answering the phone for the last few days. I was worried."

An hour later, the medical examiner arrived and took custody of the remains. When we returned to the patrol car, I felt that I needed to ask Joanie some questions about stiffs. This first death case had been so horrible; I wondered if I could stomach this job. I'd figured all bodies would be similar to the ones in the lab at Cal, but now I wondered. *Were dead body calls always this awful?*

"Joanie, was that body unusually bad? Are most of them that decayed?" Searching for the right words, I was trying to phrase the question without sounding wimpy. Gina had told me that in the FTO program you never wanted to give your training officer the sense you were squeamish. Gina's advice made me recall Mom's lack of tolerance for squeamishness. At least I'd graduated from Mom's training.

"No, that was one of the worst I've ever seen," Joanie said. "When they're freshly dead, they hardly smell at all." *Thank God.*

My questions were soon answered because an hour later we were sent to another death case. This one was an elderly woman in a Tenderloin apartment. Her health care worker checked in daily. She'd been dead only a few hours when the aide found her. Joanie was right. There was no odor to speak of and no maggots. This body wasn't creepy. The woman looked like a mannequin resting peacefully in bed.

But even this made me doubt myself. Shouldn't a scene like this make me feel terrible? I wondered if something was wrong with me. I knew most young women would have been horrified at seeing a dead person, or at least moderately upset. But I felt nothing. It occurred to me that my childhood had created some sort of detachment in me—some sort of adaptation that was unusual, maybe unhealthy, but strangely useful for my chosen line of work.

At midnight, when I unlocked my apartment door, a gust of grey smoke telegraphed Mom's presence. She was on the couch, watching the late news.

"Hi, Mom. How's it going?"

"Good. But I'm really getting sick of our government being mixed up in all this Central American crap. Sandinistas, Contras—I'm thinking of going down there and helping out." *Oh, great.* A few years back she'd mentioned joining the People's Temple, but before heading to Jonestown, she'd met John and dismissed that idea. Now I'd have to worry that she'd volunteer in a revolution and be kidnapped, or worse.

"Yep, it's crazy. I don't understand it either."

"I didn't say I didn't understand, Karen! Of course I do. I could practically teach college-level history. I said I'm sick of it!"

"Yes, I agree. Did the refrigerator arrive?"

"Yes, the delivery guy was very nice."

Dropping my shoulder bag on the floor, I moved back to the kitchen. The refrigerator stood in the center of the room, abandoned mid-delivery, many feet from the cubby. Already simmering, I returned to the front room.

"Why is the refrigerator in the middle of the kitchen?"

"Oh, well, he was so friendly. We got busy yakking. I told him he could just leave it there. He turned out to be horrible in bed though. You know. One of those one-way-street guys." She dramatically rolled her eyes.

"You had sex with the delivery man in my bed?" This was a new low—even for Mom.

"Well, I didn't plan on using your bed. We were on the couch. The bed was his idea. Honestly, it wouldn't have happened if I hadn't been stoned. After we smoked the joint, the rest is a blur. You know I seldom smoke the stuff. I'd forgotten how goofy it makes me." She giggled.

She trailed me as I stormed back to the kitchen. Maybe it was adrenaline from anger or superhuman strength from Devlin's burpees, but somehow, like the Incredible Hulk, I half-carried, half-walked the refrigerator across the kitchen and slid it into the cubby. After parking it, I stared at it, stunned by what I'd done. Then I turned to Mom, who was watching me, wide-eyed. For the first time ever, I understood I could intimidate her.

"You smoked marijuana in my apartment? Are you crazy? I'm a police officer. I could get fired if someone smelled dope coming from this place and called it in! I'm still probationary. They can fire me for anything!"

This felt unbelievable. I was grasping something I'd denied for years: Mom cared about nothing but her own immediate gratification. My hopes, desires, and needs meant nothing to her. I was so busy worrying about her, I didn't even know what my needs and desires were half the time. Had I become a cop not only because I felt I had always been one but because unconsciously I needed to arm myself to finally feel strong enough to say no to Mom?

"You need to leave now," I continued calmly, as I seethed inside. "Call John and tell him you're coming back. I am done with you." Slowly, I moved closer, looking her in the eye.

"Don't you dare tell me what to do! I don't take orders from you," she said. But she'd been backing out of the kitchen as I neared. The tide had turned. She could see my new confidence and seemed unsure what I might do next. She grabbed cigarettes from the couch. "I can't believe how you treat me! After everything I've done for you! You are the worst daughter on the planet! I'll see you in hell!" She slammed the front door for emphasis.

Collapsing back onto the couch, I crumbled into tears. All the strength I'd shown instantly disappeared. I'd sent Mom out into the November night. *What will happen to her?* My teeth chattered as if I were freezing.

I was writing a burglary report the next day when Sergeant Malone tapped my shoulder.

"There's a woman at the front counter who says she's on the list for the next academy class, and she wants to talk to a female officer about the job. I know you have about three minutes in the business, but you're the only woman working," he said.

"Sure, I'll talk to her."

When I reached the front counter, I froze. This beautiful, blond woman looked so familiar. *Where had I seen her before?* And then I knew, and took a step back. We recognized each other simultaneously.

"Janice?"

"Karen?"

She was Dad's wife, my stepmother.

"Wow, Karen, you became a cop?"

"Yes. What are you doing here?" The question came out more harshly than I intended.

"I'm scheduled for the next academy class. I start next month."

How is this possible? I hadn't seen her in years, and I never would have imagined she would be interested in becoming a cop. She had struck me as bohemian, maybe a dancer or an artist. But then again, she probably wouldn't have guessed that I'd become a cop either.

After so long, I no longer had hard feelings toward Janice. I blamed my father for turning his back on me—no one else. But

I did feel a certain degree of moral superiority. *What kind of parent would allow a teenage daughter to be homeless?* And now Janice was here asking me for advice. Well, I'd show her I was the bigger person. I'd take the moral high road. Answer her questions, mentor her through the academy, and turn the other cheek.

She called me frequently during her academy training, and we became good friends. Though I wasn't anxious to resume a relationship with my father, I did want to broach the subject of their refusal to allow me to move in when I was fifteen. I needed to understand why. Maybe she'd tell me what an amazing person I was, how truly saintlike for the forgiveness I was now showing her, or at least how mature I was not to hold a grudge. Maybe I just wanted her to feel some of my pain, some guilt, or regret. Maybe I *was* holding a grudge?

We often met for coffee and unwittingly became the first stepmother/step-daughter duo within the police department, though I never really thought of Janice as a stepmother. I had reserved that description for Jim's first wife, Sheila, as I continually tried to put names to family relationships based on affection, not blood.

"It really hurt me when you and Dad didn't take me in after Mom was sent to Napa," I blurted to Janice one day.

"What?" She seemed genuinely shocked.

"That day when I came to your cottage. I asked Dad if I could live with you guys. I told him I would help take care of Seth. He told me you didn't want me living there." I watched her face, trying to read her reaction.

"How strange," she said. "Dave told me you came over to check out the place. He said you didn't like it and you'd find somewhere else to live."

Not wanting to believe my father was a bald-faced liar, I mentally reviewed that meeting years earlier. Was it possible I had said something that made him believe his accommodations didn't meet my high standards? No, that was ridiculous. I had nowhere else to go! If my father's version of events was true, then why had I carried this resentment for so many years? After years of living with Mom's warped sense of reality, I was uncertain of so many things. Had I subliminally sent Dad the message I didn't really want to live with him?

My brain was addled. Maybe it was like with Officer Warren. Maybe my pride had made it impossible for me to ask for help when I needed it. *No, that wasn't right! I'd practically begged Dad to take me in.*

Maybe everyone was just living in their own distorted reality, changing the script as they went along to make themselves hero or victim. I'd never know exactly what happened in the cottage that day. I could make excuses for Dad. I could blame myself. I could blame him. But in the end, none of it mattered. The one thing I was certain of was that Jim had turned out to be the best parent for me, the only true parent I ever had. Dad had done me a huge favor the day he kicked me to the curb.

Joanie and I got back in the car and were almost through our shift when dispatch put out a call of a purse-snatching.

"There's a 213 in the area of Francisco and Chestnut. Meet the victim on the corner." I drove there as fast as I could. "The suspect is a white male, thirty-five years old, six feet tall, medium build, dark hair, wearing a blue windbreaker and jeans."

We were a couple of blocks away, and I was still speeding to the scene. "Slow down!" said Joanie. "Look around." Slowing to a crawl, we began searching between cars, under cars, around corners, in doorways.

"There!" shouted Joanie, pointing at a man on the corner of Lombard. I floored it to the next block. Joanie was out of the car and on top of him like some kind of stuntwoman before I had even hit the brakes. Pulling out my cuffs, I ran to help. The man looked six months pregnant. Joanie delivered the evidence from under his windbreaker as I cuffed him and led him to our car.

Another unit located the victim and brought her over for a cold show. The memory of that night at Will's drugstore when I was a robbery victim sitting in the back of a police car popped into my head. At least in this case, there was little doubt we had the right guy. We wouldn't have to worry the victim was picking the wrong person just to make the police happy.

After the woman positively identified the suspect and her property, we took him to the station. It was my job to search and inventory the suspect's property before placing him in the cell. As I led him in, he said, "What's the big deal? I didn't hurt the bitch. I just took her purse." My jaw fell open. I included his spontaneous statement in my police report. The thief's impromptu confession saved taxpayers the expense of a trial.

Joanie gave me a perfect score on my daily evaluation. Things were looking up.

The San Francisco 49ers

The 145th had reached our final two weeks of field training. My close friends had all done well, but we'd lost a few more classmates who had resigned at the strong suggestion of their training officers. Resigning was always preferable to fighting the city and risking being fired. Sergeant Meyer had been way off the mark with his estimation that one in three of us would fail the academy. We had only twenty officers left out of the original forty-seven recruits. Maybe we *were* the worst class ever.

Brian was away on a week's vacation when I rotated back to day watch for my last two weeks of training.

"It's a great sign that Brian took vacation days," said Eduardo. "If he were considering terminating you, he'd have to stay around and do the extra paperwork."

"Thanks for the vote of confidence, Eduardo." We both laughed.

I immediately liked Brian's substitute, Officer Gary Gold. He was meticulously groomed, in his late forties, tall, and attractive. He polished his brass and shoes to a high gloss and lacquered his dark hair without mercy. Officer Gold was the shiniest person I'd ever seen.

The lieutenant was addressing our lineup when the station keeper hurried in from the front office and whispered something to him. The hair on the back of my neck bristled. I always felt a wave of intuition before a Mom-related call.

"Nassberg, you have an urgent phone call on line two. You're excused to take it," said Lieutenant McNaughton. *I knew it! Not again!*

I was imagining the worst as I picked up the phone. "Hello?" My voice faltered, not sounding a bit like the cop I was supposed to be.

"Karen?" It was John. "Your mother is missing. She's been gone for five days, and I haven't heard a thing. She's taken off before, but she's always called."

John had called me on two previous occasions when Mom had hopped on a plane: once when she went to Florida, once to Boston. Both times, she'd called him and managed to find her way back without a detour to a psychiatric hospital. She usually called as soon as she reached her destination, perhaps hoping John would dramatically beg for her to come back.

"I don't know what to do," he said.

I wanted to scream at him that I didn't give a damn what he did. *Didn't I wash my hands of her when I kicked her out? Would it never end?* But I was almost a real cop now. This wasn't just my mother; this was a citizen asking for advice on a missing person. Now I was supposed to be some sort of authority on this type of thing.

"Have you called the psych ward?"

"No. I thought I should call you first."

"OK. I'll make some calls and get back to you as soon as I can." I returned to my spot in lineup and put Mom's missing-person search on hold. The last thing I wanted was to find her, especially while on duty. *Perhaps she's right. Maybe I am the worst daughter on the planet. After all, I threw her out, and now she is missing. Maybe she will see me in hell after all.*

The San Francisco 49ers, led by Joe Montana, had been on a winning streak for months. The city celebrated as the team won playoff after playoff. It was looking as though they might go all the way to the Super Bowl, but no one seemed to believe they had much chance to win. On the day of the Super Bowl, the city was completely unprepared. It had been a long time since a San Francisco sports team had won big; no one seemed to foresee that if the 49ers won, the city would go wild. Normally, for a big event, the entire department was mobilized. But this time, the city had made no special-event plans.

Officer Gold and I were scheduled to be off about an hour before the game ended. The Central cops stood in front of the station television watching the last quarter. We all hung around late, expecting an order from headquarters to stay overtime. When the order never came, we checked off, hoping to catch the end of the game at the corner bar.

"I wonder why they're not holding us over," said Gold as we waited to salute the lieutenant, reporting off. "This is going to be crazy. They're making a big mistake."

"You think so?"

"Don't go to the bar. Get in your car and drive straight home."

Before going downstairs to change, I made a cursory call to the psychiatric ward. I'd been checking every day for a week. Mom still wasn't there. I gave John a quick call, but he still hadn't heard from her either. Then I took Gary's advice and got away from North Beach.

From home, I watched the madness on television. The score was 27–21, and Dallas was leading. With fifty-one seconds left in the game, Dwight Clark caught the winning, desperation touchdown pass from Joe Montana—forever known as "The Catch." The 49ers had won their first Super Bowl, and the city, especially the Central district, went wild. A skeleton crew of cops handled near-riot conditions. I waited by the phone, expecting a call ordering me to return to the station, but the phone never rang.

The officers trying to keep the peace that night were pelted with bottles and overwhelmed by crowds. Dozens of people were hospitalized, including several cops. Many citizens were struck with rocks, and a few people were stabbed. There were several incidents of looting, and a few dozen people were arrested. By luck, no one was killed that night. I watched the melee from home, searching for my coworkers in the crowds. I worried for my classmates and wondered which of them were working.

The city officials learned from that near riot, and when a celebratory parade was scheduled for the 49ers two days later, everyone was called in. Just as I stepped out the front door to leave for my parade assignment, my phone rang.

"Karen! It's me. Mom. Guess what?" She sounded manic. "I'm in Reno, and I divorced that bastard!"

"Uh-huh," I said, keeping my tone as neutral as possible.

"Gotta go." she said. "I'm off to throw my wedding ring into the Truckee." The line went dead. I dialed John's number, wondering what to tell him. I didn't want to be the one to deliver the news of his divorce, and I wasn't even sure if she'd really divorced him. By the tenth ring, I hung up. Relieved he hadn't answered, I left for work.

Gary and I were assigned to Sergeant Kelly's squad for the parade. The entire station hopped onto Muni buses and headed to City Hall, where we met dozens of cops from all over the city. We waited in the cavernous basement, playing cards until we were deployed. The parade route looped around Market Street and ended up at Civic Center for a rally. A few hours before it began, we marched down Market Street as a platoon and found our positions behind the barricades.

The parade was thrilling. Our squad was so close to the motorized cable cars, we could practically touch Dwight Clark and Joe Montana. Everything moved along peacefully until the end of the rally, when Market Street was swarmed with people. The barricades quickly became meaningless as hordes of people climbed over them and filled the traffic lanes. Most were families and good-natured revelers, but some were looking for trouble. There were people everywhere, shoulder to shoulder. The only uniformed officer I could even see in the mob was Officer Gold, standing right beside me. I kept my right elbow tight by my hip, protecting my gun.

The radio traffic on our handhelds grew incoherent as officers began reporting looters breaking windows on Market and Fifth Street. Other cops came over the air saying they were being pelted with bottles and rocks and needed backup. Gary and I started to push our way through the crowd, heading for Fifth Street.

There are several radio codes that San Francisco cops use to call for help. Most of them are codes that mean "Get here as soon as you can, but we're not getting killed yet." But a 406 is called only when an officer has been killed or is seriously injured. Before we could make it to Fifth Street, cops all over Market Street were putting out 406 calls. In my three months of street training, I had never heard a single 406 called before. Up and down Market Street, cops were separated from their squads and fighting with drunken citizens. If an officer was overpowered and someone in the crowd got his gun, the celebration might quickly become a tragedy.

That night, Officer Gold and I responded to call after call for assistance. By the time we reached one corner, the fight was over and a new fight had started somewhere else. The scene was so confusing that we'd lost Sergeant Kelly and had no idea where the rest of our squad was. Like the military, we were never supposed to leave a man behind. The expression *squad integrity* had been drummed into us relentlessly in the academy. But normal police crowd protocol didn't prepare us for the pandemonium of that day.

After a while, we encountered another Central squad leader, Sergeant Webb. He scanned the crowd near us, searching for his missing troops. Webb was a nut—everyone knew it—but now we couldn't avoid him. He had seen us, and he called us out.

"You, Gold! Recruit! Where's your squad leader?" he demanded.

"I don't know, Sergeant. We were separated from our squad." I looked over at Gary, who was uncharacteristically silent.

"OK, you're my squad now," he ordered. Webb looked away, and Gary rolled his eyes at me. Webb's remaining four guys stood beside him, looking miserable. We assembled on the corner as someone chucked a few bottles at us. Glass shattered around my feet, and I lowered the visor on my helmet. I felt very calm, as if I had been training for this moment my whole life.

"Where the fuck did that come from?" howled Webb. He turned and fixated on a nearby bar. "Follow me!" he cried, darting across Market Street. Webb led the squad into the bar. Gary and I trailed behind him. The bar was full of older guys, guys like Jim, just sitting around drinking beer and watching replays of the game. These bar customers weren't doing a thing. *They didn't throw any bottles!* Then Webb began swinging his thirty-six-inch baton like a baseball bat, knocking patrons off stools. I gazed wide-eyed at Gary. *What the hell was this? What was the matter with Webb?*

We followed Webb, watching in horror as he hit random bar patrons with his stick, then marched us out the back door of the saloon into the alley. The other men in the squad looked at each other incredulously, wondering what they should do. We stood there waiting, our batons held ready in the port-arms position.

"We're going back in!" Webb said, turning and marching back in. His squad reluctantly followed him.

I followed Gary, who took one step inside the bar, then turned around. "We're getting the hell out of here. This is not our damn squad. Let's go." We backed away from the bar, abandoning Webb and his unfortunate men, and ran double time to City Hall, where we found Sergeant Kelly and our original squad straggling in.

Back at Central before sign-off, Gary took me aside. "Listen to me, kid. What you saw tonight . . . you never saw. You don't know what Webb is capable of. We never followed Webb. We got separated from our squad and we were trying to find Sergeant Kelly. Got it?"

"Loud and clear." Mom had taught me the code of silence early. My survival had depended on it.

A few months later, I would be called into Internal Affairs, along with everyone else who encountered Webb that night. I would wrestle with my conscience before being questioned by the investigator. In the end, Webb's stunt would eventually cost the city more than a million dollars in civil settlements.

I was sitting in the assembly room using my template to draw a diagram on an accident report. Brian, back from vacation, sat beside me drinking black coffee and working the *San Francisco Chronicle*'s word jumble.

"I always put the letters in a circle alternating consonants and vowels. The words jump out that way." It was our last day working together, so Brian had been giving me nonstop advice about everything.

One of the older cops, Vince, came in from the front office and told me I had a phone call. I was no longer panicking every time I got a call. This was becoming my new normal. When I picked up, it turned out to be John again.

"Karen? Your mother has returned home."

"What?" *Didn't she divorce him? Does he even know? Can you even still get a quickie divorce in Reno?* My questions were answered in no time, as I heard Mom in the background.

"Yes, we're divorced. But now I'm back, Karen, and it's like a honeymoon!"

"Good," I said to John. "Thanks for telling me." *Who ever knew what the truth was with Mom?* I hung up. At least now I could stop wondering if she was sleeping on the streets.

As we got ready to sign off our last watch together, I felt sort of wistful saying good-bye to Brian. He seemed sad to see me go too.

"OK, final exam. What's the goal of police work?" he asked.

"To go home with the same number of holes in you as you came to work with," I replied, as he'd trained me.

He looked at me with some amusement as we approached the lieutenant's office together for the last time. "Hey, we're throwing a bachelor party for Nick tonight, you want to come with me?" he asked.

"What? Isn't it going to be all guys?"

"It's all guys and you. It'll be fun," he said. "Come on."

I went. Forty-two men, and me. They didn't treat me any differently than the rest of the team. The jokes were raunchy, and we all drank too many shots. When Captain Taylor stood to toast the future groom, Vince used his dessert spoon as a slingshot and flung frothy chocolate mousse at the captain's Armani suit pants. It landed on his crotch. The captain turned crimson, and we howled like it was the funniest moment in the history of the world . . . which for me, right then, it was. I was a real cop, and nothing had ever been more hilarious.

Siberia

The next day Scot and I reported to Ingleside Station for our permanent assignment. We were the only rookies from the 145th sent to that station. The administration distributed new officers to the nine district stations as needed, but recruits who had "juice"—family or friends in high places—usually ended up downtown at one of the choice assignments. Scot and I were juiceless. The Ingleside district was on the southern border of San Francisco and felt like a completely different town. But at least Scot and I were going there together.

We immediately submitted the three requests for transfer each rookie was allotted. Once we turned in the requests, we might wait years for our names to come up for assignment to a new station. I requested Central, Northern, and the Mounted Patrol. Though everyone put his name on the Mounted list, the expected waiting time was more than twenty years. But I wasn't yet ready to abandon my childhood fantasy of riding with the horse patrol.

As Scot and I unpacked our equipment at Ingleside, it felt as though we were being sent to Siberia. The Ingleside neighborhood was completely unfamiliar to me. There were over 300 different street names, many only a block or two long, and it took new officers months to learn their way around. This was before global positioning systems were commonplace, and I worried we would be sent to a location I couldn't find. I studied my street guide like a nun poring over her Bible. But the good news was that I was now working in a part of town Mom had never visited.

The swing-shift crew at Ingleside was extremely young. The most senior members had only about four years' street experience. Four other women were assigned to the station, but we rarely worked the same nights.

The lieutenant assigned Scot and me as partners. Normally the bosses tried to partner more seasoned veterans with the new cops. But the guys weren't exactly lining up to partner with the new girl or the gay guy, so Scot and I were partners by default, with a grand total of eight months' street experience between us.

Our first-ever call to a gunshot wound was at a middle-class tract home on Persia Street. The dispatcher told us it was an apparent suicide, and I assumed the scene would be similar to the death scenes I'd seen during training.

The victim's mother opened the door and led us down the hallway, and there, collapsed on the ground, was a body in a pool of thick fluid. I knew it was blood, but my mind registered it as something else—*strawberry Jell-O*. The contents of a human skull poured out on wall-to-wall carpet looked exactly like strawberry Jell-O. The man's skull had been blown open with a .45 caliber handgun—a self-inflicted gunshot wound. I knew I should have been paralyzed with shock at seeing something so obscene, something surely no human was ever meant to see. Yet, all I could think of was strawberry Jell-O. *Maybe cherry. No, definitely strawberry.* In spite of the body and gun that were right in front of me, a part of my mind insisted on seeing the red, gelatinous pool as nothing more than a dessert spill.

The living room was full of the victim's family members. They were Guatemalan immigrants. The mood was somber but surprisingly unemotional. The victim's mother, soft spoken and pretty, told me her son had threatened suicide so many times that no one was surprised this had happened. She spelled her son's name for me, and told me his date of birth.

"He was a security guard," she said. "That's why he had the gun."

The estimated time for the arrival of a deputy from the Medical Examiner's office was one hour, which probably meant more like three and would feel like twenty. As the years went by, I would grow to despise the time spent waiting for the ME. Trapped between the grieving and the gruesome, time stood still. Sometimes I would try to fill the silence by encouraging the family to talk about their loved one, but experience taught me that it was easier for everyone if I just stood and waited silently, like an emotionless Beefeater guard.

When the ME team finally arrived, I introduced the deputy to the family members. After they'd placed the body on a cold metal stretcher and covered it with a tarp, the older deputy asked me to get a spoon from the kitchen. I did it mechanically, not understanding. Handing him a soupspoon from the dish rack, I wondered if he might pull a container of yogurt from his brief-case. I watched in disbelief as he stooped down and scooped the congealed blood into a plastic container. *Is it really this unscientific? Don't they have some sort of sterile tool for this?* The deputy handed me the spoon, and I rinsed it in the sink. The relatives, seated in the living room, had mercifully not witnessed the collection of the evidence.

The Ingleside was more residential than the Central, and swing-watch officers were sent to mediate family disputes almost every night. All those years of conflict-resolution training with Jim and Mom were finally paying off.

Sometimes, agreeing with an angry spouse was a useful calming technique. But I learned that feigned empathy must always be delivered with absolute sincerity. If the actor lacks the skill to play the part, he should never attempt it. The backlash was drastic if the combatant suspected the officer was faking concern.

Another useful tactic was bringing the couple together with my old Mom and Jim favorite, "It seems to me you have both been working too hard. I can see how much you care for each other and want to make life easier for each other." If I was really on a roll, I might convince the couple to hug before I left. People spent a fortune on classes to learn similar techniques. I'd been raised in a free workshop.

Scot and I whined to each other continuously about escaping the Ingleside. We both longed for the bright lights of Chinatown and North Beach, but it might take a decade before they reached our names on the Central list. We felt trapped.

After a series of purse snatchings in the Ingleside, the lieutenant called me into his office and assigned me to work a plainclothes detail with Phil, another rookie. I was excited by the idea of working undercover, if only as a decoy. Generally, the only plainclothes opportunities for women cops consisted of impersonating prostitutes and arresting wannabe Johns. The idea of arresting women who were selling their bodies to survive did not appeal to me. I had come too close to that abyss myself. And Gina had warned me against working the Vice Detail. She'd become disgusted with the job when a prospective customer offered to pay her to defecate on him, a request simultaneously disgusting and impossible to do on cue.

My undercover job was to saunter down the street near the hot purse-snatching spots, carelessly toting a handbag as bait. Phil would watch me, trolling from a distance, hoping to reel in the thief once I'd hooked him. We did this routine four or five hours a night.

"This is getting old," complained Phil on the way to our spot. "We've been fishing for two weeks and all we've caught is colds."

"Boo-freakin'-hoo. I'm the one freezing my ass off out there. You're in the nice, cozy car with the heat cranked up full blast." Cops spend a lot of time complaining; it's kind of like a hobby.

Suddenly there was frantic air traffic. The dispatcher's voice was panicky as she put out an All. All citywide radio stations were transmitting at once that an officer needed the most urgent kind of assistance.

"406 at Van Ness and Willow. Shots fired, officer down!"

The chaotic radio traffic was impossible to decipher. This call had a different feel to it than the 406 calls I'd heard during the 49ers parade. Every unit in the city came up on the air, telling dispatch they were responding.

"Code Thirty-three. Stay off of the air! Keep the channel clear for officers at the scene!"

We were responding from the opposite side of the city. Phil was driving, and though it didn't always make sense, when a police officer was shot, cops responded from everywhere. We knew it would take no less than ten minutes to get to the scene, but we had to go, Code Three the whole way, siren shrieking, our adrenaline pumping. Dozens of police cars were already at the scene as we drove up. Phil and I couldn't even get close.

Sergeant John Macaulay had pulled over a car spotted in a grocery store robbery from the previous week. The robber started firing as soon as the sergeant approached him, shooting Sergeant Macaulay, fleeing, and then later shooting himself.

John Macaulay was thirty-five when he was killed. My reaction to his murder surprised me. If he'd been my training sergeant or a beloved mentor, my story would be more dramatic, more understandable. But the truth was, I'd never met John Macaulay, and until I saw his photograph at the funeral, I wouldn't have been able to pick him out of a lineup. But there it was—death—real to me in a way it had never been before.

This was my first police funeral, the first of many I would attend. Legions of uniformed cops from all over the country stood in formation saluting the coffin as the sad wail of bagpipes sent "Amazing Grace" through St. Mary's Cathedral. A drummer, playing slowly and steadily, followed the grieving young family to the hearse. Only a zombie could walk away dry-eyed, and having grown up with a woman who had no room for sentimentality, I drank it all in like nectar.

For the first time it hit me. *People are killed doing this job.* The fraternal summer-camp high jinks of the academy were behind me now. I could no longer play at being a cop, flippantly laughing at strawberry Jell-O and stinky Camembert. These were real people, my brothers and sisters, and their lives had ended, often tragically. Taking the job seriously was the least I could do to honor them.

Just as the Ingleside became unrelentingly depressing, Scot came into work with good news. He'd made some phone calls and had somehow been able to get us both transferred back to Central. No matter how much I needled him, he never revealed how he had accomplished this. Much to my surprise, Scot had some juice. It had just taken him a while to squeeze the oranges.

What Shall We Do with the Drunken Sailor?

Being back at Central was a blessing and a curse. Much as I loved North Beach, I now constantly worried about encountering Mom. As far as I knew, she was still living on the other side of the city, with John. I hadn't seen her since the night I threw her out and hadn't spoken to her since she called upon her return from Reno. Now I worried she might return to one of her old haunts, like Vesuvio, and dreaded the possibility of my being called to remove her. I imagined everyone saying I was as awful as Devlin, a cop so mean I would arrest my own mother.

Now I was working the midnight shift with Nora, a female partner who was fast becoming my best friend, and the nights flew by as we shared our life stories. When you are enclosed in a car with someone for eight hours daily, even if you remove the life-threatening element, it is inevitable you will become intimately acquainted. Eventually, we could almost read each other's minds.

Nora had joined the department a year before me, and we had so much in common that we described ourselves as "evil twins." We loved the same books, movies, and foods, as well as everything French. We looked similar enough that the station cops often confused our names. We joked that we even shared the same mother, because Nora's mother was also a mentally unstable Anglophile.

We also shared a dislike of the dastardly Devlin, and he sometimes came up in conversation. Mine had been his last academy
class, though he'd stayed in the department for another year
before retiring. That last year, his only job was weighing officers
and ensuring they complied with fitness regulations. Between
the academy and my first weigh-in, I had lost ten pounds. I'd
looked forward to weighing in and rubbing Devlin's face in my
lack of obesity—not to mention that I'd actually been allowed
on street patrol and had not yet been killed. But when he
weighed me, he acted like I didn't even register on his radar. He
wordlessly logged my weight onto his clipboard, even asking for
my name, as if he'd forgotten. His games with me were over, and
I simply did not matter to him.

It was anticlimactic in the same way that graduating from
college had been. After telling me for years I would never go,
Mom acted like my graduation had always been a given. So, I
had to wonder, whom was I was trying to prove myself to?
Mom, Dad, Devlin, Warren? In trying to gain their respect, or
their love, I'd been driven to accomplish task after task. I was
beginning to think the very people I had resented the most were
the ones who made me the person I was becoming. I even felt a
glimmer of gratitude for them.

After lineup, Nora and I were anxious to get in the car to talk
privately. There had been a big department scandal that everyone was talking about, and I was worried about Gina. The most
recent police academy class held their graduation celebration in a
room of a local bar, the Rathskeller. My stepmother, Janice, was
one of the graduates.

It was not unusual for veteran cops to drop by this type of
party, and many from the Northern and Central had stopped by
to get a look at the new recruits. Gina was among these veterans
and had seen much more than she'd expected. A new graduate

had been drunk and handcuffed to a chair while a prostitute performed oral sex on him in front of the entire room. Now rumors were flying through the department, and somehow Gina was being cast in the role of villain.

"But how did Gina get mixed up in it? Why is everyone pissed at her?" I asked Nora. "I've been trying to call her, but she won't answer my calls."

"I heard that when she saw what was going on, she tried to stop it. She left and made some calls to the brass. Then, when they blew her off—OK, no pun intended—she called the press. Now it's all over the news, and everyone's blaming Gina for embarrassing the department," said Nora.

I felt sick. I had a free-floating anxiety about the incident. I flashed back to Officer Gold and the advice he gave me on the night of Webb's craziness.

We circled North Beach again, and dispatch came over with a disturbing-the-peace call at the St. Tropez Hotel. The name usually made us laugh and speak with French accents. The depressing hotel bore little resemblance to any Riviera resort. But tonight we weren't in the mood to joke.

"Three Adam Four, responding," Nora told dispatch.

It's been said before, but in police work, it's often the most innocuous calls that turn out to be the most dangerous. As we climbed the two flights to the registration desk, we could already hear the commotion. A booming male voice shouted, "I'm gonna kick your ass, motherfucker!"

We reached the top step and took in the scene. A stark naked, beefy, completely hairless young man was trying to pull the smaller and skinnier male desk clerk through the registration counter window. The opening in the plastic window was only eight inches high by eight inches wide, and the naked attacker was obviously frustrated in his effort to squeeze the clerk through the impossibly small hole. The bully's buzz cut, tattoos, and bodybuilder physique suggested he was a very fit member of the United States Navy. Taking this sailor down would not be easy.

One of the lingering effects of Devlin's demoralizing evaluations of my baton dance was that I rarely used my baton, mostly out of fear he had been right and that I might be inept with it. Even when I would have been perfectly justified in defending myself, I seldom used as much force as I could have or maybe even should have. I feared I would use the baton on a resistor and he'd laugh at me the way Devlin had. *You foolish faux cop! You think you can heurt me with your leeettle steeeck?* For some reason, the imaginary bad guy always had a French accent.

"Popeye" was considerably taller than Nora and I were, so we were going to use a high/low maneuver. Trying to get Devlin's famous carotid restraint on the naked sailor, I jumped up on his back, while Nora kicked in the backs of his knees. But our usual moves weren't working, and he would not go down. I was riding him around the hallway of the hotel like Secretariat's jockey. My arm was in a good position for a chokehold, but it took all my strength just to stay on his back as he ran down the hallway trying to buck me off.

Nora got to her radio and called for assistance. She grabbed at his slippery, sweaty body and somehow got one cuff on him. She pulled on the handcuff chain with all her weight, and I cinched up on my carotid hold, remembering Devlin's droning instructions, "The officer places his arm around the neck . . ." as we brought him to the floor.

When our backup team, Jess and Liam, came running up the stairs, they froze, momentarily stunned by the spectacle of a uniformed female officer riding a naked, buff young man. Jess and Liam helped us get the other cuff on before they began offering their commentary. Just out of earshot of the sailor, Liam whispered, "Ride 'em, cowgirl! You won a free beer!"

Jess, Liam, Matt, Will, Nora, and I were in the same squad and often floated between partners when our steadies took a night off. We'd all become quite close, like teammates. After checking off, we usually met at the Northstar, our corner bar. Often it was still dark out when we started drinking. That morning I proposed a toast to Devlin and his chicken hold. Though I would never love the man, I had to give him credit for teaching me some good moves.

We talked about the graduation party scandal and what might happen to the people involved. There were rumors that the chief planned to fire the whole class, and I thought about Janice. We'd spoken on the phone, and she was very worried, though she hadn't been involved in any of it. I figured the chief was bluffing. There was no way to justify firing the recruits who hadn't even known about the incident.

Every one of my squad mates would have given their lives to save mine, and I would have done the same for them. I felt I could talk to them about almost anything. But no matter how close we grew, I remained ashamed of sharing the details of my childhood. I wasted a lot of energy masquerading as a normal person, imitating the behavior of the people around me, as I had throughout my childhood. But now, as I came to love my squad, this charade was becoming exhausting. I no longer even knew what "normal" meant. And I wasn't even sure I wanted to be "normal" anymore. My childhood wish for a family like Donna Reed's now seemed ridiculous.

Matt and I had been working together quite a bit. I had been considering asking him to be my steady partner since Nora had changed her hours, but I wasn't sure he would want to work with me as a steady. One morning while waiting for the rest of the team to arrive after our shift, we sat at the bar swigging Bud from bottles. I shook out liar's dice onto the bar.

"Pair of deuces. You win again. Luck of the freakin' Irish." I handed him the leather cup and ordered him another shot. "My mother was in and out of mental hospitals my whole childhood," I blurted. I wasn't sure why that had just popped out of my mouth. I waited for a joke or a "that explains everything."

"Wow," he said. "Well, it's amazing that you turned out so great. You must be a very strong person."

What? So I told him the whole story—Mom, Dad, Jim—the full catastrophe.

"You went through all that and you graduated from college and the police academy? Most people would have just used it as an excuse to give up."

His reaction made me reconsider my story. Maybe I had underestimated my friends. Maybe my story wasn't about being a victim of my childhood. I was beginning to see that my fear of being judged by my friends was unreasonable. My brother and sister cops were compassionate and had family problems of their own. I was so used to life with a woman who saw the worst in everyone that I expected the world to judge me the way Mom did.

When we stumbled out of the bar at noon, the sunlight seared our eyes. We headed home to bedrooms decorated with light-canceling aluminum foil–covered windows.

Although Matt's words made me reconsider my shame, I still hesitated to tell him where we were going the next night when I got a call at the station.

"Karen, it's Leaf, remember? I used to work for your daddy."

I stared into the phone receiver, wondering if this was a prank call. I hadn't spoken to Leaf in a dozen years. I saw Jim two or three times a month and spoke to him on the phone all the time, but even Jim hadn't mentioned Leaf in years. It made no sense to get a call from him after all this time. And I'd never called Jim "daddy." Leaf's use of that word surprised me.

"Karen, Jim and I ran into each other tonight and had some drinks. Now I can't wake him up. I need you to come get him." Leaf gave me an address in an alley in North Beach.

"Matt, I need to run an errand. You ready to go out?" He nodded, and we headed to the car.

On the way, I thought about telling him what was going on, telling him the man I considered to be my dad was passed out in someone's garage, but I didn't want Matt to meet Jim this way, to only know Jim as a passed-out drunk.

When I found the apartment building, Leaf was waiting for me on the sidewalk. Matt read my mind and stayed in the car. Leaf hadn't changed much over the years. He still wore his hair in a long ponytail, but now it was streaked here and there with grey. He hugged me like a long-lost daughter.

"Look at you in a police uniform!" He stepped back to take in the picture of little hippie-kid Karen, as if I was a cute kid at his door on Halloween. Then he led me into the open garage. "See, he's asleep in the back seat of my car, and I can't wake him up." I looked into the sedan where Jim was curled up, snoring.

"Well, how long has he been there?" I asked.

"A couple hours."

"Is there some reason he can't sleep there?"

"Well, no. I guess not. But I just thought you should know."

I wondered why he felt this information was so necessary for me. Did he really think I could carry a 240-pound man to his apartment on the other side of town?

"OK, well, call me when he wakes up, or tell Jim to call me, and I'll drive him home if he wants." I gave Leaf a hug, which was clumsy with the bulky bulletproof vest and all the equipment hanging off me.

When I got back in the car, Matt discreetly asked no questions. I drove back to the station and went into the women's restroom. There were a few stray lockers housed there because the locker room downstairs was so small. As I walked in, I gasped, then froze: scrawled across Gina's locker in gigantic black marking pen letters were the words *snitch bitch*. I felt like I'd been slapped.

As I came out of the restroom, the sergeant at the station keeper's desk looked up from his newspaper. "A report's already been made," he said, anticipating my words.

A few weeks after the Leaf reunion, Jim took a fall and broke his clavicle. But ever the stoic, he refused to see a doctor. Barb took care of him, bringing him groceries and cooking for him. I called him often, but am ashamed to say I did not help take care of him.

He called me one afternoon, and we chatted longer than usual, reminiscing about his crazy days with Mom. It had taken me years to fully appreciate all he had sacrificed to take care of me. I had little understanding of it at the time, but he had put himself in a potentially dangerous situation. Had someone looked into our living arrangement, or had Mom made one of her sex-slave allegations publically, Jim might have had to fight a legal battle. He had been a parent to me when no one else had been able or willing, and I would always love him.

"You've always been my other daughter, Karen," he said at the end of the call.

"Someday," I said, "I'm going to take you on a really great cruise somewhere. Someday, I'll be able to thank you for everything you've done for me."

In spite of my many painful associations with the floating world, an ocean voyage was the currency I was choosing to show Jim my gratitude. It had taken me years to realize that Jim was my only real parent. He had always been my rock, ever strong.

"You've already thanked me by growing up to be you. I love you."

Two days later, the ringing phone woke me in the afternoon. Still groggy from a graveyard shift, I tripped on my way to answer it.

"Karen?" The shakiness in Barb's voice alarmed me. "Jim died this morning. That fall he took created an embolism. It happened very fast."

Shot in the gut, I never saw it coming. He was fifty-four years old.

As I hung up, the wracking sobs began and didn't stop for hours. Sobbing felt foreign; I couldn't remember the last time I had let myself completely break down. I was seized by a grief I had never experienced before.

When I stopped weeping, I felt hollowed out, empty, and lost. I wasn't sure what to do next. Mom needed to know. I should've prepared myself for telling her—reminded myself not to expect too much. Instead I clung to the idea that sharing the loss with her would give me some comfort. After all, this was death—the death of someone who'd been so important to us both.

John answered when I called to deliver the news.

"I need to speak to Mom."

He put her on.

"Mom, I have some bad news." I paused. "Jim died this morning."

"Oh," she said. "He always drank and smoked too much."

That was it. No emotion whatsoever. Icy coldness. She didn't ask about Barb, Steve, or me, or the funeral arrangements. She had nothing else to say.

I sat down and thought about her reaction for a long while, finally appreciating the depth of her narcissism. The people in Mom's realm only existed when they served her. Jim had spent years giving to Mom selflessly and caring for me, and this was her response to his death? *He always drank and smoked too much.* Any residual affection for her I'd clung to from childhood crumbled to ash with the realization that Mom was a manipulative user and nothing more. The painful truth hit me: I detested my mother.

Sheila, Barb, Steve, and I did take Jim on a last cruise. But not the one I'd envisioned. We scattered his ashes in San Francisco Bay, near Angel Island. Each of us threw a red rose on the water and watched the current carry the flowers to sea. Before we'd arrived at the scattering spot, one of the *Neptune*'s crew asked if a family member would like to pour the ashes into the Bay. We'd debated about it, finally deciding to let the professionals do it. Steve said, "I'm just afraid the wind will blow the ashes back, and I might get some Dad in my eye."

We couldn't stop laughing. Jim would have loved that.

A few days after the memorial, I returned to work in the Central four-car with Matt. He caught me up on the news. He told me Gina had taken a leave of absence and was suing the city. Although she had many friends who loved her, they could not protect her from those who'd decided to make her life miserable after the Rathskeller incident. Some had refused to respond when she'd called for backup. Now no one expected Gina to ever return to work. Losing Gina only compounded my grief over losing Jim.

I drove around in a fog for weeks, sad about Gina and bereft about Jim. Just seeing someone who vaguely reminded me of Jim reduced me to tears. *He did so much for me, and now I would never be able to repay him.* The only time he traveled to Europe was to rescue Mom and me. He'd spent less than a week in England. The only sights he'd seen were a mental hospital and an orphanage. As the years passed, I had finally allowed myself to hug him and, a few times, to tell him I loved him. But it killed me that I hadn't had the chance to do anything big for him. *And I hadn't even said, "I love you" at the end of our last call.* I was tormented by that thought.

Matt, Nora, Liam, and Jesse gave me love, support, and a few too many shots of tequila as I gradually rejoined the living. Finally, I had true brothers and sisters, people who had my back, no matter what. Lieutenant Frost had been right: when I needed help, I got it, this time without even having to ask.

Still, sometimes I wondered about how quickly things might change. I had been accepted into a family, but now I wondered if I might someday make a choice that would leave me wearing a scarlet letter or a Sharpie *"snitch bitch."* I worried I might someday see things I could not remain silent about. Now I imagined future ethical dilemmas in which I had to choose between the job I loved and speaking up about a brother or sister officer's actions. It seemed my new chosen family was as unpredictable as Mom.

The Paddy Wagon

"Listen up, men! It's hats and bats!"

"Hats and bats!" echoed from the sergeant in the assembly room to the locker rooms downstairs as we scrambled to gather our riot gear. The demonstration was nothing unusual, several dozen people opposing our latest military action in Central America. The squads were being mobilized only because the protestors had formed a human chain across the Sansome Street traffic lanes, stalling the rush-hour commute.

I never enjoyed being called out to protests. I always remembered marching in antiwar protests and walking with La Huelga as a kid, and I often sympathized with the protesters and their cause. But I had sworn to enforce the law, and I didn't have much sympathy for protesters who planted themselves in traffic lanes, potentially endangering others who might need to get through.

We crowded around Sergeant Collins, listening as he called out our assignments.

"Three Adam Ninety-two, report to Sansome and Broadway. Take the wagon."

Matt play-punched me in the shoulder. "That's us! Karen, let's hit it."

Matt was the consummate Irish Catholic police officer and a former seminarian. I had tentatively proposed being steady partners, never expecting him to say yes. When he agreed, I felt I had finally gained membership to a secret order. We'd only been partners for a year, but I knew he had my back. He'd take a bullet for me without question, and I would do the same for him.

Grabbing my helmet and long baton, I followed him to the garage. Sergeant Kelly hopped into the driver's seat. No one called it the paddy wagon anymore, but I still did, a lingering habit from our childhood games. Sometimes, when there were too many of us to squeeze into patrol cars, we used the wagon to transport cops. Riding inside the rolling tin can made me claustrophobic—a weakness I kept to myself. To the casual observer, I appeared fearless.

I jockeyed for a spot on the outside of the van. My feet perched precariously on the running board, I swung from the overhead bar as we floated over the city streets. Matt swayed from the bar beside me. We laughed as Sergeant Kelly tried to eject us by hitting every pothole in San Francisco. Through the back-door grate we mocked our squad mates, stuffed inside the wino, juicy-foot-scented prisoner's compartment.

"Clowns in a car!" I heckled.

"When was the last time you rummies took a shower? You guys reek!" Matt yelled. We both laughed. Our squad glowered. We knew we were sealing our fate; they'd make sure we rode inside for the return trip.

I heard the protesters before I saw them: "Bad cop, no donut. Bad cop, no donut!" *Always the same stupid mantra at every single protest. Why can't they change it up? Show a little imagination!*

We parked along Sansome, and I pulled my helmet from its perch atop my baton. While snapping the chinstrap, I froze, gazing into the crowd.

No! This could not be happening!

"Karen, hop off! We're here!" yelled Matt. "This is our post!"

Helplessly, I stayed rooted to the running board, as immobile as the office towers surrounding us. My hand was glued to the overhead bar as if my central nervous system had shut down command.

"Karen, what's up? We need to move out!" Matt said more forcefully. He grabbed my arm and pulled me down. Then he opened the doors to release our captive squad. "What's going on, Karen?" Matt led me to the sidewalk and gently pushed me into line with our squad against the office buildings. I couldn't speak. I wanted the ivy climbing the brick walls behind me to consume me, hide me. It had been more than two years since I'd seen her. We hadn't spoken since her careless dismissal of Jim's death, and I had sworn to myself that I would never again get sucked back into her drama. But my nightmarish premonition of arresting my mother was coming true.

Sergeant Kelly raised his baton straight over his head, signaling our squad to line up in front of him. Then he spun it overhead in a circle. I quickly pulled my plastic visor down over my eyes and marched robotically behind the blue uniform in front of me. We joined the rest of the platoon in an encirclement formation.

The protestors had chosen a passive-resistance stance. Sitting cross-legged side-by-side, they occupied all four traffic lanes. We stood around the group, holding our batons in port-arms position as the lieutenant read them the unlawful-assembly admonition over the bullhorn for the second time.

Mom looked manic, possibly homeless, her stringy, gray hair unwashed. She sat among the protestors heckling us as booking teams moved in to begin the mass-arrest process.

"You fucking pigs!" she yelled. "Get your hands off of me! Assholes! Fascist Nazis! I'll sue you!"

A wave of nausea came over me as I prayed she wouldn't recognize me. Hoping to camouflage myself in the sea of blue, I turned away from the arrest team and pushed in more tightly against Matt. I watched a beefy cop cuff Mom's slender wrists. I had the impulse to go save her.

"Get your hands off me!" she screamed. "My daughter's a fucking cop!"

And then an authoritative voice in my head said with certainty: *Do nothing!* The voice sounded so clear, it was as if Matt had said it. I didn't move.

She was still shrieking as the cops loaded her into the wagon. The heavy doors clanged shut, and Officer Maloney secured the bolt, locking Mom in. The wagon slowly rolled down Sansome Street, and I watched as it turned the corner.

"Karen, are you OK?" Matt asked. His face was full of concern.

"Yes. I just saw someone I thought I used to know." Our eyes met. He looked puzzled for a moment and then nodded. He placed his hand on my shoulder and gently squeezed.

Epilogue

In the end, I probably came closer to arresting my mother than Devlin ever did. I even had to ask myself if I became a cop because I had an unconscious wish to arrest her. It was a fair question. Yes, maybe on some level I had wanted to put my mother in a place where she could never hurt me or anyone else again. But that certainly hadn't been what I was thinking when I joined the department.

The thing I had feared all those years, the embarrassment and derision of my peers, turned out to be trivial. I had already learned that much worse things could happen in life. People die in many ways every day, but no one actually dies of embarrassment. And my perceived or imagined judgment by my coworkers became unimportant.

I had been accepted as part of a family of 2,000 members, though the family was not exactly as I had imagined. I had grown to realize that all families have conflicts. Most families have members who dislike some of their relatives, and the police family was no exception. I couldn't know it then, but over the years the police family would support me and stick with me in sickness and in health, as I worked patrol, investigations, and the Homicide unit.

Eventually, I would grow to appreciate Devlin and his cohorts, and to appreciate that police work is not a job you should take if you can be easily bullied out of doing it. And though I had no way to know it back then, the department would provide me with a loving husband who was himself the son of a San Francisco cop, making my membership into the police family legacy official. We would have two sons together, and one day adopt a daughter. I would credit Jim for inspiring me to adopt.

As my children became older, we saw Mom occasionally. She even commended me for "thriving in spite of" her. Her use of the expression gave me pause. It sounded so close to "thriving to spite her." And it was true. Mom had taken enough of my life. I would not let her ruin one more hour of it.

I used to worry that I might become like my mother, and in a way I suppose I have. The voice I heard that day on Sansome Street was so real that reporting it probably makes me sound as if I belong in an institution, which is, after all, where I started out. But ultimately, it was that authoritative voice in my head that set me free. It was as if some mysterious force gave me absolute permission to cut the cord once and for all. I won't pretend I was freed overnight, but I finally understood Mom was a bottomless pit. No matter how much anyone gave her, she never got better.

And as it turned out, Mom was just fine without me. John bailed her out after that Sansome Street arrest, and they stayed together until his death many years later.

I decided to find out what had become of Mom. I hadn't received any hospital calls for more than five years, and I had rather deliberately lost track of her, even convincing myself that at eighty-one years old, she might be dead.

A clerk at the Social Security office told me she could only say my mother was still alive; she was not allowed to give me her address. But she said she would forward a letter to Mom for me. I gave the clerk my note, not sure if Mom would ever receive it. It said "please call me," along with my phone number. Less than a week later a social worker, Martha, from a skilled nursing facility, a "sniff" as she called it, told me my mother was in Oakland.

I sat parked in front of the sniff for a long while before I worked up the nerve to walk in. Martha was thrilled to have found a family member for Mom, who had not had a visitor in the months she'd been there. When she told me my mother had almost died, I could tell by her expression she was dismayed by my apparent lack of emotion. Mom had had a stroke and was recovering from pneumonia, Martha told me. I nodded.

"It's good that you finally came," she said. "Your mom has two roommates, and they both have visitors all the time."

"Don't try to guilt me. You have no idea what I've been through with this woman." It just popped out of my mouth. I knew how cold and heartless it sounded.

"Of course. I'm sorry. I can imagine she might have once been abusive. She still gets angry at us sometimes."

I walked down the hall to Mom's room. Martha followed.

"Karen is here," said Martha. Mom was frail and debilitated. She was childlike, half the size she'd been five years earlier at our last meeting.

"Do you know who I am?" I asked.

"You're Karen." I suspected she might just be repeating Martha's cue.

"But do you know who I am?" I asked.

"You're my daughter, Karen." And in spite of myself, tears rolled down my face. I sat down in the chair beside her.

"I'm a hundred years old," she said.

"No Mom, you're eighty-one."

"Well, you're no kid yourself," she replied. Yes. Still the same woman.

My children and I visit Mom now. It no longer causes me pain to see her. And it only makes me sad when I imagine a different life for Mom. Hoping for a different life is a pointless exercise. Ultimately we must all make the best of the lives we are given.

There is no doubt in my mind that had Jim not taken me in as he did, I would have ended up on the streets. It's not hard to imagine the choices I would have had to make to survive. It is not hard for me to imagine not surviving at all. Jim saved my life.

Never doubt that the love of just one person can save a child's life, in fact, sometimes it's the only thing that can.

Acknowledgments

I am deeply grateful to all those who encouraged me to write. Thank you Christine Bronstein and NBTT. Special thanks to Stephanie Lehmann, my first editor, who whittled down thousands of words and gave me this book's title, and to the indomitable Flossie Lewis for early reading and editing, to Laura Venters, and Julia Scheeres for further editing, to Kelly Corrigan for inspiring me, and for saying, "write it for your children," to my teachers, Stephanie Losee, Rachel Howard, Caroline Paul, Melanie Gideon, the workshoppers at S.F. Writer's Grotto, and Esalen, as well as Nafisa Haji, Cheryl Strayed, Pam Houston, Steve Almond, Carol Pott, Eve Batey, Mickey Nelson, Andrea Burnett, Sam Barry and Loretta Barrett.

I am ever grateful to my book club, the Killer Angels, for being my Steel Magnolias. And to Marcia Billings, Pat Rager, Sue Holland, TT and Sue Lynch, Katrina Hodge Willis, Sven and Barb, thanks for believing. To my brothers and sisters of the 145th San Francisco Police Academy class, thank you for sharing the best and the worst nineteen weeks of my life. I wouldn't have been here to tell this or any other story had it not been for Mom, Dad, Jim, and Sheila, I am grateful to each of them for loving me as well as they were able.

But mostly I thank my husband, Greg, and children Keenan, Aidan, and Kyra for loving me and giving me the freedom to write. I love you all.

Karen Lynch is a native San Franciscan. After graduating from UC Berkeley, she joined the San Francisco Police Department in 1981. She lives in Novato, California with her husband and their three children, including Kyra, who was the subject of an essay that won the **2012 Notes & Words** national essay contest. Her memoir, *"Good Cop, Bad Daughter,"* is the story of how growing up with a bi-polar mother trained Karen to be a cop.

CPSIA information can be obtained at www.ICGtesting.com
Printed in the USA
LVOW07s1534191015

458847LV00037B/433/P

9 780988 375420